G. J. Libaridian

Liberation and Revolution

Critical Essays in Modern Armenian History

ЧԻ

Gomidas Institute
London

This is the fourth of a projected five-volume series by the author.

The first two volumes were in Armenian:

Հայաստան-Թուրքիա. Պետականություն, պատմություն, քաղաքականու-թիւն, Անտարես, երեւան, 2021 [Armenia-Turkey: Statehood, History, Politics. Antares, Yerevan, 2021] (A Turkish translation of this volume will be released by Aras Publishing in Istanbul in 2024) and Հայաստանի երրորդ Հանրապետություն. Ղարաբաղեան Հակամարտություն, Անտարես, երեւան, 2022, [Third Republic of Armenia. Karabakh Conflict. Antares, Yerevan, 2022].

The third volume was published by Gomidas Institute, *A Precarious Armenia. The Third Republic, the Karabakh Conflict, and Genocide Politics,* London, 2023.

The fifth volume. A parallel work to this volume, will be published in Armenian during 2024, by the A. Yohannisyan Institute in Yerevan: Ազատագրություն եւ Հեղափոխություն. Քննական փորձեր արդի Հայոց պատմության [Liberation and Revolution: Critical Essays in Modern Armenian History].

The author is grateful to the following for granting permission to reproduce in this volume Chapter 6 "What was Revolutionary..." Oxford University Press; Chapter 8: "The Past As Prison ..." *Turkish Policy Quarterly*; Chapter 11: "History of Third Republic ..." Presses de l'Université Laval.

ISBN 978-1-909382-79-4

For more information please contact:
Gomidas Institute
42 Blythe Rd.
London W14 0HA
England
Web: *www.gomidas.org*
Email: *info@gomidas.org*

The translations, editing and publishing of this series is supported by

CALOUSTE
GULBENKIAN
FOUNDATION

ԳԱԼՈՒՍՏ ԿԻՒԼՊԷՆԿԵԱՆ ՀԻՄՆԱՐԿՈՒԹԻՒՆ
ՀԱՅԿԱԿԱՆ ՀԱՄԱՅՆՔՆԵՐՈՒ ԲԱԺԱՆՄՈՒՆՔ

and
a generous friend
The Parsekian Foundation

The views expressed in this publication do not necessarily reflect the views of
the Armenian Communities Department of the Calouste Gulbenkian
Foundation. The Foundation's support does not constitute endorsement of any
specific opinion or perspective.

CONTENTS

INTRODUCTION

This volume offers twelve essays on modern and contemporary Armenian history, the problems of writing that history, and how that history is used and abused.

These essays selected for this volume were written over a span of 45 years. The earliest dates back to 1979 which is reproduced here without any changes: the purpose of this selection is to subject the author's intellectual evolution—academic and political-- to the test of time and to the judgment of the reader. These essays have been selected on the basis of their relevance today; many important other articles were left out because they have already been published in easily accessible venues and could not be accommodated in this volume. Nonetheless, six of the 12 essays appear here for the first time.

While written at different times and on different occasions, the essays can be read independently of each other; the collection can be seen as a whole considering the themes underlying the subjects covered.

The main theme, as the title suggests, is the challenge of modernization of an ancient people, which involved (1) revolutionizing by creating new institutions within the structures that dominated the life of the Armenian people, and (2) planning for the liberation of that people from oppressive regimes under which the two main segments were living, but mainly those living in Ottoman Armenia. These political projects aimed at transforming the Armenian people into a modern nation. The experiment in the Ottoman Empire ended when Ottoman policy turned into the Genocide. Eastern Armenia, under Russian rule, ended up with the First Republic, which was transformed into a Second, Soviet Republic, and finally in 1991, into the Third Republic.

A second theme is the exploration of a simple question, but one that is difficult to answer: How did change come to Armenian society? To what extent was it caused by internal stimuli, and in what ways was change provoked by external factors? And, at the end, what was the relationship between the internal stimuli and external factors? The question of the mechanisms for change and struggles between old and new is a natural theme that underlies almost all the essays.

Finally, this collection of essays suggests patterns of Armenian political thinking and behavior that belie a commonly held belief that Armenians learn from history. Having a long history and a long memory of historical events is not the same as having a critical view of one's history. Especially when policies based on questionable historical memory and even more doubtful lessons learned from that history produce manifest disastrous patterns of Armenian policy making. The author is still exploring such patters in their historical context and intends to share them with interested readers in subsequent publications.

The last chapter is an attempt to understand the rather uncommon experience of the author in two different dimensions. First, he wrote and taught history as a historian and then ended up being part in the making of that history. The essay is an attempt to explore the relationship between two aspects of the author's relationship with Armenian life, as a historian and then a diplomat, as a method to understand how history is written and lived.

The 12 chapters in this volume offer one way of looking at history and at ourselves. The value of history is in its ability to explain as many of the significant changes as possible. The author hopes that the reader will benefit from the interpretation offered in this volume of that difficult trajectory.

Liberation and Revolution

Critical Essays in Modern Armenian History

"NATION" AND "FATHERLAND" IN NINETEENTH CENTURY WESTERN ARMENIAN POLITICAL THOUGHT

1983

This article reveals deep antagonisms between, on the one hand, writers and thinkers concerned with the peasantry and other disadvantaged segments of Armenian society in the Eastern provinces of the Ottoman Empire, in historic Western Armenia and, on the other, urban, liberal and more privileged segments based in Constantinople and other, mostly coastal cities. That antagonism pitted the love for "nation" defined in ethnoreligious "terms" against the love of "fatherland," defined by devotion to the problems of Armenians still living in the geographically conceived historic Armenia.

Conflicts and issues that continue to plague Armenia-Diaspora relations today will find their parallels in the antagonism of the 19th century.

(Richard Antaramian's Brokers of Faith, Brokers of Empire, *published in 2020, offers a much more complex picture of the relations between the two segments of Armenian society in the Ottoman Empire in the 19th century and enriches our understanding of the problem analyzed here.)*

This article was adapted from the present author's doctoral dissertation "The Ideology of Armenian Liberation, 16th through the 19th Centuries," and was first published in the Armenian Review *(Autumn 1983).*

Nationalism has been generally regarded as one of the central concepts in the understanding of nineteenth century Armenian political thought. Taking root in the 1850s, it came to embody the concerns and goals of many segments of the Armenian people. Nationalism is also an abstract concept;

while universalizing the Armenian experience, it might tend to overshadow the exact processes which give meaning to that term at different times and in different places.

One of those processes among Armenians in the Ottoman Empire was the increasing antagonism between the privileged urban population and the dispossessed rural masses. The two segments of the population once shared a self-definition imposed by the Ottoman state, that of a *millet*—a depoliticized community whose members belonged to a single religion or religious denomination. Within this context, the termination described, in a sociological sense, the elite of the *millet*, represented by the clergy and the economically successful elements. That leadership, even when selected in democratic fashion, was limited to urban elements which by and large had no fundamental interest in pursuing the cause of the oppressed and repressed in the rural areas.

Thus, as the *millet* mechanism failed to resolve the social and economic crisis of the Armenian provinces and a political consciousness evolved among the rural and small-town Armenians, many became aware of the political implication of social and economic stratification. For the rural Armenian, "fatherland" came to replace the "nation" as the central component of Armenian nationalism. By merging with *hayrenasiroutiun* (love of fatherland, patriotism), Armenian nationalism entered a new, more dynamic phase dominated by issues relevant to craftsmen, peasants, and non-skilled workers. Through patriotism, the lower classes asserted the primacy of their own concerns in the determination of national goals beginning in the 1860s. This democratization led to the revolutionary phase of the Armenian liberation movement by the end of the 1880s and the adoption of socialism as the ideology of emancipation. Hayrenasiroutiun was also distinct from *azkasiroutiun*, love of nation. Fatherland implied a geographically defined—however vague the borders of that patria at the time—place; and a geographically defined Armenia had clear political implications.

The nationalism associated with the interests of the dispossessed classes in the provinces acquired additional potency since the laboring Armenian classes were in the Armenian provinces, where most Armenians lived; and what were rural outposts from the perspective of the Ottoman government and the Constantinople Armenian establishment constituted the historic fatherland of the Armenian people. By grounding nationalism in a historically imagined territory, love of fatherland gave the emancipation movement a political legitimacy denied to those whose love was for the abstracted cultural-religious heritage of Armenians, the *azk* or nation.

THE VIEW FROM THE TOP

In the context of the Ottoman Armenian people, the difference between *azkasiroutiun* (love of nation) and *hayrenasiroutiun* (love of fatherland) reflected not only a chronological progression in political thought but also divergent, if not conflicting, class concerns. This was most clearly articulated in the debates which took place in the capital of the Empire, Constantinople. Here, a large Armenian colony, headed by the Patriarch, was given the impossible task of representing all Armenians.

Any political advantage that proximity to the center of power could have offered Armenians in the capital was neutralized by the *amira* class's control over the patriarchate through the seventeenth and eighteenth centuries. The amira class, composed largely of *sarafs* ("money lenders"), high level Armenian bureaucrats, and a few other influential families, dominated the patriarchate.[1] Because of their tight control of the millet structure, the position of all Armenians was identified with that of the saraf.[2]

The outlook of the amira class reflected the concerns of an elite that was successful in the economic sphere but lacked political security. Their financial and often physical well being was dependent on the success of Ottoman officials whose careers or projects they financed. The amiras accepted the definition of Armenians as a religious community represented by a state-imposed church hierarchy. This acceptance or bias was construed as a non-political attitude and, consequently, not subject to any judgement by political standards. For those who championed the cause of the amira class, this "non-political" framework was articulated in the belief that "there was no solution outside the Armenian [Apostolic] Church."[3]

> It has been discussed, and it is undeniable that our people do not have, politically speaking, a national [institution] . . . but we do have an alternative through which our people will survive. The governments ruling over us have been protectors of this [alternative] institution and nucleus of union; to preserve our ethnic identity we do not need a political one. This link is the unity of religion through which all

Armenians are related regardless of their place of residence or of the state of which they are subjects.[4]

By defining the Armenian predicament as one of survival of ethnic identity, it became possible to formulate a political agenda that denied the Armenian people a political future. Political leadership, reduced in form and content, was assigned willingly to the clergy not because there was no political institution, but because there was no need for one. Unity through the Church gave the concept of nation a transcendent dimension and relegated other categories such as class and caste into secondary and expandable dimensions.

The sanctioning of the Church as the only legitimate context within which a commonness could be articulated signaled more than a mere appreciation of an old and quite flexible institution that had managed to survive the destruction of Armenian dynasties. It reflected a general view of society within which existing hierarchies in the economic and social spheres supported each other in the task of using the nation as the necessary but otherwise missing social foundation of conservative institutions.

This view was shared even by the Mekhitarists, the Catholic Armenian order headquartered in Venice and Vienna, who were instrumental in bringing about an Armenian cultural renaissance. Erudite monks from the Mekhitarist centers introduced the Armenian reading public to a large number of European concepts. Inspired by romanticism, they attempted, above all, to give Armenian identity historical roots. Yet the Mekhitarist view of Armenian culture and history had wholesomeness, a harmony which Armenian society lacked. The discrepancy was particularly evident among Armenians in the Ottoman Empire whence most Mekhitarists were recruited and where most of the Congregations' efforts concentrated. The Mekhitarists were most conscious of the cultural backwardness of Armenians and strove to educate and enlighten them. But they were careful not to transform cultural views into political trends. The Europeanization of the Armenian self-image was not intended to be a prelude to the adoption of the Western pattern of a radical-conservative antagonism in the political spectrum. There was to be an evolution in Armenian society, but not necessarily a dialectical one.

The Mekhitarists promoted a history built around heroes and villains, a history which celebrated isolated individuals and events as the embodiment of a glorious yet tragic past. In 1861 the Mekhitarists of Vienna reissued in booklet form an article first published in 1849 when Europe was in turmoil and a few Armenian young men, who studied in Europe at that time, knew that turmoil meant revolution.[5] The major portion of the booklet eulogizes some of the great figures from both Western and Armenian ancient histories. After ascribing the greatness of past heroes to classic patriotism, the author warns against the "abuses of patriotism" then rampant in European capitals. The booklet ends with a special plea to Armenians not to sympathize with these abuses or their perpetrators. To insure against such a possibility, the author defines what patriotism should mean for Armenians of different classes. For those who have wealth and power, "true patriotism" involves helping the less fortunate, respecting the law by not being whimsical, donating funds for the construction of public institutions, and not forgetting that wealth does not release one from the duties and obligations of "good citizenship." Those without money or power, the author of the article asserts,

> must respect the above mentioned [rich] Armenians and honor them as interpreters and executors of the law, as the lieutenants of God. [The lower classes] must have faith in them and must not nurture doubts without good reason. If they note any shortcomings in the upper class, they should not consider them unjust and evil or demean their names in the presence of others. Rather, to the best of their ability, they should cover up for the others' shortcomings and should praise them publicly. Even if they cannot honor the person, they should honor their rank and position, so that the respect for the rule of law is not diminished and law and order are not eroded. Those with average or no means should not be jealous of the rich and should not attempt to imitate the rich in everything the rich do. They should also not expect that the rich give all of their wealth to other causes.[6]

Cultural awakening, then, should not occur at the expense of the preservation of social harmony and national subservience for the benefit of the upper classes and the Ottoman state. Yet the author glorified Armenian historical or mythical figures like Hayk, Aram, Tigran, and Vardan who, according to legend and chroniclers, distinguished themselves by rejecting foreign rule and subjugation to the will of others. The author most likely believed that identification with the past was a sufficient source of pride to obviate the need for emulation. History was introduced to neutralize political aspirations rather than inspire them. In this manner, historical figures were abstracted from their historical reality and then offered to Armenian readers as sources of pride. Acts of heroism, self-sacrifice, and courage were introduced as manifestations of spiritual values rather than tactical means to resolve a political crisis.

MIDDLE CLASS LIBERALISM

By the middle of the nineteenth century the Ottoman Empire was brought within the sphere of the European-dominated world market system. Trade between the Ottoman Empire and the West increased tremendously, although the import of manufactured goods exceeded by far the exports from traditional industries such as dried fruits and rugs. Armenians, along with other largely non-Muslim groups, made up the merchant class that carried out this trade.[7] Gradually, in addition to the comprador bourgeoisie, the new middle class included professionals such as doctors and lawyer; literati such as writers, teachers, and editors; and small manufacturers. These groups had little involvement with tax-farming, the economic basis of the sarafs.

This new middle class began a process of secularization and democratization of Armenian institutions which performed the classical function of liberalization. Yet this middle class lacked the social legitimacy and integration within dominant institutions that the amiras had enjoyed. The economic interests of this class placed them outside the political structure as well as in opposition to it. Political power, which could have guaranteed if not promoted class interests, was not to be found in the Ottoman Empire. Aside from their timid attempts under the Tanzimat ("reforms"), the middle class made no effort to create a political power base. The economic activity of the middle class did not even have any relationship with the Ottoman elite. Thus, this new middle class was deeply alienated from the established Ottoman institutions. To make up for its alienation, the middle class developed greater reliance on the West. Merchants sought their individual economic security through the acquisition of citizenship of Western countries. They also sought to establish social legitimacy by sponsoring a cultural renaissance. Inspiration for such a renaissance came from Europe and demonstrated their inclination to act as cultural mediators.[8]

The cultural-ideological relationship between European and Armenian societies, while based upon unequal economic and political standings, was nonetheless dynamic because of the challenge the West presented to Armenians as a historical entity. The Armenian awakening was predicated by the answers to some basic questions raised by that challenge: Why did such a difference emerge between Asian and European societies? What is the substance of that difference? These seemingly rhetorical questions were asked to legitimize the overriding goals of "progress" and "enlightenment," to be achieved through education, science, learning, industry, and trade. The corollary questions were: How can Armenians close the gap between the two societies? In what political framework can they hope to do so?

The concept of nation was instrumental from the beginning in defining the Western challenge and Armenian responses to it. Certainly, in the 1860s the concept had evolved into more than a gathering of coreligionists. It included *recognition of* civilizational achievements of the past, albeit still devoid of a political context. The past was there to inspire and remind Armenians that they were once able to deal with Europeans as equals, and therefore they could expect the same in the future. The existence of a glorious past gave Armenians the right to recover their dignity. In fact, as early as in 1846 the Constantinople newspaper *Hayasdan* clearly indicated this direction of thought:

> Wake up, Armenian nation, from your death-inviting slumber of ignorance; remember your past glory, mourn your present state of wretchedness and heed the example of other enlightened nations: take care of your schools, cultivate the Armenian language, learn other useful languages and liberal sciences [professions] . . . only then can you reach the goal of happiness.[9]

Liberalism introduced a dynamic concept of nation as opposed to **its** conservative religious definition. Yet enlightenment, the ultimate in individual and social happiness, was perceived to be attainable within the status quo because it was essentially a matter of culture and civilization. One of the chief architects of the national awakening, Servichen, placed the process of change strictly within the confines of the millet structure. He stated in his 1863 opening address to the newly elected National Assembly of the Patriarchate:

Our duty is not only to protect our religion bequeathed to us by our ancestors but also to use all means for the single purpose of developing the national spirit: a spirit which is the lone factor in enlivening the nation and which we will try to reconcile first with the spirit and the course of our times and second with national obligations toward our benevolent government by rejecting foreign intervention.[10]

Nahapet Rusinian (poet, publicist and physician) even considered banning the word "political" from the Armenian language to ensure the proper interpretation of national goals.[11] The best nation, argued a writer following the Zeytoun rebellion, is one which respects the authority of the state and the best defense of people's liberties is obedience to the laws of the land.[12] The cultural definition of a national awakening was shared by most liberals and enthusiasts of education. For instance, the students of the Noubar-Shahnazarian school in Constantinople espoused literature, the most expressive mode of culture, as the ultimate solution: What Armenia needed was "not heroes, but geniuses; it does not need soldiers of arms but soldiers of Light. . . . We will produce Madame de Staels and Lamartines."[14]

In the context of this national awakening, education and literacy became overriding concerns. The National Constitution insisted on free education for all Armenian youth.[14] Societies were also established to educate *bantoukhd*s (migrant workers from the provinces) in Constantinople. They, in turn, were expected to return to their villages and spread literacy there. Literacy was the solution to poverty. The *Parekordzagan* (Benevolent) Society of Constantinople took the more practical step of setting up a model farm in Cilicia through which they educated local farmers in scientific agriculture.

Most Constantinople Armenians were concerned with the goal of bringing education, progress, and enlightenment to the capital. The liberal creed of Armenians there was overwhelmingly an urban one. During a debate on the unequal distribution of deputies in the Armenian Assembly, the respected liberal oriented *Masis*, the newspaper founded and edited by the French educated Garabed Utujian, defended the preeminence of Constantinople:

Constantinople must have priority since, firstly, it is the capital of the state; secondly, it is the center of the national [Armenian] administration. The Patriarch is there, the progressive and educated elements of the nation are there. In one word, the great strength of the nation is there.[15]

In this view, urban dwellers were the only subjects who needed to be educated in order to give substance to the idea of enlightenment. The nation, as understood by Constantinople Armenians, could have prospered in and by itself in the capital. The strength of the nation, based upon the unity of goals such as progress and enlightenment, would be secured when each class accepted its own function in society. According to *Masis*, the upper class was responsible for the care of the poor; the middle class was to submit to and cooperate with the upper class; and the lower class was to accept thankfully what was given to them by the other classes.[16] Unity, the ultimate precondition for happiness, would be achieved when moral and financial virtues were spread.[17]

THE "HAYASDANTSIS"

For a long while the provincial Armenians shared the urban social vision based on communal harmony. Karekin Srvantsdiants, a clergyman who devoted his whole career to the welfare of the rural Armenian population, was hopeful for the future. He believed the common good could be achieved by people caring for each other: the rich helping the poor, the healthy caring for the sick, the older assisting the younger, and the fortunate looking after the unfortunate. He founded his vision on a specific version of "patriotism," however. In 1861 he declared patriotism "the real root of all good," and defined the "good" to be the welfare of the community. He thus pointed out common misconceptions that should be corrected:

> I feel sorrier for those who, although educated, hold the idiotic opinion that one's fatherland is where he was born. . ... They say "Here is our fatherland, where we acquired wealth, where we have properties and inheritances. I must work for this place; I must labor for the education of my children and progress of the city. We owe it to ourselves that our children grow happy. Thank God we have our churches and masses, beautiful sceneries, spots of entertainment, and the means to have a good time. And we feel secure. This is our fatherland, the comfort which we seek."[18]

The criticism of this diasporan mode of thinking and its culture also led to a further distinction between *hayrenasiroutiun* and *azkasiroutiun*. While the first advanced the people as the dominant and dynamic force, the latter focused on the concept of nation as an abstract and timeless entity. Quite early in his career Srvantsdiants pointed out that culture, however enlightened, cannot supplant the love of the fatherland, i.e., a sense of history and of the individuals that assure its continuity. Thus, "true patriotism" required a change in focus:

> Our fatherland is where our history, our heroes and saints are. It is the
> people there that make our fatherland real with their sufferings. It is
> they who need and are worthy of assistance. Had it not been for the
> *hayasdantsi* [native of Armenia], Armenia would have turned by now
> to a thing of the imagination.[19]

Mgrdich Khrimian was instrumental in developing a critical look at urban perceptions and values. Khrimian was a self-taught clergyman born in Van who identified himself with the interests of the provincial Armenians. He began as a teacher and ended his career as Catholicos of All Armenians. As a young teacher he encouraged his students to look at the past, which for him began with the Bible, to legitimize change. The Bible allowed him to be critical of all existing political authority within an accepted framework. Through his student, Srvantsdiants, he asserted: "God did not create the enlightened soul so that it is kept in the dark, and he did not condemn any nation to slavery. Let us become like Adam [in the Bible]."[20] Another one of Khrimian's students proclaimed: "Only national history gives life to dead souls."[21] The student presented a long list of Armenian heroes from Hayk to Tigran; he expected this knowledge to have a liberating effect on all Armenians. Khrimian himself used history effectively to recreate the dilemma of the nation. In an imaginary conversation between a "glory-seeker" and a "patriot," Khrimian presented the quintessential Armenian political issue.

> Glory-seeker: Was it not the patriotic Vardan who got into something
> above his head and caused the death of thousands of young men? The
> Patriot: For the welfare of my people I am willing to sacrifice
> everything. If Armenia had not been covered with the blood of young
> men, the Armenian people would not have blossomed now.[22]

By elevating the welfare of the people above all other considerations, Khrimian began a shift in Armenian political thought—from an abstract nationalism to a concrete populism, although he was not to be the one to articulate the populist program. Much of the implied advice in these discussions was obviously directed at the Armenian leadership in Constantinople; this advice was also not heeded. Gradually it became clear that conflicting interests rather than harmony dominated the Armenian community. By the sixties, the contrast between urban and rural life became a major theme in Armenian journalism. At the height of the debate on the ratification of the National Constitution, Khrimian's Van-based monthly journal published an imaginary dialogue between a city dweller and a peasant. While the article highlighted the importance each group had for the economy and general welfare of society, the primary purpose of the dialogue was to present the case for an equitable—if not proportional— share of seats for provincial Armenians in the National Assembly. To the scorn shown by the urban dweller, the peasant responded, "your laws are like traps in which the poor and the weak peasants are caught. You suck our bloods like spiders through bribery, restrictive measures, prohibitions, and other forms of injustice."[23] In his dialogue, the city was the home of money-seeking hypocrites who professed but did not live by the liberal creed; of a power-hungry clergy; of journalists who were more impressed by the parliamentary rhetoric of Gladstone than the utter poverty and wretchedness of most Armenians surrounding them; and of middle class parvenus who spoke loudly of philanthropy but spent most of their money on dresses—believing, meanwhile, that they had saved the nation by having organized dances.[24]

During the debate on the National Constitution Bishop Khrimian had shared the view that "Constantinople must be the focus of Armenian political power since it is the seat of the Sultan." Nonetheless Khrimian had invited Constantinople Armenians to make Western Armenia the focus of their attention.[25] In 1862, Srvantsdiants was wondering whether any of Khrimian's messages had any value for the millet. In an article in which he discussed the government's torture practices, Srvantsdiants asked:

> Does the government have the right to torture? Of course not. But who is objecting, who is knocking at the government's door? Where are the intermediaries, where are the modern leaders, the leaders of the nation? Thank God we have them, but they are being cautious.[26]

Khrimian made bantoukhds and the provincial masses the focus of his attention. His efforts merely earned him the label *"hayasdantsi vartabed"* or "the priest from Armenia." *Hayasdan* (Armenia) was thus reduced to a locale like so many others.[27] While the label intimated a provincialism unbecoming of urban intellectuals and bourgeoisie, the reduction of Armenia to a mere geographic entity enabled "the enlightened" to regard Constantinople as the proper location for the rebirth of the nation. For Mateos Mamourian, an editor and novelist from Smyrna (Izmir), who once chaired the National Assembly's Executive Committee, nothing should have been expected from the millet leadership anyway, since its leaders were too busy fighting each other.[28]

Nonetheless, for the majority of Armenians in major urban centers the capital city continued to represent "the strength of the nation" while historical Armenia was an alien place. The literati of Constantinople devoted much time to discussing administrative details, resolving conflicts related to churches, charities, and schools. They called their efforts the *azkayin kordz* or the business of the nation.

The program for progress and enlightenment proposed by the literati and the middle class of the capital acquired its legitimacy from contact with European cities and cultures as well as from the conviction that such a program had universal validity. It is not surprising, therefore, that the liberals applied their agenda for attaining enlightenment and progress to the provinces without consideration of the issues raised by the rural Armenians. The inherent values of the ideology and Constantinople Armenians' need for legitimacy became important factors in the belief of the urban liberals that their program provided a fundamental solution to the ills plaguing the rural population.

This belief was further encouraged by the spirit of the Tanzimat which led many to believe the Porte was ready to support essential administrative and judicial reforms. In fact, the Armenian National Assembly in Constantinople, in a daring and imaginative act, elected the *Hayasdantsi* Khrimian as Patriarch. Khrimian began his brief tenure in Constantinople by encouraging provincial Armenians to submit reports on their social and economic problems to the Assembly. They followed his advice. Activist teachers and clergymen in the provinces helped communes articulate grievance-filled reports which poured into Constantinople. Based on these reports, a final study indicated that, in addition to not having benefited in any way from the Tanzimat, provincial Armenians were heading toward economic ruin and suffering increasing social deprivation and dislocation—

a process leading to the disintegration of Armenian collective life in the historic homeland as well as to total dehumanization. The report also made recommendations—to end the obvious inequalities in taxation, justice, and religious intolerance—which, if enacted upon by the Porte, would alleviate the desperate situation. Furthermore, rather than denying the authority of the central government, the report asked the Porte to strengthen its position with regard to provincial governments to guarantee that local officials follow directives sent to them from a capital now interested in reforms.[29]

The Assembly was divided on the question of actually submitting the report to the Ottoman government. Some thought it would invite the Porte to question the loyalty of Armenian leaders, hence affect their privileged position in the capital. At the end, a milder version of the report was presented. Ultimately, it was discarded by the government and conveniently forgotten by the Assembly.[30]

Khrimian also sought, without success, a revision of the National Constitution in order to give provincial Armenians a larger share of representatives in the Assembly. The Constitution had ensured an absolute majority control by the Armenians of Constantinople. The Patriarch realized that without proportional representation the cause of the provinces would be lost. He realized that the Constantinople bourgeoisie acted only in the interest of its own security and perception of Ottoman institutions. Moreover, he fought for the creation of a second, a *kaghakakan* ("civil" or "political") council which would deal specifically with provincial issues. The existing council provided by the Constitution was composed of Constantinople Armenians who interpreted "political" to mean largely non-religious matters, such as schools and orphanages.

Khrimian resigned in 1873. His support of provincial Armenians made him an enemy of many influential Armenians in Constantinople. His enemies accused him of arbitrary rule, hence of opposing the Constitution.[31]

They also charged that Khrimian spent too much money on bantoukhds, neglected the prestige of the Church, diminished the power of Constantinople in favor of the provinces, and supported the cause of the poor and oppressed at the expense of others. His critics disapproved of his closing the prison of the Patriarchate where opponents could be jailed by the order of the Patriarch or the Assembly. They were dismayed at his refusal to use the state police to secure Armenian compliance to millet decisions. Finally, he spoke so much of the conditions and problems of the provinces, remarked an opponent, that he "endangered the nation."[32]

Khrimian's brief term became a test of Armenian liberalism among the middle class. The limitations of that liberalism were clearly exposed by its timid and reluctant approach to the question of reform. By acquiring the privilege of playing democracy in the capital, the Armenian intelligentsia and middle class assumed responsibility for absorbing the shocks of social discontent in the poverty-ridden villages of Western Armenia.

Thus the failure to achieve concrete reforms remained the more fundamental cause for Khrimian's resignation. The expectations that the millet system, however democratically designed, could be used to mediate a change in the structure of the Ottoman state were a subversion of the purpose for which the millet system had originally been established. The temporary enthusiasm of the Assembly in pursuing the cause Khrimian advocated had stretched to the limit whatever ambiguity one could read into the role of the millet. The 1863 Constitution of the Armenian millet spoke eloquently of the rights and responsibilities between the Armenian collective and Armenian individuals, but it disregarded the more essential relationship between the Armenian individual and the Ottoman state while asserting that "in particular circumstances [the Patriarch] is the medium of the execution of the orders of the Ottoman Government" with regard to the millet. The reverse—the right of the Patriarch or the Assembly to represent the interests, and especially the complaints, of Armenians as a collective— was not inherent in the document; it depended on the goodwill or political mood of the Porte.

A BOURGEOIS NATION

The urban enlightened continued the quest to reconcile its ideology of progress with the difficulties inherent in the situation. They believed a solution was on hand when Western powers temporarily assumed the sponsorship of reform in the Ottoman Empire through the Treaty of Berlin in 1878. Confident that the Ottoman state could be coerced into implementing reforms in the Armenian provinces, the usually timid liberal Armenian community poised to lead the reforms; after all, no other segment of the people was better equipped to apply European concepts among Armenians.

While a number of writers expressed reservations with regard to the usefulness of Article 61 of that treaty prescribing the reforms in the Armenian provinces, others wanted to see in it the ultimate opportunity for the realization of the liberal political program. The most important and effective spokesmen for that position were Patriarch Nerses Varjabedian and Bishop Maghakia Ormanian. Varjabedian had a vested interest in presenting the result of the Congress of Berlin (and at San Stefano before that) as a success: after all, he was responsible for undertaking the Armenian diplomatic initiatives toward Russia, first, and then the Great Powers. Ormanian was a highly educated, concerned, and ambitious clergyman. Soon after the Treaty of Berlin was signed, the two clergymen put forth a vision which constituted a close approximation to a bourgeois program of nation-building. In lectures and booklets they argued that the international concern for Armenia assured a rush toward the exploitation of its natural resources. Varjabedian was convinced that British capital would soon invade Western Armenia. The immediate task of the nation was to ensure that Armenian capital from coastal cities and Europe gained ownership and control of resources in Armenia and, by bringing progress and enlightenment, assure a better life for all. The nation was invited to send to Armenia its best industrialists and doctors, teachers and preachers, financiers and bankers. Capital and culture, until then viewed as Western commodities, were to be Armenianized to achieve what the diplomacy of begging had started.[33]

Ormanian emphasized the need for social harmony if the program is to succeed. Unity became the panacea for the problems of an inherently impotent institutional structure.[34] Ormanian argued that the Church was best equipped to bring about that unity.[35] He further argued that Armenianism should begin to break away from an abstract, intellectual context, and the promised reforms provided that opportunity. "If a person is inspired by the question of reforms," he stated in a lecture, "he would not consider it below him to labor [in Armenia], he would not consider it worthless to do commerce there or help the arts [crafts] flourish, or be a landlord and landowner there."[36] Ormanian developed his ideas further in a lecture in 1880 on the responsibilities of the youth. He urged provincial

Armenian youth to learn reading and other technical skills. But it was important that Armenians do the teaching because, he argued, if the Europeans did it, they alone would benefit from it. Ormanian exhorted, "Those who know how to establish their interests in that land . . . the land will know how to reward its benefactor. Blessed are those who will be the first to undertake that task, since not only will they have given content to patriotism and be praised for it, but also because they will reap the profits of their endeavors and labors."[37]

Except for a few highly motivated teachers, history does not record an influx of capital or of men to the provinces, neither Armenian nor British— not until the revolutionaries. The waning of Western concern and increase in Ottoman oppression produced only a loss of interest in the provinces among the liberals. The capital community finally made its peace with the Porte when the Patriarchate and the Assembly agreed not to meddle in affairs which were outside the state's sanctioned jurisdiction. Thus, the millet leadership could present *takrirs* ("petitions") regarding churches and monasteries, but not political matters.[38] The Assembly expressed its intention to remain within its prescribed limits by requesting that Ottoman censors cease the publication of the Constantinople-based newspaper *Meghou*. The editors of this maverick newspaper had dared to criticize the Assembly for its inaction regarding the status of Armenians in the provinces.[39]

THE POLITICIZATION OF CULTURE

The ethnic identity of Armenians in the provinces was rooted in the historic land on which they lived. The residents of Van did not need to labor at cultural edifices or intellectual definitions to assert a link between themselves and history. Dead heroes and living legends served to integrate the physical environment of mountains, valleys, and rivers into the cultural environment that included ancient fortresses and medieval monasteries. The peasants' link to the land of Armenia was neither culturally inspired nor politically negotiable. Rather, it represented the most basic relationship between man and nature. The land was their source of livelihood, just as it had been for their ancestors throughout the centuries. This identity was not, therefore, in and by itself an acceptance or rejection of Ottoman rule, just as

Armenians' attachment to the land was neither a threat to nor a confirmation of Ottoman territorial integrity.

The politics of rural people revolved around survival, which hinged on the basics of land, water, harvest, and taxation. The goal of the peasantry was to create an environment where the preservation of traditional norms was possible as well as desirable for each successive generation and where change was manageable. All else was judged within this context. Irrelevant national or international politics were reduced to legend. Legends included words uttered by kings and foreign potentates, words which were adjusted instantly into local terminology. These legends were measured against accepted local wisdom, which was ready to analyze and amplify the significance of events that had relevance to their own affairs. Whether there to oppress or to assist, the outsider had to adjust to the world of the peasant and, to some extent, become a part of it. Culture had meaning only if understood in the widest social sense. As such, it could not be removed or alienated from politics through bureaucratic or legal definitions.

The religious-ethnic definition of the Armenian, imposed by the Ottoman system and glorified in the capital, had not really pervaded the depths of consciousness of Armenians in the provinces. To be sure, the millet was still the structure through which civil matters were formally regulated; Armenians continued to adjust to and explain in this context the routine policies and daily practices of the ruling Ottomans. But in the provinces, especially in those areas with the least amount of formal cultural development, political-economic oppression meant cultural oppression. The corollary was also true. Cultural enlightenment was understood as political change; cultural pride was not dissociated from political self-respect. The middle class and clergy, on the other hand, continued to believe that culture, economy, and politics were distinct activities as alien from each other as their professions often were from the course of Ottoman policies and developments. The provincial Armenian, totally dependent on domestic laws, practices, and conditions, could not afford such delusions. The patriotism of the Armenian peasant and town dweller (who often lived not so distant from rural life), consisted of a simple attachment to a land invested with historical and spiritual significance. Patriotism was a natural part of their identity. The new, culture-laden *azkasiroutiun* of

Constantinople had been a distortion of the patriotism, *hayrenasiroutiun*, of the provinces.[40]

This patriotism was injured before and after the Russo-Turkish War of 1878. Fires of suspicious origin destroyed the Armenian market sectors in a number of cities, including that of Van in 1876. Confiscation of Armenian land by Turks and Kurds became a common occurrence in the Diarbekir and Van provinces. But it was the war itself that most devastated the economy and fueled the patriotism of provincial Armenians. Ottoman armies passed through Armenian provinces as if the latter were being conquered anew. The armies destroyed crops, treated civilians cruelly, and made extraordinarily harsh demands for provisions which turned a requisitions policy into officially organized looting. Western Armenians were filled less with the celebrated sympathies toward the Russian armies than with outrage against the Ottoman soldiers. It was as if the Ottoman state sought to punish the Christian Armenians for the sins of Balkan peoples.

It was to these devastated people that a few urban liberals such as Mgrdich Portukalian and Mardiros Sareian came to speak of enlightenment, progress, and national pride following the Treaty of Berlin. Their words could be absorbed by the rural population only in the context of its own, yet unarticulated, political agenda. Consequently, as soon as Western pressure decreased, the Porte adopted a policy of systematic repression under the aegis of Sultan Abdul-Hamid II. Sultan Abdul-Hamid II lacked the commitment to social and political reforms that some of his predecessors had. He perceived his role primarily as the embattled ruler of a once-powerful empire now threatened by foreign encroachments. The millions of subjects of different religious and ethnic backgrounds whose welfare depended on his policies were significant only in relation to the higher and narrower goal of the survival of his state and the preservation of the status quo. He was open to modernization in those areas which strengthened the army and the power of the state. Thus the government was extremely sensitive to any signs which might have signaled the rise of a political consciousness among Armenians. It therefore established strict censorship on all publications and scrutinized the activities and words of any element that might have given independent articulation to Armenian discontent.

Ultimately, the efforts of the government backfired. Its attempts to prevent the politicization of culture through the suppression of culture radicalized discontent. Names of historical figures such as former kings, once devoid of any emotional charge, acquired political significance when uttered against the laws of censorship. Ordinary people were transformed into heroes and martyrs for having used words such as *azadoutiun* (freedom). For the new heroes, the act of imprisonment, exile, or torture by a hated government became more ingratiating than the original infraction of the law.

Eventually, these incidents acquired a historical significance. But in the eighties they were still isolated cases which no one interpreted as the beginning of a revolution. Nonetheless, at that time it was clear that the situation in the Armenian provinces was rapidly deteriorating and the community was threatened on many fronts. In a long and bitter piece of correspondence to Mateos Mamourian in November 1883, Bishop Karekin Srvantsdiants, who once dissuaded his compatriots from converting to Russian orthodoxy to secure protection, noted:

> Although it is the compatriots in Agn who do not let me leave, the state of national affairs in Constantinople and confused situation on the roads also are considerations in my decision to stay here a while longer. Let conferences, plenipotentiaries, 16ers and 61ers [reference to those supporting Article 16 of the Treaty of San Stefano and Article 61 of the Treaty of Berlin] give and take, let writers and editors beat their drums without coming to their senses, without recognizing the ones who are actually pulling the strings and watching them fight, and without realizing who is in fact benefiting from the noise we are making. We see the paths of the foreigners and follow them, although our purpose is to reach our fatherland. The path of the foreigner leads to the city of the foreigner; yet we get there, we get tied down there, and then we tell our nation that that is the path to the fatherland. Even more amazing are those who knew the foreigner well and used to point out its traps to the nation, warning us to run away; those same [individuals] are sitting today in the halls of congress [of the foreigner] as agents from within and from without. There is no need to write their names; the ones who were close to you, you know well; the ones at a distance you called them glory-seekers. How many have we seen of the devoted who turned devotees of profit and glory, self-denying and

patriotic ones who, in the name of the Armenian Question, sought personal benefit and glory; those who secured their cuts from the funds collected for the starving only declare themselves benevolent; those who opened schools for the benefit of their relatives and, having robbed the nation through fundraising, closed down the schools, leaving to the nation only the blame for their own acts and the deficit of their spending. They planted a Catholicos in Sis [The Cilician Catholicosate] and now are forcing the fruits of that action down the throat of the nation; they assign the glory of Zion to the Patriarch [of Jerusalem], but his debt to the nation. The prelates they have assigned to the largest sees, the nuncios and directives they forwarded have resulted in parishes and districts that remain unattended and in people subject to oppression; a number of Armenians are rotting in prison, others are trampled upon by bandits; these [Armenians] are denied protection since speaking on their behalf and supplication are being left unanswered by the *parekhnam* ["the one who takes good care," benefactor—an adjective used for the Sultan]. Fallen materially and exhausted spiritually, times such as this I do not believe Armenians have had to endure. The wheel of 61 turns in many directions and some of the children are running behind it, falling in ditch after ditch. The wheel is turning North. Finally, the Catholicos [of Etchmiadzin] too has decided to act [but] the commotion on that subject is meaningless. The murderous and roaming tribes from Russia are filling the Armenian province on this side; Armenians, cut off from the land and from the hope of land, are forced out . . .[41]

Beyond the hopelessness it conveys, the letter suggests a relationship between corruption in community institutions and inadequacy at the diplomatic level. Most importantly, it constitutes a summary of the criticism directed toward the liberal program of the Armenian middle class from the perspective of provincial Armenians and a few urban radicals.

By 1881 the right of Constantinople to lead Armenians was challenged radically. Arsen Tokhmakhian, a student who toured the provinces and published his thoughts, reasoned:

The Western intelligentsia is in Constantinople. They are fine people, writers and rhetoricians. But they are living in an imaginary world. They are solely concerned with the Patriarchate and the National Assembly. They declare each other great men and geniuses. But what have they done to deserve those adjectives?[42]

Khrimian and the provincial intelligentsia of the sixties and seventies were unable to shed their original belief in goodwill and benevolence inspired by an unadulterated Christianity. Others were more willing to project the existing conflicts and divisiveness into the past and learn new lessons. Tokhmakhian argued that a cohesive, undifferentiated, and idealized history that failed to relate the desperate present to the distant and glorified past was an obstacle to a clear vision of the future:

> Ancient Armenians have never lived, never ruled as one nation, as children of one fatherland. They were divided into many tribes which eroded each other's strength in incessant struggles. ... The turning point at which one can speak of an all-national idea came when the nakharar [nobility] and dynastic houses were eradicated from within, leaving behind the sorry consequences which are still with us...[43]

Tokhmakhian too wanted to glorify Armenians, but he had a different group in mind:

> What has kept our nation going is the working class, not religion. It is the nation that has kept religion, and suffered because of it; while the Church was unable to keep the old colonies, the peasant was able to preserve the nation. ... I beg you to turn your attention to and study all aspects of the life of the peasants who constitute the root of nationhood; [I beg you] to know him and the world in which he lives, which is called fatherland.[44]

It was obvious that by the early 1880s the Armenian millet, the Ottoman state, and Western powers had failed to fulfill their promise of reform for the majority of Armenians living on their historic lands. While the search for alternative strategies began earnestly with the founding of the newspaper *Armenia* in Marseilles by Mgrdich Portukalian, a shift in political terminology had already taken place. Patriotism had come to signify a whole range of new problems. The role of nationalism itself, and therefore its historical value, had changed toward a radical direction.

---

1. H. M. Ghazarian, "Arevmtyan Hayastan" [Western Armenia] in *Hay Zhoghovrdi Patmoutyoun* [History of the Armenian People], Ds. B. Aghayan, et al., eds., (Yerevan, 1964) V, pp. 20-25; also, by the same author, *Arevmtahay sotsial-tntesakan katsutyounu 1800-1870 tt* [The socio-economic condition of Western Armenians during 1800-1870]

(Yerevan, 1967), pp. 377-378; Sarkis Atamian, *Armenian Community: The Historical Development of a Social and Ideological Conflict* (New York, 1955), pp. 29-30.

2. Louise Nalbandian, *The Armenian Revolutionary Movement: The Development of Armenian Political Parties through the Nineteenth Century* (Berkeley and Los Angeles, 1967), pp. 43-45; Mikayel Varantian, *Haygagan sharzhman nakhabadmoutiun* [Prehistory of the Armenian movement] (Geneva, 1913), II, pp. 73-94.

3. Garnik Gouzalian, *Hay kaghakagan mtki zarkatsoumu yev H. H. Dashnaktsoutiunu* [The development of Armenian political thought and the A. R. Federation) (Paris, 1927), p. 42. In Eastern Armenia, Sedrak Manandian expressed the same view: "How should we cover it up? We are all fanatic lousavorchagans [members of the Apostolic Church]; we consider Armenianism and the creed of the Lousavorich as one, since that is our national peculiarity;" quoted in Gouzalian, p. 87. See also Mikayel Varantian, *Haygagan sharzhman nakhabadmoutiun* (Geneva, 1912), I, pp. 287-291.

4. H. Chamourjian-Teroyents in *Erevak* (Constantinople, 1861), no. 109.

5. H., *Khosk vasn hayrenasiroutyan* [Discourse on Patriotism] 5 (Vienna, 1862).

6. Ibid., pp. 23-24. In other publications the Mekhitarists expressly criticized Balkan and Italian national movements as well, and, generally speaking, democratic tendencies in political movements. See also Ghazarian, "Arevmtahay hasarakakan hosankneru" [Western Armenian social currents] in *Hay Zhoghovrdi Patmoutyoun*, V, p. 428.

7. A. J. Sussnitzki, "Ethnic Division of Labor" in Charles Issawi, ed., *The Economic History of the Middle East, 1800-1914* (1967), pp. 114-125; Stanford J. Shaw and Ezel K. Shaw, *History of the Ottoman Empire and Modern Turkey* (London, New York, Melbourne, 1977), II, pp. 242, 244.

8. See, for example, James Etmekjian, *The French Influence on the Western Armenian Renaissance, 1843-1915* (New York, 1964); Nalbandian, pp. 32-34.

9. *Hayasdan* (Constantinople), July 27, 2846. See also V. Ghukasian, "Arevmtahay lusavorichneru yev *Hayastan* tertu" (The Western Armenian Enlighteners and the Newspaper *Hayastan*), *Banber Yerevani Hamalsarani*, 2 (1969), pp. 214-224. The concept of national development as a prerequisite for progress is also discussed by Guzalian, p. 59.

10. Varantian, II, p. 6.

11. Ibid., p. 66.

12. Dj. Aramian, *Zeytountsik yev lousavorchagan hayk* [The People of Zeytoun and Apostolic Armenians] (Constantinople, 1867).

13. Varantian, II, p. 261.

14. Avedis Sanjian, *The Armenian Communities in Syria under Ottoman Dominion* (Cambridge, 1965), pp. 40-41.

15. *Masis*, July 5, 1861.

16. Ibid., December 31, 1859.

17. Ibid.

18. Karekin Srvantsdiants, "Hayrenasiroutiun yev hayrenik" [Patriotism and fatherland] in *Ardzvi Vasbouragan*, 3(1861), p. 92.

19. Ibid., pp. 93-94.

20. *Ardzvi Vasbouragan*, 1 (1862).

21. Ibid.

22. Ibid., 10(1862), pp. 289-308.

23. Ibid. pp. 289-308.

24. Much of satirist Hagop Baronian's writings depict not only the superficiality of the claims of westernization of an essentially "oriental" community in Constantinople, but also the use of that claim to ignore the appeals of Armenians in the provinces.

25. *Ardzvi Vasbouragan*, 1(1857), pp. 1-3.

26. Ibid., 3(1862-63), p. 79.

27. Khrimian Hayrig complained that the Armenians of Constantinople knew more about Europe than about Armenia; see Saroukhan, *Haykakan khuntirn yev azgayin sahmanadroutiunu* [The Armenian Question and the National Constitution] (Tiflis, 1912), p. 61. An 1850 geography textbook has scant reference to elements of Armenia's geography in a general chapter on Asia; Agheksander Vardapet Baljian, *Ashkharhakroutiun yev hrahanks* [Geography and Exercises], (Vienna, 1850), pp. 123-134.

28. Rouben Berberian, "Hay masonnere yev 'ser' otyagu Bolso mech" [Armenian masons and the "Love" Lodge in Constantinople], *Hairenik Monthly* 5 (1937): 80-81. The novelist Raffi thought the National Constitution was a weapon in the hands of the Ottoman government to distract Armenians from their real problems; see his *Amboghchakan Gortser*, (Yerevan, 1958, IX, p. 263.

29. Varantian, II, 50-63. For a detailed presentation of this report, see Lilian Etmekjian, "The Armenian National Assembly of Turkey and Reform," *Armenian Review*, 1 (1976), pp. 38-40.

30. L. Etmekjian, pp. 42-43.

31. The charges of anti-constitutional behavior were leveled against Khrimian when he based some of his actions on the "spirit rather than the

letter of the Constitution." The patriarch's resignation speech included the response to the charge: "The pages of the Constitution are even gentler than the petals of a rose; if you handle them rudely, they will fall apart. ... I want to embrace the Constitution, but I do not want to press it so hard as to strangle it."

32. Hayk Ajemian, *Hayots Hayrik* (Tiflis, 1929), p. 452.

33. Berberian, pp. 158-160.

34. The lecture was printed in booklet form under the title *Mioutiun hayoutyan* [Unity of Armenians] (Constantinople, 1879). The lecture was delivered in Scutari, for the Grtasirats Mioutiun, or Education Society.

35. Ibid., pp. 24-38.

36. Ibid., pp. 39-42.

37. The lecture was delivered in Constantinople on February 24 and published the same year as *Hay yeritasartoutian* [To the Armenian Youth], p. 39.

38. Rafik Hovannisian, *Arevmtahay azgayin-azatagrakan sharzhoumneru yev Karini "Pashtpan Hayreniats" kazmakerpoutyounu* [Western Armenian Liberation Movements and the "Defenders of the Fatherland" organization of Karin (Erzerum)] (Yerevan, 1965), p. 205. The instruction was given in 1880. Reporting that the Porte would no longer accept takrirs on provincial Armenians, the satirist Hagop Baronian wrote: "I suggest that a letter be forwarded to Kurds to inform them that henceforth they should spare our property, our lives, and our honor and violate only our religion." See Baronian's *Amboghdjakan gordser* (1962-1977), IV, pp. 447-448.

39. Berberian, p. 125.

40. This explains, at least in part, the unusually enthusiastic reception in the provinces accorded the adoption of a National Constitution in 1863. The Bolsetsis knew what they were getting; the provincials did not make the necessary distinctions between millet and state to avoid disappointment. Rafik Hovannisian, p. 220; Ajemian, p. 556; Ardag Tarpinian, *Hay azadakragan sharzhman oreren* [From the days of the movement for Armenian liberation] (Paris, 1947), p. 118.

41. Srvantsdiants to Mamourian, November 1, 1883; in *Divan hayots patmoutyan*, G. Aghanian, ed., (Tiflis, 1915), Xm, pp. 451-454.

42. Arsen Tokhmakhian, *Hayreniki pahandjneru yev hay goughatsin* [The needs of the fatherland and the Armenian peasant] (Tiflis, 1881), p. 7.

43. Arsen Tokhmakhian, *Masis lerneri haravayin storotner* [The southern slopes of the Masis mountains] (Tiflis, 1882), eBook 1, pp. 21-23.

44. Tokhmakhian, *Hayreniki pahandjneru...*, pp. 60-61.

2

SOVIET ARMENIA

1979

This paper was prepared for a conference on the South Caucasus that convened on May 15, 1979. The conferences was co-sponsored by the Kennan Institute for Advanced Russian Studies and the US International Communications Agency and took place at the Wilson Center in Washington DC.

The idea of such a conference, the first ever in the US capital at least, belonged to then President Jimmy Carter's National Security Advisor, Zbigniew Brzezinski, who was also the convener of the event. Being an Eastern European scholar himself, born in Warsaw, Poland, Brzezinski was much more familiar with the nationalities question within the USSR. Others, scholars, diplomats, and experts, were familiar with the history and politics of Eastern European countries, but much less of Armenia, Azerbaijan and Georgia. US politicians even less so.

The conference was organized, in fact, to familiarize US congressmen, their aides, and officials in various bodies in the executive branch with the neglected region. The South Caucasus republics, along with the Central Asian ones, were considered irrelevant, often referred to as Russia and their inhabitants Russians. Brzezinski wanted the US Government to know the differences in nationalities, however small, and the political and strategic significance of such differences in the future.

There were seven speakers. Anaïde Ter-Minassian, from Paris, covered Armenia with this author; Ronald Suny covered Georgia; and Audrey Altstadt and Tadeusz Swietochowski covered Azerbaijan. For some reason, most of the questions from the audience following the presentations were related to Armenia and Armenians.

The conference organizer was Paul Henze, Brzezinski's deputy. As the reader will note, my paper referred to the rise of anti-Turkish national sentiment in Soviet Armenia. At the end of my presentation, Henze asked me the following interesting question: It is clear that Moscow is encouraging anti-Turkish Armenian nationalism; should not Moscow be concerned that some day Armenian nationalism may be turned into anti-Soviet nationalism? I was ready to answer many questions, and I did. But I was not ready for this one. As Dashnaktsakans, members and sympathizers, we had only recently moved from the anti-Soviet to the anti-Turkish camp.

I met Paul Henze again by chance 25 years later. Neither of us had forgotten the question. The course of history had made it impossible for us to forget it.

History showed, also, that many of the other themes covered in this paper continued to be relevant. The question of Karabakh is the most prominent among them. Most significantly, history revealed that the switch from anti-Soviet to anti-Turkey executed by the Dashnaktsoutiun had, among reasonable explanations, some that were less than respectable.

Eastern Armenia formally entered the Soviet Union in 1922, a year after the dissolution of the post-First World War independent republic. Soviet Armenia is the smallest of the constituent republics of the USSR (30,000 km^2). It has a population of 2.5 million, 88.6% of which is Armenian. This represents only 62% of the total Armenian population of the USSR, however. Another million, or 26% of the 3.5 million total, live within the jurisdictions of Georgia and Azerbaijan, largely concentrated in major cities or historically Armenian districts. The remaining 350,000 are scattered across Soviet territories outside the Caucasus. In all, Armenians constitute 1.5% of the Soviet population.[1]

Along with the other Soviet peoples, Soviet Armenians have lived through the trials and tribulations that have characterized the history of the USSR since its birth: civil war and famine, forced collectivization and a rapid pace of industrialization, the Stalinist purges, and great losses during the Second World War. Throughout many centuries of cohabitation, furthermore, they have shared with other Caucasian peoples political and military misfortunes that befell the region, as well as cultural traits which have transcended frequent antagonisms. Finally, for the century and a half that the region has been part of a Russian empire, and Armenian political thought and intellectual development have followed closely those in Russia.

These general comments serve to set the framework within which Soviet Armenia's history has evolved. Yet the understanding of the problems facing its people requires consideration of the peculiarities of the Armenian case: the consciousness of a political and cultural past forged over millennia; a history closely linked with the territory and people of the larger portion of the historical homeland, Western Armenia, now Eastern Turkey; the burden of that history placed on the survivors and descendants of the First World War Genocide that depopulated Western Armenia; the existence of a large Diaspora both inside and outside the Soviet Union, all of which is compounded by the realization that because of its small size, what is left of the Armenians might be unable to survive as a cultural unit.

Hence, Armenian perceptions of a Soviet Armenian state are based on the evaluation of the degree to which the current status constitutes a rampart against cultural assimilation, and the degree to which it can bring the Armenian people as a whole closer to the goal of political and cultural survival, the two being mutually-reinforcing.

There is justification in the often-made assertions that the Sovietization of the republic provided the best available defense against pan-Turanian imperialism and Turkish expansionism, which in 1920 could have resulted in the decimation of the Eastern Armenian population as well; and that six decades of association with the USSR have provided the material means for a small land to develop a diversified modern economy, and the conditions for its people to develop culturally and acquire a decent standard of living.

Indeed, the economic development of Soviet Armenia has been impressive, even by Soviet standards. Whereas the average increase in production in the USSR has been 113-fold between 1913 and 1973 (117-fold in the RSFSR), Soviet Armenia's production has multiplied 222 times.[2] The unified Transcaucasian energy chain has secured a steady supply of energy for the growing needs of the republic.[3] And participation in the economic development of the Soviet Union has allowed diversification, and provided markets which would have been otherwise difficult to acquire.

The rate of urbanization has been equally dramatic. Compared to a 10% urban population in 1931, 59% of Soviet Armenia's people now live in cities, slightly higher than the all-Union average of 56%. Furthermore,

Soviet Armenia has one of the highest rates in the USSR of workers in the sciences, and in professions with higher education.[4] One might also add that the Armenian SSR has posted a 41% increase in its population between the most recent census years, 1959 and 1970. The average of 3.72% annual increase constitutes the fourth highest in the USSR.

Gradual progress has also been marked in the cultural realm since de-Stalinization. The quantitative increase in printed material has been accompanied by the tackling of wider and somewhat more liberal themes by artists and writers. The Soviet Armenian language has been gradually cleared of common words transferred from the Russian. Equally significant is the fact that during the last two intercensal years, of all the major ethnic groups in the USSR, the rate of increase in the use of the mother tongue as a first language was highest among Armenians (1.5%).

More important, perhaps, has been the more permissive attitude toward the attempts in Soviet Armenia to reintegrate the Soviet Armenian experience with the Armenian past. An early measure in this respect came in 1956, when the Soviet government allowed the election of a Catholicos of All Armenians—the Supreme spiritual head of the Armenian national church—to the vacant see at Etchmiadzin in the Armenian SSR. Vazgen I, Catholicos since then, has enjoyed a wider berth of movement and easier access to his people than was allowed since 1921.

Similarly, in 1965, on the fiftieth anniversary of the Genocide of 1915, there were subdued official commemorations in the capital, Yerevan, and a monument was erected near the city in memory of the victims. Since then, republican leaders have institutionalized government participation in this most symbolic and emotional of Armenian ceremonies each April 24. In recent years, the new First Secretary of the Communist Party of Armenia, Karen Demirchyan, has led the official delegations and masses of marchers to the monument.

Since 1956, references to places, events and people tied to the history of Western Armenia have abounded in Soviet Armenian literature. Historians have dwelled at length on the human and political consequences of the Genocide. They have also taken guarded steps in rehabilitating selected moments from the Armenian Liberation Movement against the Ottoman Empire before the First World War, ignored until now because it was led by parties which communists have always regarded as nationalists and competitors for their leading role before the Revolution.

Nevertheless, the changes described above have not dispelled the more critical view of the Soviet Armenian state. It has been equally valid to assert, for example, that Sovietization has forced Armenia back into an orbit where an independent pursuit of national interests is impossible; that the degree of autonomy allowed has been conditional upon decisions made in Moscow; and that, finally, Armenian culture has fallen in danger to being subsumed by the dominant Russian one.

> The fear of loss of national identity is even more real in Armenia than in other Soviet republics. Despite the many achievements, and underlying the statistical evidence, loom phenomena which have created apprehensions within official and non-official circles alike.[5] The high rate of population growth and the large increase in the number of those using Armenian as a first language are due primarily to immigration from other Soviet republics and the Diaspora. In fact, since 1928, the birthrate among Armenians has declined steadily from 56 to 22.1 per thousand in 1970.[6] Also, of the fourteen non-Russian "Union Republic" nationalities, Armenians rank lowest in their preference for marital endogamy within their own republic.[7]

Furthermore, the continuing creation of a Soviet Diaspora presents further problems. Although 97.7% of the Armenians in the republic use their mother tongue as a first language, only 71.5% of those in the province of Rostov do so, and 35.5% in Moscow. When one realizes that there are as many Armenians with higher education living outside as there are inside the republic—the trend among Armenian professionals, unlike the Georgians, is to move where opportunities arise—then the future of that Soviet Diaspora becomes more problematic. Most communities outside the Republic lack facilities for the preservation of the Armenian language and culture. Also, for reasons of cultural and political nationalism in Georgia and Azerbaijan, existing Armenian educational institutions have become subject to severe local pressures. Both neighboring republics, as seen earlier, account for large and old communities.

The USSR is the heir of the Russian Empire, and as it was during tsarist times, Russian is the *lingua franca* of the Soviet Union. To a large extent this is natural, given demographic and geographic realities. More than at any given time, however, opportunities for recognition and promotion on the all-Union level require the use of Russian for most professions, while economic interdependence growing out of regional imbalances in natural and manpower resources mandate the universalization of values consecrated in Moscow. Yet the fear of loss of national identity, presaged by the use of Russian as a first language, is more than an unavoidable complement to industrialization. Rather, it is a matter of conscious policy, pursued through administrative changes in educational laws and an increasingly open campaign for the more efficient teaching and widespread use of Russian.[8] As is well known, the draft submitted for final approval of the new Constitution of the Armenian SSR deleted the provision in the previous law which recognized Armenian as the official language of the Republic. The language provision was reinstated in the new Constitution (1978) only after massive demonstrations occurred against a similar Proposal in Tbilisi for the Georgian SSR.[9] Even then, the new law provides for the "protection" of Russian and other languages within the Republic (Article 72).

While the fear of assimilation seems real, it is not regarded as clear a shortcoming in Soviet policy as the status of Armenians in the Autonomous Republic of Nakhichevan and the Autonomous Province of Nagorno-Karabakh. Both were historically Armenian districts. The first continues to have a small minority of Armenians while the second has an 80% Armenian majority. These districts were causes of war between the Armenian and Azeri republics prior to Sovietization.

In 1921, with Soviet control of the Caucasus in the balance and relations with Turkey at a critical point, the Soviet Russian government ceded both districts to the Azeri Republic. This, despite a 1920 decision by the Soviet Azeris to return these districts to Soviet Armenia.[10] Armenians have consistently charged that Azerbaijani authorities have pursued a policy of cultural oppression, economic discrimination, and ethnic depopulation against their Armenian inhabitants.[11] It is reported that in 1962 a petition signed by Nakhichevan Armenians detailing specific charges was sent to Secretary N. Khrushchev, with no apparent results.

Similarly, discriminatory practices reached such proportions in Karabakh that in 1969, Soviet Armenian leaders were reportedly in Moscow to register their complaint and request the incorporation of the district in the Armenian SSR. Their request was denied.[12] In 1975, many Armenians were ousted from the Communist Party in Karabakh, or imprisoned on charges of nationalist agitation contrary to "the principles of Leninist friendship of peoples and proletarian internationalism."[13] Having silenced all local opposition to the *status quo*, authorities in Karabakh and Azerbaijan declared the issue resolved to the satisfaction of all concerned.[14]

These declarations, printed in an official publication and including derogatory statements toward the Armenian SSR, prompted one of Soviet Armenia's most respected novelists, Sero Khanzatyan, to dispatch a letter of protest and indignation to L. I. Brezhnev. Khanzatyan, a member of the Communist Party since 1943, reminded Brezhnev that "nothing hinders the development and strengthening of the solidarity between proletarian classes more than injustice against a people." He reiterated the demand for the return of Karabakh in the name of the same principles which had been called upon to justify the current situation. A commentary which accompanied a copy of the letter to the Diasporan press asserted that the systematic policy of forcing Armenians to leave the region through social, economic and other forms of oppression is tantamount to genocide according to the definition in the U.N. Convention on Genocide, to which the USSR is a signatory. The unknown author further revealed that according to an official survey, Armenians in Karabakh wanted nothing more than to see their land under the jurisdiction of the Armenian SSR.[15]

Armenian territorial aspirations have been even more evident against the Republic of Turkey. These entail Turkey's eastern provinces, which were once inhabited by Armenians, and where a large number of Soviet Armenians trace their roots. Soviet permissiveness toward the manifestation of strong feelings on this issue by symbolic gestures has been counter-balanced by an actual policy of improving relations with Turkey. Only twice in Soviet history, in 1917 and 1945-6, have leaders of that state come close to reviving the historical antagonism between Russia and Turkey. The more consistent pattern has been to win the trust and friendship of Turkey through continued assurances of non-aggressive purposes and economic assistance. Whether this policy has been pursued in order to discourage Turkish alliances with the West, or to accommodate the sizable number of Turkic peoples within its borders, the fact remains that Soviet policy has in no way reflected the expectations of one of its constituent peoples, the Armenians, that reparations be made for the human, material, and territorial losses suffered during the First World War.

Unusual manifestations of Armenian nationalism in Soviet Armenia can be seen as the expected outbursts of long-repressed hopes which are being externalized, but not reflected in actual policy. Such an outburst occurred in 1965 when the official commemoration of the fiftieth anniversary of the Genocide was interrupted by young demonstrators in Yerevan. They demanded action "to recover their lands" rather than ceremonies to honor the victims.[16] It is probable that the major reason for the removal that year of Y. N. Zarobyan as first secretary of the CP of Armenia was due to his inability to prevent and deal effectively with these demonstrations.[17]

Subsequently, illegal activities have carried on. In 1969, 1970, and 1973-74, Soviet Armenian courts tried, convicted, and imprisoned a number of activists— grouped under a "National United Party"—for having advocated the idea of a united and independent Armenia, and for having formed cells to achieve their goal.[18] Three of the leading members of that group were executed by a firing squad in January 1979 after a secret and unpublicized trial in Moscow. They were charged with having planted an explosive in a subway of that city two years ago.[19]

To achieve a *modus vivendi* between official policy and Armenian aspirations, however, as a general rule, the Soviet state has relied on bureaucratic methods of oppression, rather than the massive violence of the past. Still, the Soviet government has difficulty in determining the extent and form of nationalism that is considered harmless. Hence, it has not hesitated to press the full power of the state against such manifestations it considers threatening. There has been a barrage of criticism aimed at Armenian chauvinism, nationalistic tendencies, and disregard for Marxist-Leninist principles in the interpretation of Armenian history. The guardians of the faith have not spared writers and artists who have deviated from the norms of "socialist realism."[20]

Others have been subjected to varying forms of censorship and silence. The interesting fact regarding this latest wave of repression against intellectuals is that the works of its victims have displayed more humanism than nationalism. Moreover, a half century of oppression and abnegation within the new empire have strengthened that nationalist sentiment. As a consequence, there seems to be a growing cooperation between activists in Armenia and other parts of the Union, especially in Russia and the Ukraine. And at least for some, the national issue has been reintegrated within the larger sphere of problems faced by Soviet society.

An Armenian *samizdat* has proliferated in Yerevan, and a committee has been formed there to monitor the implementation of the Helsinki Accords.[21]

In addition, a number of Armenians have been involved in dissident activities in the Soviet Diaspora.[22] Even the "National United Party," once adherent of an exclusive nationalism, has eliminated from its program a strict ideological opposition to communism to pursue its goal of independence within the context of other forms of opposition to the present Soviet state.[23] Soviet Armenian nationalism embodies, then, an unwillingness to accept the injustices of the past, the oppression of the present, and fears of future assimilation. While the ethics of modernization and development has had a dampening effect on the political concerns, that nationalism remains less abstract, and far less idealized than that among Diasporan Armenians.

The Armenian Diaspora, itself largely the product of the events in the Ottoman Empire, shares with Soviet Armenians the burden of the past, as reified by the Genocide. And more imminently than in the Soviet Union, Diasporan Armenians live the agony of assimilation. Hence the national heritage, both cultural and political, have become the two factors which have brought the two segments closer after years of isolation, widespread anti-Soviet activity, and divisions within the Diaspora regarding attitudes toward a fragmented, Sovietized fatherland.

But the increasing communication and understanding within the Diaspora on the one hand, and between the Diaspora and Soviet Armenia, on the other, are due to three additional factors. Firstly, even the most anti-Soviet of the organizations, the *Dashnaktsoutiun* (the Armenian Revolutionary Federation, or ARF), has come to collectively accept what was sensed by many on an individual basis: that given the alienation of Western Armenian lands, the lack of progress toward their liberation and the increasing reality of assimilation, cultural survival and political nationalism needed tangible concepts more than abstract slogans and pride in a past. Soviet Armenia, despite its shortcomings, is seen as that reality. Soviet Armenia's cultural viability has infused fresh blood into a stagnating and disintegrating Diaspora through tours in communities abroad by artists and writers; by visits to Armenia by thousands of Diaspora Armenians each year; and Soviet Armenian invitations to groups of teachers, students and eminent individuals to spend time in that country.

Secondly, to support the claim that Soviet Armenia is a homeland for all Armenians—a claim which is useful to leaders in Moscow as well—authorities have had to make serious concessions to Armenian cultural nationalism: Soviet Armenia has had to reflect its Armenianness at least as much as its Sovietness. The Diaspora has become one of those tools by which Soviet Armenian leaders have been forging their unique brand of "national communism." In recent months they have gone beyond the exportation of culture and taken the unprecedented step of sending planeloads of material assistance to the Armenian community in war-torn Lebanon.

Thirdly, the continued support of Western governments for the Republic of Turkey have undermined the enthusiasm of Diaspora Armenians toward the foreign policy of countries such as the United States. Armenian national parties in the Diaspora, unlike Soviet Armenians, have been free to formulate political-territorial demands against Turkey. For a long time, these policies were pursued within the framework of Western diplomacy. But now even the human rights campaign is seen as a foreign policy tool, since it is applied selectively, and has even ignored the plight of the Armenian minority in Turkey.[24] And although there is the remote possibility that the Soviet Union might someday take up the Armenian cause for its own reasons, political leaders in the Diaspora have one less reason to make anti-Sovietism the basis of their policies. Without accepting the assumptions and values of Soviet communism, Diaspora Armenians are sharing with Soviet Armenians the frustrations borne out of political impotence as well.

Soviet Armenia, like her Caucasian neighbors, displays a strong nationalism rooted in history and concerned with the future. This gives the region its unique position in the USSR. Although these nationalisms have clashed in the past and are at conflict in the present, they have become mutually-reinforcing in their dealings with higher authorities in Moscow. Furthermore, it is difficult to assess whether the selection of republican leaders with Soviet, rather than local experience will reinforce or weaken these nationalisms. It is clear so far that because of the position of the Caucasus and the existence of the Diaspora, Armenian leaders have mastered the art of interpreting their actions as being beneficial to Armenia and the Armenian people, as well as the USSR and the Soviet people. There is also no doubt that the limits of that duality are defined in places other than the Caucasus. The space within which these leaders have moved might be endangered when the struggle for the succession to the present soviet leadership is over.

1. Unless otherwise indicated, statistical information regarding Armenians in the Soviet Union and Soviet Armenia is derived from the latest All-Union Census in the USSR in 1970. As usual, one must approach any statistical information, particularly from the USSR, with caution.

2. *Sovetakan Hayastan Amsagir* [Soviet Armenia Monthly] (Yerevan), no. 6 (1976), p. 4.

3. *Ibid.*, no. 7 (1978), p. 37.

4. For these and other comparisons see B. D. Silver, "Levels of Socioeconomic Development Among Soviet Nationalities" *American Political Science Review,* Vol. IV (1974), pp. 1618-1637.

5. See M. K. Matossian, "Communist Rule and the Changing Armenian Cultural Pattern," E. Goldhagen, ed., *Ethnic Minorities in the Soviet Union* (New York, 1968), pp. 185-197.

6. Khodjabekian, Haygagan KhSH Bnakchutiunu yev ashkhadankayin resoursneri verardatroutyan arti himnakhntirneru, Yerevan, 1973, p. 48.

7. L. V. Chuiko, *Braki i razvodi* (Moscow, 1976), p. 76.

8. See, for example, F. P. Filln, ed. *Russkii iazyk kak sredstvo mezhnatsionalnogo obshcheniia* [The Russian Language as means of Communication between Nationalities], Moscow, 1977.

9. *Sovetakan Hayastan* (Yerevan daily), April 15, 1978; *Christian Science Monitor*, April 28, 1978. On the question of minority languages see also S. Grigorian, "A Note on Soviet Policies Toward the Armenian Language" *The Armenian Review* Vol. XXV, No. 3 (Autumn 1972), pp. 68-76. For two contrasting views on the impact of language reforms in 1958-59, see H. Lipset, "The Status of National Minority Languages in Soviet Education," *Soviet Studies*, Vol. XIX, No. 2 (October 1967), pp. 181-189; and B. D. Silver, "The Status of National Minority Languages in Soviet Education: An Assessment of Recent Changes," *Soviet Studies*, Vol. XXVI, No. 1 (January 1974), pp. 28-40.

10. *Pravda*, December 4, 1920.

11. *New York Times,* December 11, 1977.

12. *Aztag Shapatoriag*, no. 6 (1969), p. 95.

13. *New York Times*, December 11, 1977.

14. Sarada Mitra and Adel Haba, "We Saw the Brotherhood of Nations," *Problems of Peace and Socialism*, Vol. XX, No. 6 (June,1997), esp. pp. 18-19, 25.

15. Both documents were first published in *Zartonk* (Beirut daily, organ of the Armenian Democratic Liberal Party), October 15, 1977.

16. V. Dadrian, "Nationalism in Soviet Armenia..." p. 247. Less violent nonetheless unusual demonstrations occurred in Moscow as well; see V. N.

Dadrian's "The Events of April 24 in Moscow—How they Happened and Under What Circumstances," *The Armenian Review*, vol. XX, no. 2 (Summer, 1967), pp. 9-26.

17. M. K. Matossian, "Armenia and the Armenians", Z. Katz, ed., *Handbook of Major Soviet Nationalities* (New York, 1975) p. 158.

18. Cited in *Azdak Shabatoriak*, no. 17 (1971), pp. 272-274; no. 26 (1974), pp. 419-421. For a statement by the leaders of this group containing the objectives and by-laws of the party, see "Le Parti National Unifié en Armenie sovietique" *Haïastan* (Paris, monthly), no. 391-392, April-May 1978, pp. 38-40. The renewed national fervor might have caused the removal of yet another first secretary of the Communist Party in Armenia, A. Kochinyan; see "Soviet Armenian Chronicle," *The Armenian Review*, Vol. XXVII, No. 1 (Spring 1974), pp. 102-103; no. 3 (Autumn 1974), p. 325; no. 4 (Winter 1974), pp. 435-37.

19. The news of the opening of the trial, the verdict, and the execution were announced in one report by the Tass Agency on February 1, 1979. According to A. Sakharov, the charges against the three were false, since none of the accused were even in Moscow during the bombing incident.

20. The most vehement criticisms have come so far from the First Secretary and Secretary of the Central Committee of the Communist Party in Armenia, K. Demirchyan and K. Dallakyan, in speeches delivered to the Central Committee on January 30, 1975 and October 19, 1975; see *Grakan Tert* [Literary newspaper] (Yerevan), February 7, 1975 and *Sovetakan Hayastan*, October 21 and 22, 1975.

21. *Haiastan*, no. 381, May-June, 1977, p. 19.

22. P. Reddaway, ed. *Uncensored Russia—The Human Rights Movement in the Soviet Union* (London, 1972), pp. 103, 151 passim; idem, *The Trial of the Four*, comp. P. Litvinov, (New York, 1972), pp. 399-405; and G. Sanders, *Samisdat—Soviet Opposition* (New York, 1974), pp. 368, 372.

23. "Le Parti National Unifié . . .", *Haiastan*, pp. 38-40.

3

ARMENIAN EARTHQUAKES AND SOVIET TREMORS

1989

This article explores the relationship between the December 1988 earthquake in Armenia and the political situation created by the Karabakh movement. Natural disasters reveal the vulnerabilities of political regimes and, at the least, weaken their foundations. In the case of regimes that already have weak foundations, natural disasters may accelerate their demise.

The article was first published in Society *(March 1989, no longer published). It was written at the request of the journal's editor, the well-known sociologist Irving Horowitz.*

The earthquake that struck northern Soviet Armenia on December 7, 1988, forced General Secretary Mikhail Gorbachev to cut short his visit overseas. This unusual gesture was appreciated by everyone as a sign of care. The general secretary placed his concern for human lives above other considerations by his tour of the ravaged area, and his statements that the Soviet government would do everything in its power to assist in the rescue and relief efforts. It did not take long, nonetheless, for political considerations to enter decision-making in many areas. Gorbachev was seen on television shaking his finger, scolding Armenians for their questions on issues other than the earthquake, and for their charges that Armenian orphans were being removed from Armenia to other parts of the Soviet Union.

It was unavoidable that the rescue and relief effort would be politicized. The region has been in turmoil for ten months, resulting in the deportation of 200,000 Armenians from Azerbaijan. And Gorbachev has refused to apply *perestroika* to the nationalities policy, thus jeopardizing his entire reform program. In addition, the magnitude of the devastation was such that even a smoothly-functioning bureaucracy would have been overtaxed; and the USSR is not known for its bureaucratic efficiency. The Soviet Union's civil defense capabilities proved to be inadequate. Even the general secretary's goodwill was not sufficient to accelerate adjustments.

For the first time in its history, the Soviet government allowed massive help from other countries into stricken areas, and gave access to newsmen with cameras. Many reporters started relaying information and pictures from the stricken area within a few days of the disaster, and questions were raised about Soviet capabilities and intentions. An engrained Soviet reluctance to provide full information, and the basic ignorance of most reporters concerning Soviet and Soviet Armenian societies, raised questions about Soviet capabilities, if not Soviet intentions.

On the one hand, Western reporters, especially those from the United States, were particularly inclined to notice and report those dimensions of the relief efforts that were inadequate and/or chaotic. These reports seem to have triggered secretiveness, defensiveness, and a tightening of the availability of information, as evident in earlier patterns of Soviet reaction. On the other hand, American reporters tended to accept without question the assumptions and judgments underlying Moscow's attack on Armenians when it criticized them as being insensitive, corrupt, uncooperative, and nationalistic. The central government may have been truly offended by the mistrust Armenians felt toward Moscow. But its attacks on Armenians may have also been a means to deflect the growing criticism of the inefficiency and disorganization of the rescue and relief effort.

The following specific facts and events exasperated and politicized the situation to a degree that was unnecessary, and certainly unhelpful to the rescue and relief effort:

- Political refugees in an earthquake zone: Large numbers of earthquake victims were those who found refuge in the Leninakan/ Kirovakan area prior to the earthquake. That increased the number victimized by the earthquake, including the death toll.

- Images of orphans and the feared end of the nation: The Soviet government showed it was, at least, insensitive to the trauma induced by the earthquake and the prior Armenian experience with trauma—the Genocide—in immediately soliciting or welcoming applications for the adoption of Armenian children from non-Armenian Soviet citizens in other parts of the USSR.

- Eliminating credible sources: The government used the earthquake to neutralize the new Armenian political movement by detaining six or more members of the Karabakh Committee, individuals with a significant degree of credibility in the eyes of the public.

- Continuing deportations: The government has failed to condemn continuing attacks on Armenians in Azerbaijan. Only on the fifth day after the earthquake did it make a vague reference to possibly allowing the now-twice-victimized Armenians from Azerbaijan to return to their homes as a partial, but natural solution to the refugee problem.

- The brothers and sisters in Karabakh: The government used the earthquake to equate the quest for justice and self-determination in Karabakh with immoral or insensitive behavior. When Armenians stated that they did not want to forget their brothers and sisters in Nagorno-Karabakh and in Azerbaijan, Gorbachev accused them of using the earthquake for political purposes. It may very well be that for Armenians, it was the government that politicized the tragedy by using it as a pretext and cover to arrest the leaders of the Karabakh Committee.

- The demonization of the victims: The government has refused to allow journalists and reporters who understand the issues and who could report accurately on them to travel to those parts of Armenia and Azerbaijan where "ethnic strife" is taking place. On the other hand, media members who were allowed into the earthquake zone, many of whom were unqualified to speak on earthquakes or on Soviet politics, have broadcast reports that are denigrating to Armenians. These reports depended mostly on specially-prepared government media reports. Both Soviet and Western attitudes are predicated on the West's enchantment with Gorbachev, as well as the propensity that central authorities in any system tend to have in viewing constituent parts as burdens, as obstacles to their concentration on larger issues, and as nuisances for the achievement of great deeds. Armenians may have by now become an abstraction, acceptable to Moscow if they accept Moscow's definitions of them as non-thinking victims to be pitied, but not to hold Moscow accountable. At different times since the earthquake, a variety of official sources have blamed Armenians for everything from the damage caused by the earthquake to bringing about the failure of *perestroika* and leading the government to bankruptcy. While the impact of the earthquake on the Soviet economy has yet to be assessed, the way the question is articulated predisposes both Soviet and world public opinions against Armenians. This is seemingly the least political-sounding tool used to deny Armenians their collective humanity, and to undermine the legitimacy of their political rights and demands.

•   Karabakh Organizing Committee: During the past ten months the Karabakh Committee had raised most of the issues now being debated in connection with the earthquake. In addition to its demand that Nagorno-Karabakh be reunified with Armenia, the Karabakh Committee, or Organizing Committee, had articulated concerns in four other areas, all of which have a direct impact on the handling of the earthquake:

(1) The committee's demand on behalf of large numbers of Armenians to close down the Metsamor Nuclear Plant has now become a necessity.

(2) The committee's substantive critique of corruption becomes all the more significant given the problems with the construction of buildings that collapsed, the health care delivery system, and the nonexistent civil defense mechanism.

(3) The committee's critique of the government's arbitrariness and bureaucratization acquires new value as bureaucracy, once more, seemed to be hindering an efficient relief effort, thus increasing the death toll.

(4) The committee's demand for the democratization of social and political institutions is directly related to the government's inept treatment of the issue of orphans and refugees.

People mistrust the state, particularly the information it provides and the judgments it makes, in sharp contrast to the continuing credibility of the Karabakh Committee. Rescue and relief efforts and evacuation and other orders would have been better received if these actions had been explained properly and had received the informal support of the committee. Instead, committee members were jailed, and institutions and individuals in government reverted to their more familiar, yet unworkable, arbitrary, and bureaucratic decision-making. Even where the state makes the correct decision, implementation is made difficult because a significant number of

Armenians do not believe that these institutions have their interests at heart.

The mistrust that Armenians had of the central government apparently intensified, rather than decreased, with Gorbachev's visit and his subsequent behavior. That mistrust has become a major factor in the way Armenians have come to regard Soviet decisions.

Dimensions of Relief

As soon as the magnitude of the impact of the earthquake became known, many individuals and organizations within and outside the Armenian community realized that a major relief effort would be needed. The United States and international agencies with experience in, and responsibilities for such disasters were best equipped to organize such an effort.

Armenian organizations whose goals include relief, such as the Armenian Relief Society, the Armenian General Benevolent Union, and the Armenian Missionary Association of America, responded quickly. They were joined by the Armenian Assembly and other groups throughout the United States. The first three groups had previously cooperated in securing a United States government grant to the Armenian community in war-torn Lebanon. Armenian organizations, already overwhelmed by calls for information from the media, were swamped with calls from their own members and others offering help.

In preparedness, experience, and magnitude of actual relief, the world response, and even the American response, was more significant and immediate than the Armenian. It was a tragedy of biblical proportions with little political significance, at least at first. In addition to governments and relief agencies, individuals offered financial help, organized fund drives, and volunteered to go to Armenia to assist in the rescue and relief efforts. The result has been an outpouring of goodwill and benevolence that has not been seen in this country since the Ethiopian famine relief.

American relief has not yet reached the Ethiopian level, but Armenians have surpassed by far their Lebanese relief effort. The outpouring of effort and donations is a strong indication of the vitality of the Armenian community, the presence of a traditional support system, and the significance Soviet Armenia has for the Diaspora. Reinforced by the increasing openness of the last three years, that significance increased with the growing number of Soviet Armenians now in the United States who have family ties to both American-Armenians and to Armenians in the earthquake zone.

The response was also magnified by the memory of the Genocide newly revived with the pogroms and mass deportations of the Armenians in Azerbaijan, and with the excruciating images of outstretched hands begging for bread behind relief supply trucks in once-proud Leninakan.

The rescue and relief operations were soon politicized. On the international level, this disaster marked the first time the Soviet Union has been willing to accept external relief assistance of any significance. While there were scientists and doctors who were allowed to help in the Chernobyl situation, the Soviet Union managed on its own the rescue, relief, and relocation programs.

Gorbachev's immediate acceptance of outside help in all respects was a generous and courageous act, but it also exposed the weaknesses of the Soviet civil defense and health systems. However, the goodwill expressed by Gorbachev to provide all possible assistance, as well as by Ronald Reagan and other world leaders, could not be translated immediately into an original and coordinated program of assistance. Among the factors affecting the relief program were:

(1) jurisdictional issues within the United States, where foreign disaster relief is coordinated by the State Department

(2) a centralized bureaucracy and government in the Soviet Union where every action must be approved by levels of authority who are protective of their prerogatives

(3) fears of security breaches in an earthquake affected area that also constitutes the international, military, and strategic borders between the Soviet Union and NATO (Turkey)

(4) pressures for immediate action versus the State Department's policy of first assessing needs in order to assure appropriate response.

In spite of these hindrances, much relief and rescue assistance was accepted from the West, including from the United States.

Earthquake relief was also politicized with respect to the relations between the Soviet government, which is directly responsible for the relief, and the Armenian population both in the affected areas and in Yerevan. The already-strained relations created by anti-Armenian attitudes in Moscow and by Armenian expectations from Moscow was compounded by apparently well-meant, but possibly insensitive decision-making in Moscow regarding the rescue and relief operations. Questions such as the continuing operation of the nuclear power plant, Metsamor, and charges of corruption in the construction industry—questions that had been raised earlier by the Karabakh Organizing Committee—were compounded by arbitrary and bureaucratic decision-making that affected both the dispersement of orphans and rescue and relief operations.

A serious problem of credibility with the Armenian people continues to affect the degree of understanding and cooperation between Moscow and the Armenians. A defensive and exasperated central government may be determined now to neutralize the Karabakh Committee, charged with "hampering relief efforts."

Yet a third area in which the earthquake has been politicized is in the arena of an economically successful, but politically impoverished Diaspora dynamics. An increasingly sophisticated worldwide campaign against Turkey's denial of the Genocide, the Karabakh movement since February 1988, and the mass deportations of Armenians from Azerbaijan in November 1988 made obvious the need for major Armenian-American organizations to overcome petty differences and to institutionalize and generalize a minimal degree of coordination and cooperation. Progress in this area has always been momentary, and limited.

Until the 1970s, a large constituency saw divisions within the community in terms of the two political parties and two Apostolic Churches which, separated since 1933, have now become entrenched and institutionalized. By the 1970s many of the divisions beyond the church had become irrelevant. A consensus has evolved, for example, on how to view Soviet Armenia. The politics of the fear of assimilation has created *de facto* common denominators in actual programming. As a consequence, political parties found it much easier to issue joint communiqués and to cosponsor events. Where that did not happen, it was generally because of local traditions and the personalities of leaders rather than burning political or ideological differences.

The past year brought new objective realities that made other issues almost irrelevant. A better-educated, better-integrated, and more secure community turned to existing organizations for leadership, guidance, and their ability to absorb its energies. Once alienated, a significant part of that revived community gave the organizations a new look as Armenian issues were internationalized. This development amounted to a reevaluation of community life.

It is probably fair to say that while most organizations were always overworked, few were ready to really provide a viable forum for the participation of individuals not used to the routine of community life. That routine had evolved from matters often unrelated to the larger society. In the absence of real challenges, petty quarrels had become major conflicts between, and within organizations, while the idea of a battle against assimilation had become an unmeasurable series of slogans. The campaign for Armenian issues had been reduced to a reproduction of institutions, structures, and values, and to a duplication of efforts. The dynamics of community life had little to do with events of an international scope.

Most organizations were geared toward action in the internal arena. For these organizations, legitimation within the community continued to be the centerpiece of all strategic thinking. Those poised to make an impact on the outside world were involved more in internal politics than pursuing a program to affect the world community's thinking and attitude toward clearly-defined Armenian goals. Often jumping from issue to issue, major organizations spent much energy and time reacting to statements and events without having overcome the limitations of an ideology peculiar to the victimized and colonized.

There has been much progress since the 1950s. Organizations are now often staffed by paid employees; there is much more professional know-how, and most offices have acquired state-of-the-art technology. In specific areas, such as the ethnic press, relations with non-Armenian entities, and the audio-visual media, there has been an introduction of professional concerns and values into the Armenian context. And some visible progress has been made toward a rational deployment of resources in areas relevant to contemporary concerns.

The national organizations lacked an agenda that was clearly thought out, an agenda assessed and strategized in the context of the larger realities.

The balance of power that was overwhelmingly against Armenians was translated into a crass realism justifying the absence of long-term thinking—a pattern that continued to make Armenians feel comfortable in their limitations, and in their fleeting sense of satisfaction of their imitations of the famous and glamorous.

While organizations often differed in their stated goals and priorities, their obsession with acquiring legitimacy within the community and claims on exclusive loyalties produced three interrelated results:

(1) All organizations seemed to be saying and doing the same things. Competition for the same kind of loyalty became fierce. Immediate success and recognition became critical at the expense of long-term programs.

(2) Many members of the community who had much to contribute became alienated.

(3) Critical parts of the stated goals of organizations were unfulfilled.

Diasporan conditions, including the absence of a state, may always pressure organizations into assuming responsibilities otherwise not theirs, or into a reactive politics. Yet the Armenian Diaspora is already a few generations old and experienced. Its members have started wondering if existing organizations have the capability of coping with the next round of issues, let alone the ability to foresee them.

As the earthquake hit, one of the first concrete and universal experiences of many Armenians was the question of where to send contributions toward relief. While those members of the community who clearly identified with one or the other of the "sides" knew the charity through which they would make their contribution, most Armenians unaffiliated with any major organization were lost. Armenians and their American friends expected to find a "natural" place to send their contributions, and many assumed there would be at least some coordination of the effort toward relief from a natural disaster. No one imagined that there could be serious differences on whether to send relief or whether anyone here would be making decisions as to what was needed. No such coalition existed, nor has one evolved as of this date. A number of meetings that took place at the instigation of major organizations produced little—primarily because the convening group assumed that they would guide, or even dominate the coalition.

Personal and organizational egos continued to function the same way as they did before the earthquake. While no one doubts the grief each felt, and the dedication each had to the relief effort, that spirit was not translated into a process of transcending one's prejudices toward others. The intolerance toward one or the other side of many of those espousing "unity" and "coalitions" appeared to be as strong as ever. Without impugning sinister designs to anyone or to any organization, there have been, and continue to be attempts, perhaps unconscious, to turn earthquake relief into the pedestal on which individuals and organizations seek to achieve a preeminent position within the community.

Different organizations have displayed strength in different ways; however, no single individual or organization can handle all aspects of fundraising and relief work for the earthquake. The magnitude of the short- and long-term assistance needed is beyond the capacity of the Armenian people in Armenia, and in the Diaspora. No single organization commands the respect and loyalty of all important segments of the community, and no organization has emerged within the last year that can reasonably vie for that position without creating strong reactions, and without harming efforts.

On the other hand, Armenians in the Diaspora have strong attachments to Armenia, and can contribute in ways that are not accessible to others. There is a consensus that the Diaspora must have its voice heard in the process of rebuilding Armenia. In this process, it may also be able to overcome its divisions and to redefine its agenda.

The expectation of the community that organizations involved in relief and reconstruction should coordinate their efforts is increasing. The failure to coordinate will result in the more complete alienation of segments of the community valuable for their diverse talents, relative youth, and large numbers.

Recently, there have been rumors that Catholicos Vazgen I of Etchmiadzin and Catholicos Karekin II of the See of Cilicia will be making a joint fundraising tour in North America. This will certainly be an encouraging event. However, the failure to translate that spirit into a mechanism for solving long-standing disputes between the two jurisdictions may leave this community in even worse shape.

· No formula exists at this point for achieving such a goal. Ultimately, cooperation involves a process of education and experimentation, because it implies changes in normal behavioral patterns and reactions. But discussions within and outside the community regarding the first steps toward a coordinated effort have resulted in these suggestions.

- Whatever the forum in which coordination takes place, no prejudice can be shown against any existing organization. No organization that wishes to participate can be arbitrarily excluded because of personal obsessions with one or the other of the organizations.
- All decisions will be taken on the basis of a rational discourse as to what is to be done and who is best qualified to do it, rather than upon artificial balancing acts that have failed before, and which have continued to paralyze progress.
- No single organization can dominate. Major or otherwise critical organizations and institutions will inevitably play larger roles as they display more expertise, provide more experienced leadership, convey larger perspectives, and pledge more resources.
- No organization or institution will be expected to lose its identity, structure, or independence in disagreeing with the larger group.
- In order to begin the process, it is not necessary that all organizations participate, although every care must be taken to invite and respect all.

Structurally, the ideal can be realized gradually. In order to have a successful beginning which helps build trust, this approach might be considered:

- A forum can begin with a limited goal, rather than a maximal approach. Here, the relief and reconstruction work can and should be the first goal.
- A simple mechanism of representation, such as a council of presidents, may provide the basis of the first forum.
- The purpose of the forum may also be limited at first to such work as the exchange of information, the subsequent coordination in specific relief areas, and, ultimately, coordination in the rebuilding process.
- The effort may be limited geographically at first, although regional councils of national organizations will have to participate with the authorization of their central executive and policymaking bodies.
- The presidents' council may be successful if the presidents have received some authority from their executives and memberships to make decisions in well-defined areas on behalf of the organizations.
- A steering committee that devises and proposes policy and action could assume responsibility for the direction of the efforts.

- The steering committee should include individuals whose achievements and talents are universally respected, and who transcend "sides," to ensure that decisions are not distorted by partisanship.

Ultimately, even the best-conceived structural designs, the most clever organizational charts, and the most imaginative by-laws will not be sufficient to produce a coordinated effort unless there is an overwhelming sense that this disaster must be faced together, and unless those in a position of authority make a conscious and rational decision that they will act on that sense of urgency, rather than react to ingrained fears that cooperation may benefit the "other." The cost of non-cooperation will be great, deep, and long-lasting. It will affect all community organizations. The impact of the absence of such an evolution on community structures and values in the Diaspora may be as lasting as the loss of lives and hopes in Armenia.

Like other events of this magnitude, whether man-made or natural, the politics of the earthquake in all spheres may haunt us as much as the images of its victims if we do not begin to work now toward transforming ourselves, and our institutions.

4

MGRDICH KHRIMIAN: REVOLUTIONARY TRADITIONALIST, OR CONSERVATIVE REVOLUTIONARY?

2013

A presence that towered over the second half of the 19ᵗʰ and early 20ᵗʰ centuries, Mgrdich Khrimian is one of Armenian history's best known and least studied figures. A complex character, Khrimian emerges at the same time as a revolutionary and enlightened clergyman and a patriarchal character keen on preserving traditional mores and values.

This article, first presented as a paper at the 2013 Annual Meeting of the Middle East Studies Association in New Orleans, USA, is an attempt to identify and explore these contradictory dimensions of the larger than life character as well as an invitation for scholars and researchers to dig deeper into his life and work than has been done so far.

Mgrdich Khrimian (1821-1907), Ottoman-Armenian clergyman from Van, primate, writer, publisher, bishop, Patriarch, diplomat, abbot, exiled leader, and Catholicos of All Armenians, is one of the most mentioned but little studied characters in Armenian history. A dominant figure of the second half of the nineteenth century, Khrimian is not as yet fully understood or explained.

Khrimian is seen as a precursor of the Armenian revolutionary movement in the late Ottoman Empire. He supported reforms in what were known as the Armenian provinces of the Ottoman Empire, the introduction of new technologies in agriculture and printing, and the education of girls. Yet he did little to challenge the established order within the church which he served so faithfully, a church that was responsible for much of the obscurantism of his time, and unlike other clergymen, a church he served with authentic faith.

There are too many paradoxes that require explanation.

1.

Five episodes that mark Khrimian's presence in history:

1. Patriarch of Constantinople, 1869-1873
2. War famine relief after 1877-78
3. The Conference of Berlin in 1878
4. The confiscation of Armenian Church properties in the Russian Empire between 1903-05
5. And less known, during the time he was Catholicos of All Armenians, the 1906 General Church Council at Etchmiadzin.

1.1
Khrimian the Patriarch, 1869-1873

With much anticipation, Bishop Khrimian was elected Patriarch of Constantinople in 1869. Within the hopeful environment of the Ottoman *Tanzimat* reforms and the Armenian "Constitution" they inspired, Armenians in the provinces welcomed the news with enthusiasm, as did those elsewhere who had cared for the problems of rural and small-town Armenians.

Khrimian came to Constantinople to push for reforms in the provinces, where most Armenians lived. Indeed by 1871 he produced a major administrative, judicial, and economic reform plan that was presented to the Porte, with divided support from the Armenian National Assembly.

While Khrimian and his supporters thought this step to be in line with the spirit of the *Tanzimat*, at the end this was seen by the Porte and its allies within the Armenian National Assembly as an attempt to reverse the role of the millet. The Patriarchate was established initially by the Ottoman state in order to facilitate the top-to-bottom management of Armenians as a non-Muslim community, that is, from Sultan to Patriarch down to the common Armenian subject.

Khrimian and his allies were trying to reverse the flow and use the Patriarchate to get the voice of the commoner to the Sultan.

The conservatives in the National Assembly accused Khrimian of "endangering the nation" and circumventing the Armenian Constitution. He gave up on his efforts on behalf of reforms when the Port clearly told him that "political" issues, i.e., those which touched the social, economic, and legal dimensions of the lives of Armenians as subjects of the Ottoman Empire, were not the business of the millet and its leadership. The end of this phase of Khrimian's life also marked the end of any attempt by the Armenian millet leadership to attempt to use the patriarchate as a mechanism for reform in the provinces directly through the Sultan's government, until at least 1908.

The Armenian National Constitution failed the test of becoming the mechanism by which real change in the provinces would be made possible. Many in the capital and elsewhere came to see Khrimian as a troublemaker, though that attribute enhanced his position as the voice of the poor, oppressed, and downtrodden.

1.2
Famine Relief in 1877-1878

Khrimian's second major appearance was as one of the main figures organizing and implementing famine relief in 1877 and 1878. The famine had been a consequence of the Russo-Turkish War of the same period. Khrimian distinguished himself as a caring, fair, and non-discriminating relief organizer. He used the funds raised mainly among Armenians in the major cities of the Ottoman Empire to provide relief not only to Armenians, but also Muslims, most of whom were Kurds, first in the region of Van, but later further north as well.

Obviously, this mission, accomplished with relative success, increased his stature in the provinces, given the paucity of available resources.

1.3
The Congress of Berlin, 1878

Khrimian is best known for his quasi-diplomatic mission to the Congress of Berlin in 1878. His mission, entrusted to him by his successor, Patriarch Nerses Varzhabedian, was to preserve Article 16 of the Treaty of San Stefano (which promised Russian reforms in the Armenian provinces) at a conference that was aimed at revising it.

Khrimian failed in his mission, unable even to take part in the deliberations.

Even more important than the mission has been the sermon, which Khrimian delivered in a number of churches upon his return, known as the "Sermon of the Iron Ladle."[1] Khrimian compared the congress to a traditional meal where guests were invited to serve themselves. Various peoples had iron ladles, said Khrimian, and were able to serve themselves. Armenians had a paper ladle and received nothing.

This analogy was seen by many in his time, and later as well, as an invitation by Khrimian for Armenians to take up arms. Armenian organizations willing to take up arms indeed appeared less than a decade after 1878. And Khrimian is seen as the precursor of the revolutionary movement.

Khrimian lived until 1907, but had very little to do with the revolutionary parties. It is said that Hnchakians went to him early in their history to get his support; Khrimian refused. The Hnchakians expressed surprise. One of the leading Hnchakian leaders, Roupen Khanazad, relates a conversation he had in 1889 with Khrimian, during which Khanazad presented his party's aims and projects:

> "So, what is it that you want to do, liberate Armenia?" he [Khrimian] said half inquisitive, half mockingly.
>
> "Do you know how to make a dynamite? Can you explain it to me?" asked Khrimian.
>
> After listening to my explanations on the manner to prepare nitroglycerine, bombs and on their use, with a somewhat disappointed voice Khrimian said:
>
> "The way you explained it, the maker of the bomb too can be harmed. The Armenian nation is too small, there should be very few Armenian victims."
>
> I smiled and started again to convince him that no nation has achieved freedom without a great number of victims, without big losses. How could Armenians be the exception?
>
> "All that you are saying is good and well, but the Armenian nation is small; I am afraid that by the time freedom arrives, there will not be much left of us."[2]

The Ottoman government exiled Khrimian to Jerusalem in 1890.

1.4
Confiscation of Armenian Church properties in the Russian Empire

We next see Khrimian at Etchmiadzin as Catholicos of All Armenians, elected in 1892 and consecrated in 1893. His Catholicosate brought no major changes and he is generally seen as a conservative church leader and manager. Khrimian displayed much care for the large number of Western Armenian refugees that crossed the border and ended up in Etchmiadzin as a result of the 1894-1896 massacres in the Eastern provinces of the Ottoman Empire.

Nonetheless, the relative calm of Etchmiadzin was shattered when in 1903 the Russian government decided to confiscate Armenian Church properties throughout the empire. This unwise edict awoke the elderly patriarch's instincts for resistance, no doubt encouraged and strengthened both by a popular movement and organized party resistance against the move. Two years later, the Russian government relented and the properties were returned.

1.5
General Church Council in Etchmiadzin in 1906

A lesser-known, yet significant event during Khrimian's Catholicosate was the general Church Council that convened in 1906. Formally, the purpose of the council was to initiate reforms intended to modernize and democratize the church. The council did produce a series of steps in that direction, and some of that spirit survived the closing of the council.

Yet, the manner and reason of the closing of that council is as important as the changes it produced. The fact is that the council convened at the insistence of the *Dashnaktsoutiun*, which was then thoroughly entangled in the first Russian Revolution. Other than the noble purpose of reforming the most important Armenian institution itself, the Dashnaktsoutiun (Armenian Revolutionary Federation) aimed at establishing its own influence on the church through an increase in power for the lay membership of the church, just as had occurred in Constantinople in the 1860s.

Most significantly, the council meetings were presided over by Simon Zavarian, one of the founders of the Dashnaktsoutiun. To some bishops, the council was going too far in divesting the church of its properties and the clergy of their prerogatives. The Russian police intervened and dismissed the council, surely with the tacit support of Catholicos Khrimian.

Khrimian passed away the next year at the age of eighty-six.

2.

The trajectory of his life was long, and he participated in many of the defining moments of Ottoman Armenian history. Yet these two facts do not explain the larger-than-life place Khrimian occupies in the Armenian political imagination. There does not appear to be any other clergyman to come close to the iconic place Krikor Naregatsi of the 10th century holds.

There seem to be three dimensions that distinguish him from others—and not just clergymen—and make him larger than life.

2.1 The "Hayrig" factor

Khrimian had a unique talent to connect to the common people and their problems, especially those in the rural areas and small towns of historic Armenia, and to give those problems a common sense voice. His articulation of these problems, his intimate knowledge of the workday and life of a peasant, and his willingness to make these the center of his attention as a matter of belief and not of politics, earned him the title "Hayrig" long before he was elected Patriarch. Indeed, it was his being Hayrig that propelled him to the position of Patriarch.

By becoming a prolific author, he also ensured his position among the liberal bourgeoisie, and in general, among the rich and educated. Other than Archbishop Maghakia Ormanian, another Patriarch of Constantinople, and excluding a few other scholar clergymen, Khrimian is not matched in recent times for his output on social, economic, and national issues in general.

But more on his writings later.

Suffice it to say that Khrimian had a genuine sense of the ravages of injustice and oppression, and an instinct to secure charity for the poor. And he was able to articulate this in his daily encounters, his weekly sermons, his pleas to Armenian and Ottoman authorities, and in his writings, with a genuine eloquence that made the most of the transitional stage of the written Armenian language from the classical to the vernacular, using the power of the former and the actuality of the latter.

2.2

Hayrig and his self-image

Simply put, Khrimian had a very high opinion of himself. He endured rejection, exile, and humiliation with almost good humor and accepted honor, respect, and the elevation to the highest position in the Armenian Church with quasi-humility. All because he saw himself as a biblical patriarch in the sense of the Old Testament, which he referred to quite often.

In his writings he referred to himself in the third person. He was not averse to maintaining the legend that had been created around himself as Hayrig. By behaving according to that legend, he compelled his interlocutors—whether of the time or now—to treat him carefully, if not gingerly. Before becoming Patriarch, Khrimian published two periodicals with titles that the people later used to refer to him: *Ardzvi Vasbouragan* (Eagle of Vasbouragan, 1855-1856) and *Ardzvig Darono* (Eaglet of Daron, 1863-1865), Vasbouragan and Daron being two of the provinces in the south of historic Armenia where he served, respectively, as abbot and prelate of the Armenian Church.

He had a vision of humankind and life, and how Armenians and others should live, and those visions gave him a sense of self-importance to the point where more often than not in his writings, where he combined the fictional with the real (even for a child to see), he referred to himself as "Hayrig." I say children because they were important in his mind; few clergymen or even lay writers have addressed children. One of his most revealing pieces, *Babig and Tornig*, is a lengthy lecture/sermon/advice from a grandfather to his grandchild. (The in-between, the father, is missing, because he is a migrant worker away from home in the Armenian heartland.)[3]

He thought his mind was large enough to encompass a worldview, beyond the places where he had lived. He was sure his knowledge of both Armenian and general history gave him a degree of legitimacy he could not but confer upon others.

2.3

Khrimian and his writings

Khrimian's collected works, published in New York in 1929, include fifteen items across 870 pages. (The volume does not include articles he authored in the journals which he had published.) This is where we have to turn to explain the paradoxes that characterize his life and politics. The long and phenomenal life he had, the important positions he held, his involvement in some of the most important events of Armenian history, have made him a hero, though possibly intimidated historians from asking too many questions.

Khrimian had no formal education but he was well informed and well read, and amazingly so. He knew world history—in the tradition of what we used to call Western civilization. He knew Greek and Latin classics and many of the more modern philosophers, from Plato and Aristotle to Virgil and Descartes. Since he did not know any languages other than Armenian, vernacular and classical, we can assume that his knowledge came from translations of these and other works by the Mkhitarists in Venice and Vienna.

But the one that speaks to his heart is the Bible. The New Testament completes the old and corrects its mistakes, Khrimian believed, but that did not stop him from relying on the patriarchs of the Old Testament for old-time wisdom and parables.

What distinguishes Khrimian's oeuvre from the works of others is the scope, comprehensiveness, ambition, and coherence of the worldview it projects.

Throughout his life and at many critical points Khrimian addressed issues, from the creation of the world through the natures of man and society, authority and government, the concepts of right and wrong, equality and justice, etc., and their places in the human condition. It would require more time and space to cover his philosophy of man and life, history, and the world. Here I will touch only upon some of the salient notions regarding society and authority, and the tension between his idealized view of humanity and realization that we are far from living that idealized life.

Khrimian accepts the fact that there are those with authority and those without. Hierarchy is part of life, he argues, and that is how God ordained it, beginning with the family where the father rules. With the development of history, the family model was eventually extended to clans, tribes, peoples, and empires.

Inequality is born from this hierarchy. Inequality is part of God's design; it is one of the unchanging divine rules. He wrote,

It is the duty of the people to recognize and believe that the staff of governing authority is extended to earth from heaven; its upper end is attached to the stately throne that governs the universe, and the other, lower end is established in this world. That is the reason why Saint Paul says, "Governing authority is from God."[4]

It is the dynamics created by inequality that constitutes the energy in the dynamics of change and progress. It is divine power that has established inequality. If all men had been equal, we would be like animals. Without inequality there would be no competition, and we would not have developed the ideas of justice and of responsibilities and rights. We would be savages like those "in Africa or distant places in America."[5]

There would be chaos without authority, he argues. He takes on what he calls the "liberals," who wish to do away with governments and armies. Even America, he states, the land of least inequality, has a government, has a president, albeit elected, an army, and laws by which citizens must abide.[6]

One cannot create equality, he insists, not only because it is undesirable but also because it is not practical. We could divide up the land equally among all peasants, he imagines, but how would we create equality among urban dwellers? What would we divide up?[7]

Thus the poor must accept their condition and strive for a better life; and subject nations must accept their status and not try to subvert the system. Subjects of empires have the right and even the duty to demand fair treatment. In this respect, he expects the wealthy to be charitable and dominant imperial governments to govern by a sense of justice and fairness. Khrimian sidesteps the possibility that the wealthy may not be so charitable and the ruler not so benevolent and fair, two facts he knew to be true.

God's laws for nature are unchanging, believed Khrimian, and all creatures know their limits; he wished ardently that man too would know his place.[8]

And yet, while precluding any radical action to change the system, Khrimian does inject a less fatalistic note regarding the origin, nature, and future of governing authority.

First, he establishes that although ordained by divine law, inequality has had some negative consequences, what we would nowadays call collateral damage. He argues that "authority and governments are born from inequality among men in life, from the spirit of troublemaking [*khrovararoutiun*] and the intense desire for domination and power."[9] He argues finally, that empires have, just as individuals, their biological life cycles. They are born, they grow, and then they die; after all, time took care of the Macedonian, Roman, Babylonian, and Assyrian empires.[10]

Leaders need to serve, and people must learn to demand justice and fairness, he recognized. In his well-known "*Takavorats Zhoghov*," ["Meeting of Kings"], Khrimian creates a parable similar to those in the Bible and elsewhere to make complex concepts simple.[11] Khrimian sets the stage, in which the potentates of Europe are gathered and they are answering the question: "What disturbs your sleep?" While all mention major political upheavals, wars, and rivalries, in the end it is the king of Belgium who says he sleeps very well because his throne is based on the love his subjects have for him.

He also ascribed most of the crisis provincial and rural Armenians were suffering to provincial/local Ottoman authorities. He blamed Kurds for their depredations and unlawful, exploitative behavior toward Armenian farmers, but essentially blamed the lack of attention the authorities paid to the education and settlement of Kurds. Instead of weakening the central authorities, Khrimian was calling on them to increase their presence in the provinces in the spirit of the Tanzimat.

Khrimian has a curious addendum to his 1871 Report on the social-economic crisis in the Eastern provinces:

> Having forgotten and most important point in my report, I hereby present it as an addendum. When Kurds are recognized within the state as a subject people, and at the same time they are, by creed, co-religionists with the main Muslim population, it is the responsibility of the state to gradually integrate them within civilization, and it is their [the Kurds'] right to demand as much.
>
> We know, the Kurd is eternally contented with his current status and does not ask for education. But not only religion but also the requirements of the state and of humanitarianism demand that Kurds too be considered worthy of the benefits and education of the state. Therefore, one of the powerful and natural means [for the implementation] of reforms is that local authorities care for the education of the children of Kurds, at least for the children of those called nobles, the "*tossouns.*" [These] could be admitted into the schools known as *Mektebi Reshidiye*, established with the

governorships, for them to receive the necessary education. Because only by providing the necessary education will it be possible to soften the beastly behavior of the Kurds and integrate them within civilization and, thus, to turn them into a loyal people for the state and the country.[12]

Education for all is, indeed, Khrimian's panacea, at least in the short and middle-term. His solution to the crisis could be summarized in three points: (1) education, including for girls, since they will be mothers and are in charge of education of all children, (2) industrial progress, including modernization of agriculture, and open shops/factories to produce modern agricultural tools, and (3) Armenians staying on the land and returning to it when they are educated, rather than moving to big cities or to other countries.

Poverty is caused by laziness, ignorance and lack of education, Khrimian stressed. Not knowing how to read, write, do accounting, or household management causes poverty.

> But what is it that we need? What is the strong remedy that will lift the mind and spirit of the people from its idleness induced stupefaction and lethargy and lead to an active life? That which was necessary for the Western nations. That is, enlightenment and science.[13]

Progress was to be gradual, and no sudden change should be expected, he insisted. Peace and stability were of supreme value; these would allow for progress to be made over time. Always relying on the Bible for the legitimation of his views, he addressed the questions raised regarding God's management of Armenian affairs by addressing God,

> Lord, you knew beforehand that the world and the thrones are torturing us, and for that reason you told us to pray and beg for your kingdom alone. In ignorance, people are asking for Saul.[14]

At the end Khrimian appears like a patriarch of the Old Testament, torn between fate and his own judgment.

He appears to be in constant and private conversations—even negotiations—with his maker, in whom he wanted to believe until the end, and wrote as if he did.

While the emphasis changes, the spirit of his writings does not greatly change with experience and harsh realities, both those in which he participated and others that he witnessed. He was also in constant negotiations with fellow Armenians and Ottomans, the Great Powers and the small ones, because none were behaving as God intended them to do. He saw reality as a challenge that must be overcome, a challenge to his ideal of an Eden on earth.

He should probably be seen as a transitional figure and would be no less important for being such. One who responded to changing circumstances, but who also defined the responses to these changes. A radical within the political spectrum of his early years, a conservative for many in his later years. Which means that at best, these terms are relative to time and to the attitudes of other players.

Many then, and even more now, see him as the vanguard of a revolutionary movement. But his writings, spanning six decades, provide us a glimpse of a very non-revolutionary approach to the very unequal relationship between Armenians and the Ottoman state. Slow progress through education, economic stabilization and pressure, where feasible, to change circumstances. These seem to be the constants in his life, notwithstanding his foray into international diplomacy and realization that (a) Armenians did not have the resources to make a difference, but (b) had every right to be disappointed.

Though less anxious than in his earlier years, Khrimian continued to rely on religion for his positions in his old age, and seems to have found a way to legitimize a conservative approach to religious formulas. Though his positions were considered liberal compared to others early in his career, he certainly appears to have been quite conservative, or possibly more circumspect, than others who took up arms, in part ascribing their tactics to Khrimian's famous sermon. His interpretation of power relations in biblical terms might have been a subterfuge for his circumspection in challenging the state directly. It was a circumspection conditioned by his understanding of the real power of the state and the character of the Ottoman regime.

His personality defies the classical and more recognized types of conservatives, liberals, and radicals. In fact, he crystallizes the impasse in which Armenians found themselves in the Ottoman Empire. His life and works project the background against which options were presented:

Tanzimat's success or failure, the success or failure of the Armenian Constitutional era, the advantages of appealing to the Great Powers (or not), and the option of using revolutionary means to achieve reforms (or not).

But at the very end it is a sense of powerlessness that dominates his thought, justified by a blind, if not forgotten faith in God.

What Khrimian seemed to have internalized fully from one of his heroes, Movses Khorenatsi, is the latter's famous Lamentation.[15] In his poem dedicated to Khorenatsi, Khrimian appears to be offering a corollary to Khorenatsi's lamentation text:

Որբն է միայն դիւր սփոփանք [Only lamentation brings a soothing consolation].[16]

In Khorenatsi, the lamentation reads more like an indictment of Armenian institutions—feudal lords, military and church leaders and judges—whose policies based on narrow self-interest led to the fifth century destruction of the Armenian state. Khorenatsi does not seek the reasons for the loss of Armenia's sovereignty in the behavior of other states and dynasties, or even in God. In his lamentation fourteen centuries later, Khrimian is less focused. Khrimian came close to emulating Khorenatsi's exquisite rhetoric, but not his historical reasoning. Khorenatsi may have had a stronger and more real memory of statehood than Khrimian, whose concept of Armenia was an idealized, historicized, and abstract concept, but no less a dream for him. Khorenatsi did not have the problem of Armenia's loneliness; Khrimian did. Other nations will not cry with us, he assures his compatriots, crying and lamenting being the key words in this discourse.

To show the impasse at which he himself and Armenians had found themselves, Khrimian ended one of his poems with a solution worthy of an Italian opera, though probably truer than any such dramatic scenario. An Armenian woman is known for her bravery and fighting ability, and is being chased by threatening Kurds. She kills her son and throws herself down a cliff while begging God's understanding for the murder she had just committed in order to avoid being raped. Khrimian presented the story as one that should be emulated.[17]

I consider this paper as an impressionistic one that might suggest areas of deeper research. What needs further research is also (a) the impact of his positions when they were sermonized and written, and (b) the processes that were at play when, following his death, scholars and the general public interpreted, filtered, and adopted his various positions.

---

1. Haig Ajemian, *Hayots Hayrig* [Father of Armenians], (Tabriz, 1929), pp. 511-513.
2. As related by Haig Ajemian, in *Hayots Hayrig,* p. 596.
3. *Ampoghchagan Yerger Khrimian Hayrigi* [Complete Works of Khrimian Hayrig], (New York, 1929), pp. 637-776.
4. "Sirak yev Samouel," *Ampoghchagan Yerger,* p. 437.
5. Ibid., p. 424.
6. Ibid., p. 431.
7. Ibid.
8. Ibid., pp. 416-421.
9. Ibid., p. 428.
10. Ibid., pp. 429-430.
11. "Takavorats zhoghov," *Ampoghchagan Yerger,* pp. 781-788.
12. "Dzrakir Parenorokmants," [Plan for Reforms], *Ampoghchagan Yerger,* p. 864.
13. "Sirak yev Samouel," *Ampoghchagan Yerger,* pp. 451-455.
14. "Haykoyzh," in *Ampoghchagan Yerger,* p. 277.
15. "Ողբամ զքեզ հայոց աշխարհ," [I lament you, Armenian land/world] "Movses Khorenatsi," *Patmoutyoun Hayots,* M. Apeghyan and S. Haroutyounyan, ed. (Yerevan, 1991), p. 358.
16. "Voghpatsogh Khorenatsin," *Ampoghchagan Yerger,* p. 846.
17. "Tiutsazn Garinei hishadagin," *Ampoghchagan Yerger,* pp. 810-813.

5

IDEOLOGY AND REALITY: HNCHAKIAN PARADOXES AT BIRTH

2012

The Social Democratic Hnchakian Party is known as the "mayr gousagtsoutiun" or "mother party" for being the first full-fledged political organization in modern Armenian history. The self-proclaimed Marxist socialist SDHP or Hnchakian Party has struggled throughout its history to reconcile its lofty ideal of making Armenia and Armenians part of the perceived universal socialist future for humanity and the harsh realities from which it was trying to save Armenians. Its attempts to reconcile class and nation relied on an ideological maneuver that exposed, time after time, the paradoxes that were evident as soon as they tried to turn thought into action.

While there have been scholars who have dealt with the problems posed by this party for historians, we lack a critical history of the organization that played a crucial role in the Armenian revolutionary movement and its impact on the course of Armenian history until 1914. Fortunately, researchers within the younger generation, such as Varak Getsemanian, have started to produce excellent and enlightening work.

The article below, originally presented as a brief paper at a conference held in 2012 in Los Angeles on the occasion of the 125th anniversary of the founding of the party, is an attempt to identify such paradoxes as a means of understanding the conflicts within the party and the decisions it made over the years.

INTRODUCTION

Modern Armenian history is rich with personalities and groups that have adopted or expounded on ideologies that compensate for their inherent strategic vulnerabilities. In their coherence and seeming universality, ideologies provide intellectual and spiritual strength to those upholding them when they are, in fact, weak and lack the necessary resources to bring about change on their own. In their attempts to act according to ideologies, such individuals and groups run counter to realities on the ground and some way or another come to terms with them, more often than not creating paradoxes that they learn to live with.

This article will discuss three of the major paradoxes dealing with the early years of the founding of the Social Democratic Hnchakian Party (SDHP, Hnchakians), the first Armenian political party, beginning in 1887.[1] These paradoxes appear to dominate the gap between the worldview of the founders of the party and the relevance of that worldview to Western Armenian/Eastern Ottoman realities, to the Church, and to Marxist ideology. These paradoxes explain much about the difficulties the Hnchakian Party faced, as well as those that challenged the Armenian people following the Congress of Berlin in general.[2]

These paradoxes are relevant for our understanding of (a) how the Hnchakians perceived issues at the time, (b) how they proposed to resolve them, and why they thought they could resolve them, and (c) how the Armenian polity resolves problems today.[3] The following are the paradoxes this article will focus on:

1. The founders of the Hnchakian Party that proposed to save Western/Ottoman occupied Armenia were Eastern/Russian Armenians; as far as this author has been able to determine, none of these founders had ever been in Western Armenia. Their sense of the circumstances under which Ottoman Armenians were living— circumstances that required "salvation"—derived from newspaper articles, reports by others who had visited the region, or through personal correspondence.

2. The Hnchakian Party adopted Marxist ideology—rather, what they understood to be Marxist ideology—that placed class struggle above all else as the mover of history and the means to achieve socialism; yet the party advocated the independence of Armenia, an otherwise classic nationalist goal.

3. True to the Marxist interpretation, the Hnchakian Party program shunned religion and the Church as a real agency in the future

development of history; in fact, there is no mention of religion or church in the party program. Yet their first actions were closely linked to the Armenian Church, seeking to benefit from its privileges within and trying to engage it as an ally against the Ottoman state.

RUSSIAN AND OTTOMAN ARMENIANS

It has been noted before that it was Russian Armenians who founded the first Armenian political party, one that proposed to save Ottoman Armenians.[4] There have been a number of explanations for this phenomenon, such as the idealism of youth (the founders were all university students) and the increased interest among Russian Armenians in Ottoman Armenian life following the 1877-1878 Russo-Turkish War and the treaties of San Stefano (February 1878) and Berlin (July 1878).

Yet there is one dimension in this story that has not been really appreciated. That is, Russian Armenian youth with close understanding of the Russian populist movements that were primarily peasant oriented and readily saw the problem in essence as a problem of rural Armenians, the basis of Armenian society in the historic Western Armenian territories.[5] Some historians have noted the connection of Russian Armenian university students, founders of the Hnchakian and the Armenian Revolutionary Federation (ARF or Dashnaktsoutiun) parties, to the People's Will (Narodnaya Volya) secret organization in Russia without recognizing the agrarian crisis in the rural areas as the basis of the origins of the Armenian Question. This dimension was not one the Great Powers cared about, nor did the relatively stable Armenians in Constantinople or other major Ottoman cities. This is not to say there was no recognition by urban liberal intellectuals, some segments of the middle class, and a few clergymen from the provinces of the threat to the communal base of the rural Armenian economy. But for the founders of the Hnchakian Party that dimension constituted the basis of Armenian grievances.

It is important to note that this agrarian dimension of the problem in Ottoman Armenia has been lost to the parties in question as well as to most historians. Under the traumatic effect of the Genocide, what has survived for most urban Armenians, including historians and inheritors of the parties, is the nationalist and existential aspect. Soviet Armenian historians who, similar to the founders of the Hnchakian party, imagined and wrote within the sphere of a socialist ideology, recognized the agrarian dimension more readily.[6]

The question arises: why did a national party not arise among Western Armenians with the same concerns? The answer may be logistical. The Ottoman state had a dominant presence in Ottoman Armenian life; any organization that was based in Ottoman territory would be easily discovered and destroyed. There were also too many Armenians who thought it was not possible, wise, or beneficial to oppose the state. It was not difficult for the state to make use of all of these Armenians and the internal spy system to make the rise of an Armenian national political party based in the Empire impossible.

It is also possible that Ottoman Armenian political thought had not reached the point where it could imagine radical action such as an armed opposition, rebellion, or revolution. In most areas where Armenians lived, non-Armenians and Muslims were either dominant or overwhelming. Power relations here and any sense of "justice" depended on the submissive relationship the most conservative Armenian elements and institutions held with Ottoman and local authorities. The reform movements—Ottoman and Armenian millet-based—did attract the most daring but the absence of a political imagination beyond what the Ottoman Armenian leadership could offer could not easily attract the youth that was radicalized by the time the Hnchakians were ready to call for a radical approach. The reformist movements took Ottoman rule for granted in a society where the Church had the dominant role, a role that was also circumscribed by the state.[7]

Meanwhile, as we shall see later, underlying an established tradition of Russian Armenian interest in Ottoman Armenians and their plight was a territorialization as well as a historicization of Armenian identity, bringing that identity closer to modern nationalism. Within that perspective, borders were irrelevant.[8]

Thus, being Russian or Ottoman Armenian was altogether irrelevant, as far as the founders of the Hnchakian Party was concerned, in their quest to resolve the problem of their brethren across the border. As noble as it sounded, such an attitude tended to disregard the real differences between the two segments of the Armenian people, differences that compelled the party founders and organizers to make adjustments later in their strategy. When no adjustments were forthcoming, the party split, as in 1896, after the 1894-1896 massacres in Ottoman Armenia. One wing, made up predominantly of Ottoman Armenians, split from the "mother" party to constitute the "Veragazmyal" (Reformed) Hnchakian party; the latter accused the party leadership of having emphasized socialism too much at the expense of the existential struggle needed in the Ottoman lands. Such emphasis, they noted, gave the Armenian struggle an unduly anti-Western character that, in turn, made the movement suspicious in the eyes of the Great Powers, all anti-socialist.

MARXISM AND ARMENIAN INDEPENDENCE

What distinguished political parties of that time from organizations devoted to specific causes or sets of goals is the adoption of a worldview or an ideology as the basis of the organization's strategy and, to some extent, tactics. The world view or ideology a party adopted was fundamental because it is through its prism that the party will (1) define the struggle they will be engaged in, including their enemies and potential partners, (2) interpret the forces and factors that affect the environment within which they will be functioning, (3) determine the solution they will be seeking to the problem, and (4) thus design the strategy they will be following to achieve their goals.

The founders of the Hnchakian party were followers of the Marxian worldview, or what they understood to be the Marxist view. That is an ideology that considered class struggle as the prime mover of history; looked upon the exploitation of the majority of the people by a minority class as the main problem; and a classless society, through class struggle, as the solution to that problem. On many levels, Marxian socialism was the antithesis of the nationalist worldview that regarded the nation as the ultimate and absolute value.

The Hnchakian founders' experience in Russia, mentioned above, was a major factor in their adoption of socialism, at the time the most progressive and liberationist ideology, particularly appealing to the weak. The universalist perspective and appeal of Hnchakian socialism is also the reason why the party's name did not include the term "Armenian." Thus, as a matter of belief, albeit couched in scientific garb, according to SDHP, history had always moved because of class struggles, and to succeed in one's struggle, one had to have the support of the logic of history—thus neutralizing one's relative weakness in power relations. Thus, one not only sided with the class that was destined to win in history, but also the morally right one. The moral underpinnings of class struggle had an eschatological progress. Humanity had moved from the very bad toward the better; and it was bound to reach the best, and the best strategy to be part of history was to participate in it the right way; classless society, inevitable because socialists had understood the positive laws of social development, would constitute the ultimate in human progress. The Hnchakian ideologues took for granted that Armenians were part of humanity and subject to the same laws as the rest.

Logically, therefore, the Hnchakian program should have called upon Armenians in the Ottoman Empire to wage class warfare as members of the exploited classes against all exploiters regardless of their ethnicity or religion. Instead, they called upon the establishment of an independent Armenia.

The manner in which these two goals—socialism and independence – were reconciled was quite ingenious, and it constitutes a precursor for national liberation movements later in more than one continent: the relationship between empire and oppression and exploitation of subject nations as a class. The Hnchakians separated the two seemingly conflicting goals by spreading them over time. Independence was an immediate goal, while socialism was the ultimate goal. The Hnchakians were erudite enough to understand that the struggle on the basis of scientific socialism could be waged in capitalist societies that also had a proletariat, although a peasantry—the experience they were exposed to in the Russian empire speaks to this—could be a substitute for an industrial proletariat. But they asserted that the Ottoman Empire was too backward to be the scene for a class struggle; thus, the goal of waging socialist struggle itself required that an Armenia be created, one where capitalism and other prerequisite conditions could exist for the long-term goal of waging class struggle and creating a socialist society. In that way, Armenians would be participating in the making of future humanity on the right side of history.

This paradox becomes even more intriguing when the arrangement between nationalism and socialism is projected into the field of action. In seeking resources for the creation of the first goal, independence, the Hnchakians appealed to all layers of Ottoman Armenian society. One of these was the "princes" of Zeytoun, the impoverished local leaders of a mountainous district in Cilicia that had retained a degree of autonomy within

Ottoman dominion. Zeytoun was one of the very rare areas where one could see remnants of the Armenian nobility as well as a fighting spirit reminiscent of the past. Armenians imagined the 1862 Zeytoun Rebellion against the Ottomans as the first sign of the political and military renaissance of the ancient and independent Armenian people. In fact, that rebellion was primarily one of the last acts of a dying Armenian "feudal nobility"— represented by the mainly impoverished *ishkhans* (princes), who wished to preserve their privileges and were able to summon the defensive instincts of the population under their administration against the centralizing policies of the Ottoman Empire in the throes of reform. The Hnchakians made great efforts to win the very old and very conservative Zeytoun leadership to their side, the side of a battle for the independence of an Armenia, because it was a readymade resource that could be used for the short-term goal.

It is not all that clear that the Hnchakian leaders were conscious of the paradox at this level. They certainly were aware of the major conflict between nationalism and Marxian socialism; they would also become more sensitive to that after the 1894-1896 massacres, when many Western Armenians who had rallied to the SDHP, believing in its immediate goal, challenged the relevance of socialism for the Ottoman Armenian condition. The founding fathers and one mother of the Hnchakian party do not seem to have been aware of the dangers of ideology "going native," when it made concessions to national history and local mentalities, and sacrificed—from an ideological point of view—the ultimate goal to promote tactical gains. One important advantage ideologies have over simple political programs is that they are internally coherent. Real conditions and experiences are filtered and turned into elements that sustain a system of interpretations and projections or constructs for the future. Ideologies do impose new realities; they also bend because of realities on the ground.

A key dimension in the Hnchakian' ideological conundrum was that, while the individuals were enamored by socialism, as an organization the object of their concern was "the Armenian people." It was not the working class of the Ottoman Empire or of the other empires where Armenians lived; it was not the Armenian working classes and peasants in any of those places. The historical category they were trying to "save" was the Armenian people. Furthermore, their program called for the independence and reunification of all three segments of historical Armenia: territories under

Ottoman rule, the major part of historic Armenia; those under Russian rule; and those under Persian rule. That they started out with Ottoman Armenia was a tactical decision dictated by the existential threat to the Armenian people posed by the situation in that part of historic Armenia.[9]

HNCHAKIANS AND THE CHURCH

The Hnchakian program, as eventually published in the *Hnchak* monthly, does not mention religion or the Armenian Apostolic Church that had emerged as the dominant Armenian institution in Armenian life for centuries, since the collapse of the Armenian kingdoms. Maybe this was a way for Hnchakians to manifest their ideological purity or devotion to the most universal of values, socialism. In fact, establishing a political party was a form of rebellion against that dominant Church; in essence, the SDHP was a challenge to the religious institution's claim, taken for granted until then, to speak for Armenians. By creating a new institution, the Hnchakians were also creating a new principle of legitimacy. The absence of the Church and religion from the program indicated that the party, both as a new institution and as the bearer of a new worldview, had no use for religion or for the Church.

Yet, at the first encounter between Ottoman authorities and field workers sent to the Ottoman Empire to spread the new gospel, in 1889, the field workers sought sanctuary in the Armenian church of Trebizond. Their first political action, the demonstration against the Ottoman government at Kum Kapu in July 1890, began with a bizarre act: The leaders of the demonstration invaded the church of the Armenian Patriarchal seat in Constantinople, interrupted mass, and asked the Patriarch to lead a demonstration against the Ottoman government at Kum Kapu. Patriarch Khoren Ashekian refused. He was roughed up, physically; unwillingly, he did proceed at the head of the angry demonstrators, mostly migrant workers from the provinces, the lumpen proletariat of Constantinople, although they did not know that term. Following this unprecedented action, the Patriarch offered his resignation, which was rejected by the Ottoman government. As one can guess, the leaders of the demonstration were imprisoned.

It is significant that a political party that starts out by ignoring religion and Church decides to make itself known by trying to make use of the Church, to garner the Church's legitimacy, rather than organizing an activity that would more closely reflect its ideology. One could argue that once the idea of an independent Armenian state was adopted, albeit as an ostensibly short-term goal, then the party leadership would permit itself to use any tactical means available, including the Church and remnants of the feudal lords. The question is, at what point does the tactical become the dominant definer of a party. The issue would haunt the Hnchakian Party for a long time to come.

One explanation for these paradoxes is the connection of the birth of the Hnchakian Party—as well as soon after of the Dashnaktsoutiun—to the internationalization of the Armenian issue through the Treaty of San Stefano in February and the Treaty of Berlin in July 1878; that is, the birth of the so-called "Armenian Question." Once Armenians, i.e., at that time the Church, gave up their hopes for internally inspired reforms in the Armenian provinces that could be implemented through the Ottoman government, eyes were turned toward the Great Powers that assumed responsibility for pressing the Sultan to implement reforms required by the 1878 Treaty of Berlin. Yet a decade passed and the Armenian Question was practically forgotten. The Hnchakian party was the expression of both the frustration of Armenians with the non-implementation of a reform program and the perception that the internationalization of the Armenian issue could and should be used as a strategy to achieve the tactical goal of independence. The Church, specifically the Patriarchate of Constantinople, had been the mechanism for the internationalization of the Armenian Question; and in the Balkans, former Ottoman territories had escaped the Sultan's rule through rebellions and the shedding of blood. Hence the assignment of important roles to the Church and the princes, two institutions that were not only ignored in the party program but were also were implicated to be historically regressive forces within the framework of the advent of socialist society.[10]

WHAT IDEOLOGIES ARE AND DO

On a deeper level, though, ideology constituted a source of power, real and/ or imagined, for the weak. For the Hnchakians, as later in more practical terms for the Dashnaktsoutiun and to a lesser extent Ramgavars, ideology was a way of participating in (a) Western, European ("civilized") discourse, and (b) in positivist thinking: history is moving forward toward a better future, progress was inevitable. By that logic, it was time for Armenians to join the march of history. There was, therefore, hope for Armenians; they only needed to be on the right side of history.

Ideologies and systems of thought have the advantage of providing wholesome explanations of the world around you, of forces that control your life, that help you understand where you can be part of the making of your own future, where you can become an agency of that future. But that which is their advantage, their wholesomeness and coherence, is the vulnerable point of ideologies. Socialism and Marxism explained capitalism and to some extent the kind of imperialism that evolved out of capitalism. So, the Hnchakians could understand the large forces and interests at play, in principle. But no ideology or system explains everything at every level; not accurately and fully for all instances. That which explains everything, it is said, explains nothing. Ideologies, especially those that have predictive power, provide the impression that one understands the complex processes around you, that one's decisions—derived from a correct understanding of the laws of history—are bound to produce the end that the ideology predicted. Thus, one relies on the illusion that somehow one is in control of one's destiny even though one is being massacred.

Ideologies also endow adherents with a sense of empowerment that energizes and leads to acts of heroism. Yet in case one's resources are not sufficient to produce the desired change, those acts are celebrated as acts of martyrdom and produce a sense of martyrdom and victimhood that can be mistaken for success.

The Ottoman Empire was characterized as the "Sick Man of Europe", implying that it was weak. The Ottoman Empire was weak, indeed, but only relative to any of the Great Powers. But it was not weak relative to some of its subject peoples, such as Armenians. And it provided a number of opportunities to Armenians to have a false sense of being right; they had, after all, followed the dictates of an ideology, as if the purpose of the struggle was to be faithful to the ideology.

THE AFTERMATH

It is not the purpose of this article to trace the Hnchakians' ideological equivocations following their birth in 1888. But it is useful to mark a few significant moments. As indicated above, the Hnchakian party split in 1896, following which it lost its position in the revolutionary movement to the Armenian Revolutionary Federation that had manifested a more flexible attitude regarding ideology. Both wings of the Hnchakian party continued to be present in the Armenian political spectrum. The "mother" party, as the Hnchakian Party is called, did find some way to manifest its socialist identity by being more alert to the nationalist dimensions of Young Turk, especially the Committee of Union and Progress (CUP, Ittihad ve Terakkı), ideology and organizing Armenian workers in Russian cities and Baku later on. But they, just as the Dashnaktsoutiun, continued to be dogged by the duality of their cause: born to save Western Armenia and Western Armenians, they felt at home in the Russian Empire.

In 1909, the Hnchakian Party dropped its goal of establishing an independent Armenia in the Ottoman Empire: The Young Turk Revolution of 1908, it argued, indicated that you could have a bourgeois revolution in the Ottoman Empire and an independent Armenia was no longer necessary for the party's ultimate goal to be pursued. That optimism gave way to severe pessimism by 1911 as the CUP failed to deliver on the promise of the Young Turk Revolution. In 1915, 20 Hnchakian leaders were hanged in Constantinople for having plotted the assassination of Ottoman government leaders.[11] By that time, the Hnchakians had already made their peace with the Church as well, although the Patriarchate was more under the influence of the Dashnaktsoutiun. By 1915, Marxism had become negotiable, even for the mother party, and the Church proved to be incontrovertible.

The Genocide beginning in 1915 became the great equalizer. Paradoxes, policies, and ideologies became irrelevant. Armenian political parties left their original liberal ideas and progressive ideologies under the ashes of Western Armenia. The weight of the past – including that of specific policies and overarching conceptualizations in a diasporan setting that was constantly shifting demographically and geographically – have made ideologies irrelevant. Generally speaking, past ideologies were better forgotten.

Much of the movement toward liberalized thinking—socialism should be counted as the most progressive in this direction[12]—would give way to more traditional attitudes, as Armenian institutions, including the political parties, adopted "preservation" of culture and identity as the new agenda.

The party whose founders included a woman, Maro Vardanian, said to have contributed significantly to the ideological grounding of the party, never produced another woman as a leader, although it is possible that there remained more women rank-and-file members in the Hnchakian Party than in any of the others.

Nonetheless, the Hnchakians did continue, as ideologically motivated parties tend to do, to find solutions to its paradoxes. At the end of its political prevarications and to conclude the first phase of its history as a party in historic Armenia, on August 1920, the Hnchakians decreed the "Act of Self-Government of Cilicia," an act that lasted a few days only;[13] there had also been a Ramgavar declaration of independence by Mihran Damadian, once a Hnchakian leader, later a Ramgavar activist. Furthermore, the Hnchakians returned, in a way, to its ideological origins and in 1921 recognized Soviet Armenia as the realization of its ultimate goal.[14] Soviet Armenia was both socialist and an Armenia, even if less than independent. Now made up largely of Western Armenians, there was no longer a paradox; more importantly, there was no longer a Western Armenian population to save: they had been massacred or turned into refugees elsewhere.

Strangely, it was Western Armenian Hnchakians supporting an eastern Armenian state. Henceforth, the Hnchakian Party considered it its patriotic duty to support Soviet Armenia. Western Armenia, as territory, was not a matter of strategic considerations or struggles: in foreign and security policy issues that meant following the USSR line. That issue was raised briefly in 1945, but more resolutely after the 1960s, when the Soviet Union needed legitimation of the Soviet government in Armenia through nationalist rhetoric; communist ideology and the building of socialism were no longer adequate to maintain any semblance of legitimacy. Support for Soviet Armenia also meant strong support for the All-Armenian Catholicosate in Etchmiadzin in the Diaspora in the battles with the American and Dashnaktsoutiun supported encroachments by the Catholicosate of Cilicia, in Lebanon since 1921, against the Mother Church's jurisdictions in the diaspora.

CONCLUSION

Today it is difficult to visualize, even for a historian, the important role ideologies played in the rise of the Armenian revolutionary movement. One reason—the diasporization of Armenian life—was mentioned above. A second reason may be that 19th century style positivist ideologies have been discredited. Thus, we really lack systematic studies of the role of ideologies in the minds of Eastern Armenians who, unlike their equally idealistic Western Armenian brothers, reached out to guns through a different intellectual process than the early fedayees.

As indicated above, socialism, as the ideology of the Hnchakian Party and later the Dashnaktsoutiun, was also used as a critical tool to understand the wider forces around them, both economic and imperial. Diasporan agendas are not open to interpretations beyond those "sensed" by Armenians; an "ideology" is too big a word and too large a world to be relevant. Ideologies have been replaced by "national visions." One universalist ideology that survived the longest is the communist one, entrenched in Soviet Armenia for some seven decades. But that too lost its luster by the 1960s and power by the late 1980s. By the 1960s the Communist Party of Soviet Armenia, as those elsewhere in the USSR, too had to call upon national history, identity and issues to preserve a sense of legitimacy.

These and related issues require a much more detailed investigation than is intended in this article. But there is no doubt that these ideologies, however conflictual and full of paradoxes, were significant in the minds of not only those who adopted them but also of others, watching them. The Ramgavar Party would be created in 1908 as a counterbalance to the Hnchakian Party and Dashnaktsoutiun, to represent the interests of the Armenian bourgeoisie. The founders of the former clearly indicated that they were creating the new party to oppose the socialism, as well as the revolutionary methods, of the two existing parties.

The shifting fortunes of ideologies became evident in the first major conflict in the post-Genocide diaspora: To support or to struggle against the Communist party rule in Soviet Armenia. The Hnchakians, as mentioned above, and the Ramgavars, joined hands to support the new, Soviet Armenia; the first as a matter of ideology, the second as a matter of practicality. The Dashnaktsoutiun opposed it. For decades, along with the churches they controlled, these three parties scrounged for ideological groundings for their positions. That battle led them to fall in a new trap, the Cold War, the ultimate "ideological" struggle. While domestically all parties and institutions subscribed to the new religion of preservation of culture and language, they turned over the reins of their intellectual bearings to the dictates of the East-West confrontation. Their initial connection to what one may label as universally valid ideologies was now mediated by forces even less accessible to them than what they had in the Ottoman Empire.

Universal ideologies became altogether irrelevant to Armenian political thought after the collapse of the USSR. One might say the rise of the Genocide recognition campaign after the 1970s overcame any remnants of differences between the parties; it also dominated the way Armenian political parties, including the Hnchakian Party, connected to the world. And since the birth of the Third Armenian Republic in 1991, ideologies have been replaced by "orientations," Eastern/Russian versus Western/European. The position of the first group is consolidated by the essentialist interpretation of the Genocide, i.e., that Turks killed Armenians because they were Turks and that Armenians were victims because Armenians are always victims; and, therefore, Armenians are under constant threat of annihilation by Turkey, as Turks are still Turks and Armenians are still Armenian.

Therefore, fate has determined Armenia's future to be with and, if necessary, under Russia. That is the Russian orientation, supported by and large, in so many words, by all three political parties of the Diaspora and, of course, the remnants of the Communists and those plagued with nostalgia for the Russian or for the Soviet. The Karabakh Committee that led Soviet Armenian to independence, transformed into the Armenian National Movement, representing the only revival of an alternative, self-determining agenda that looked to a future of Armenia as a liberal, European style democracy in peace with all its neighbors. That is the closest we have come to a new ideology, however limited to the Republic of Armenia. The future of that vision is very doubtful, even in Armenia.

The greatest paradox is that ideologies, intended to bring the Armenian people closer to progressive humanity or the "civilized world," probably helped Armenians become victims or accept the victim status. Ideologies were transformed into shells because of the Genocide and loss of the connection to the universal, with one exception: opposing Armenian political parties aligned with opposing international forces that could only use the Armenian people, as they had done in the Ottoman Empire. Instead of participants, Armenians were now only victims of history.

The specter of the Treaty of Berlin still dominates.

---

1. As important as the Armenagans (established in Van in 1885) were, they can best be characterized as a political organization rather than as a party; they also never became a national organization. They espoused some important values but did not develop a national program of action.

2. This article does not intend to present a history of the Hnchakian Party. Prior to the publication of this volume and other sources mentioned here, there have been four works that are significant for that history: Hagop Turabian's sketchy three-article series in 1916; Louise Nalbandian's unpublished MA thesis at Stanford University, 1949 (limited to the issue of the introduction of socialism in Armenia, to 1947); Hnchakian leader Arsen Kitur's two volume history in Armenia (Beirut, 1963), a somewhat tentative and uneven work; and Soviet Armenian historian Ashot Hovannisyan's important article on the origins of the party. Please see the bibliography for full details on these works.

3. The basic tenets of the Hnchakian Party can be found in the leading article of the first issue of the official organ, *Hnchak* ("Hratarakoutyan masin" [Regarding the publication], November 1887), the leading article of the second issue ("Brnapetoutyoun. Heraga yev motaka npatakner yev mijotsner," [Despotism. Distant and immediate goals and methods], *Hnchak* No. 2, January 1888), and *Tzragir* [Program], *Hnchak*, combined issues Nos. 11-12, Oct.-Nov., 1888.

4. Russian Armenians will also establish the second party, the Armenian Revolutionary Federation in 1890.

5. For the Great Powers, the Armenian Question was a subheading of the Eastern Question, i.e., how to divide up the Ottoman Empire and who would get Constantinople.

6   See for example, H. G. Vardanyan, *Arevmtahayeri Azatagroutyan hartsu* [The Question of liberation of Western Armenians], 1967, Yerevan, and A. A. Hambaryan, *Eritturkeri azgayin yev hoghayin kaghakakanoutyounu yev azatagrakan sharzhoumnern Arevmtyan Hayastanoum* [The nationalities and agrarian policies of the Young Turks in Western Armenia], Yerevan, 1979.

7. See Gerard J. Libaridian, "The Changing Armenian Self-Image in the Ottoman Empire: Rayahs and Revolutionaries," in *Image of the Armenian*

History and Literature, Richard G. Hovannisian, ed., 1981, reproduced in Gerard J. Libaridian, *Modern Armenia*, 2004; and Gerard J. Libaridian, "The Ideology of Armenian Liberation. The Development of Armenian Political Thought before the Revolutionary Movement (1639-1885)," unpublished Ph. D. dissertation, UCLA, 1987.

8. Kristapor Mikayelian, one of the founders of the Dashnaktsoutiun, would later characterize the borders between the Russian and Ottoman Empire as being drawn by bandits.

9. This was an approach that "real" Marxists, Bolsheviks, would reject. Their point of departure would be the class struggle and would, at best, relegate ethnic/national identity to a tertiary role. There were also Marxists who would be recognized as "Specifists," who considered that under some circumstances, such as when an ethnic group was targeted for exploitation and/or oppression, special consideration should be given to the ethnic/national unit as such within the framework of class struggle. See Libaridian, *Modern Armenia*, pp. 89-112.

10. *Ibid.* The Dashnaktsoutiun would deal differently with this issue. Less ideologically constrained, it assigned all members of Armenian society, from the rich to the poor, the priest and the merchant, the teacher and women a role in the struggle that was shaping up. Of the historical Armenian political parties only the Democratic Liberal or Ramgavar Party assigns the Armenian Church as such an important role in Armenian life. Bolsheviks later would find another solution: the national question was an imperialist plot; in the specific case of Armenians, the question was framed wrongly; besides, it could not be resolved, not even by Russia, but especially by Russia, because Russia too was an imperialist power whose interest colluded but also coincided with those of Western imperialists states. Thus, only by changing Russia, and after Russia, the world revolution, could the Armenian Question be resolved.

11. See Gerard J. Libaridian, "What Was Revolutionary About Armenian Revolutionary Parties in the Ottoman Empire?" pp. 82-112, in *A Question of Genocide*, R. G. Suny, F. M. Göçek, and Norman M. Naimark, eds., 2011.

12. See Nigol Shahgaldian; unpublished Ph.D. dissertation; "The Political Integration of an Immigrant Community into a Composite Society: The Armenians in Lebanon, 1920-1974," Columbia University, 1979.

13. Antranig Genjian, S. D. Hnchagian Gousagtsoutiunu yev Giligian Inknavaroutyan Aktu, 1919-1921 [The SD Hnchakian Party and the Act of Self-Government of Cilicia]; Beirut, 1958. The term "inknavaroutiun" may also be translated as "autonomy."

14. The Hnchakian Party would return to Armenia's independence in 1991.

6

WHAT WAS REVOLUTIONARY ABOUT ARMENIAN REVOLUTIONARY PARTIES IN THE OTTOMAN EMPIRE?

2011

Historiography still lacks a systematic critical study of Armenian revolutionary parties individually or as a history of the revolutionary movement. Possibly because these are considered sacrosanct as is the case with the Armenian Church, or because scholars do not want to wade in murky waters and invite the wrath of these institutions. As indicated earlier in this volume, that may be changing with a younger generation of scholars.

Meanwhile, it is worth looking at some of the basic questions that must be answered as part of the demystification process which must be one of the conditions for the production of comprehensive histories.

This essay was first published in R. G. Suny, Muge Gocek and N. Naimark's 2011 volume A Question of Genocide, *and is being reproduced here with minor editing. The essay asks a simple question that is also the title of the essay. More of than not the answer to the question has been (a) the adoption of armed tactics as a means to achieve (b) radically new goals. These two dimensions of the revolutionary movement are certainly significant and relevant. Yet, when placed within the context of the period and environment within which the revolutionaries functioned, there is much more to consider as revolutionary. The essay below is an attempt to identify such other dimensions that were as significant and relevant in the impact the movement had on those who assessed the impact of the movement, including the Ottoman rulers.*

Armenian political parties were founded at the end of the nineteenth century for the purpose of giving a new direction to their Armenian constituents. They spoke, negotiated, and made decisions on behalf of the Armenians; and they sought to dominate the Armenians cultural and religious institutions while transforming their collective identity. Alternately called "nationalist" and "secessionist," these parties were considered separately from the political order of the Ottoman Empire, as though they were alien to the state's body politic. Often overlooked is the fact that these parties were active players in Ottoman political life, so active, in fact, that by 1908 they were widely considered as having replaced the church as the main intermediary between the Ottoman authorities and their Armenian subjects. They worked with Young Turk and other Ottoman organizations, took part in Ottoman elections following the Young Turk Revolution in alliances with other Ottomans, held seats in parliament, and deliberated on matters relevant to the whole empire.

Even less recognized is the fact that participation of Armenian political parties in Ottoman politics arose from their ideological underpinnings and programs, even though they have been seen, by and large, as "nationalist" and anti-state. The shadow cast by the genocide is so vast that it obscures to this day our sense of the choices that were available to the leaders of the Ottoman state, and, to a lesser extent, to the Armenian parties, prior to that event. The Ottoman leaders had the option to work with Armenian and other groups to solve the problems of the Ottoman Empire and, in the end, they decided not to. The Armenian parties could have acted strictly on an anti-state platform or, as the church did, not act at all. Instead they strove toward conditional cooperation.

Official Turkish historiography portrays these parties as independence-seeking terrorists, as if the pursuit of independence were blameworthy in and of itself. This depiction is cited as the reason why "Armenians" represented a threat to the Ottoman state and to Turks in general, and, by implication, were deserving of massacres, or worse. Turkish condemnation of Armenian political parties is based solely on the rhetoric of the writer rather than on the words and deeds of those being judged. The problem, simply phrased, is that historians and others who have tried to tell the story of Turkish/Armenian relations toward the end of the nineteenth and early twentieth centuries have been unable to imagine a common history, one that accounts for the complexities each found in its situation and the areas where common thought and action evolved.

Scholars must apply a more integrated approach if the critical period of Turkish/Armenian relations leading to the First World War and the genocide are to be accurately reconstructed. Unless we understand and assess adequately the "lines of contact" between the two political forces—Turkish and Armenian—in the waning decades of the Ottoman Empire, we will continue the sad situation of writing two separate histories: one of the "Armenians" and the other of "Turks," a situation that perpetuates the polemical views of the past that have dominated the literature on the subject.

This chapter does not aim to present a history of the revolutionary parties; nor is it a history of their relations with the Ottoman state. Rather, it is an attempt at delineating boundaries of political imagination developed by Armenian revolutionary organizations at their inception, boundaries created and crossed by ideology and praxis.

"ARMENIANS" AND "TURKS"

In the context of late Ottoman society, the terms "Armenian" and "Turk" are adequate, denoting ethnic categories in their most inert, essentialist sense. "Turks" and "Armenians" are individuals and groups whose actions cannot be explained strictly by their ethnic identity. Various groups of "Turks" and "Armenians" adopted different, and at times opposing policies different times and under different circumstances. Being Turkish or Armenian cannot be equated with having predetermined, self-evident, and immutable political agendas. Similarly, terms such as "nationalism" and "revolutionary" are problematic when substituted for precision.

To understand the evolution and character of Turkish-Armenian relations within the Ottoman Empire, it is necessary to make another clarification. Armenians are commonly referred to as a "minority," but what does it really mean? The term first came to be used after World War I to describe ethnic or religious groups in emerging nation-states. Empires did not have minorities; they had peoples who had been conquered. Such terminology ascribes a large degree of inevitability to the ultimate domination of an undefined "majority" and takes for granted that right to majority's supremacy This ahistorical approach is useful if the historian wishes to reduce Armenians to a mere ethnic or religious group, easily categorized as a victim (or a threat).

For more sophisticated analysis, however, the term "minority" introduces confusion and places limitations on the contexts within which Turkish-Armenian relations can be understood. Furthermore, it is not clear in what geographic context Armenians can be described as a minority. Armenians certainly did not consider themselves a minority within historic Western Armenia, even if numerically they did not constitute a majority. (In fact, no ethnic group constituted a majority at that time.) When a people live on their historic lands, they may be or feel privileged or oppressed, conquered or dominant, but not a "minority" in the sense of the post-World War I nation-states.

Of the various terms chosen to describe the Armenian political parties under discussion, "revolutionary" is one that the parties themselves used. One question we should ask, then, is: What was revolutionary about these parties? This in turn leads to others: What problem or problems did they try to resolve? And if they constituted a threat, whom or what were they threatening? What, in fact, was the character of the conflict with which historians and others struggle?

The parties in question are the Social Democratic Hnchakian Party (established in 1887, Geneva) and the Armenian Revolutionary Federation or *Dashnaktsoutiun* (1890, Tbilisi).[1] These are the parties most closely identified with developments in the Ottoman Empire and most commonly discussed by scholars who study Turkish Armenian relations prior to the First World War. The question concerning the "revolutionary" nature of these parties is critical for our understanding of their ideologies, strategies, and actions. Within such a context, we can also analyze their attempt to reshape the perceptions of Armenians, both by others and themselves, as well as their self-conscious distancing from institutions that had previously spoken on behalf of the Armenians in the Ottoman Empire. These differences between the political parties and these institutions characterized both what was most promising and most risky in the former's undertakings.

The establishment of these parties was part of an effort to turn Armenians into more active participants in their own history and the history of the Ottoman Empire. The founders' idea was to transform Armenians from objects of history into participants, which required no less than the transformation of the Ottoman Empire itself. In trying to achieve this goal, these parties also assumed responsibility for their choices, decisions that must be assessed in the larger context of Ottoman state priorities and the Great Powers intervention in Ottoman affairs.[2]

> The first program released by the Hnchakian Party stated: "The situation of the Turkish Armenian people is today the sickest. And it is the responsibility of the whole of the Armenian people to cure that disease today."[3] The lead article of the second issue of *Droshak,* the Dashnaktsoutiun organ, begins with the following assertion:
>
>> Any political party undertaking a struggle for an ideal can hope to achieve success or failure [sic] only when the following two conditions are present:
>>
>> 1. When the people, on whose behalf the struggle is being waged, understands that that struggle is necessary and participates in that struggle directly or indirectly, at least through its best representatives.
>>
>> 2. If the means and methods selected to wage that struggle correspond fully to the present realities and the demands of circumstances of the historical moment.[4]

The second point was an indirect criticism of the positions articulated in the issues of the party organ *Hnchak.* As I will show, even the revolutionaries did not agree among themselves.

REVOLUTIONS AND REVOLUTIONARIES

Many sources cast the term "revolution" in a negative light, suggesting potential for violence and recklessness, as opposed to a quest for change. Additionally, since a "revolution" challenges the concept of state, it is, by definition, contemptible to those who place the interests of the state above all. This view still prevails in current debates concerning the Ottoman Empire and its relations to its Armenian population; the Young Turk and Kemalist revolutions are considered acceptable, because they saved the state; the "Armenian" revolution is not. I pose the question about the "revolutionary" nature of these parties in a somewhat neutral sense: more precisely, I am concerned with what was radically new in the ideas, ideologies, goals, and behaviors of the parties in question; what made the founders of these parties use the term "revolutionary" to describe themselves; and how the closely related question of the "loyalty" of Armenians can be assessed within this perspective.

THE PARTY SYSTEM

The first, and possibly most revolutionary innovation introduced by the Hnchakian and Dashnaktsoutiun parties was the establishment of a political party structure in Armenian life, that is, their attempt to redefine the Armenian population as a political rather than a religious community. The Armenian Apostolic Church had dominated the political scene for centuries, owing its primacy to the disappearance of Armenian statehood and the "feudal" system that had defined political life in Armenia's early history. The church was assigned the role of speaking on behalf of the Armenians in the Ottoman Empire due to the *millet* system established by the Ottoman sultans, a religion-based system that regulated the communal life of non-Muslim communities such as Christians. In doing so, the Ottoman state was also able to limit the areas in which Armenians had any kind of self-governance or voice, while providing for extraterritorial self-government in many civil matters.

Smaller political groups had formed earlier, the *Armenagans* (1885) being the most prominent among them, and they can be partly credited with introducing the idea of parties as an alternative mechanism for the Armenians expression of grievances in the Ottoman Empire. Yet none had been able to develop the political scope and momentum to become nationwide parties that could supplant the church as the Armenian mouthpiece.

Despite the formally high position in which the church and its leader, the patriarch, were held in the eyes of Ottoman administrators, it became increasingly evident that their power was limited and, depending on the grievance, also useless. When the millet leadership, once democratized in the 1860s, attempted to reach beyond the confines of church-related affairs (clergy, churches and monasteries, properties, civil affairs, and to some extent education) to deal with social and economic problems plaguing the poor Armenian population in the provinces, the Porte made it clear that such concerns were not within the mandate of the patriarchate or the structures in its control. Archbishop Khrimian, the hero of the common people, resigned in frustration in 1873, accusing the government and the leaders of the Armenian community in Constantinople of blocking every effort at putting the plight of the provincial Armenians at the center of the National Assembly's agenda. Later, in 1878, when he returned from Berlin disappointed with the results of the Treaty of Berlin, Khrimian gave a number of sermons in Constantinople and the provinces. He explained that the reason why Armenians had lost ground in the treaty was that the weapon they were using to bring about change was made of paper, and that to take a share of the "soup" being offered in Berlin an "iron ladle" was needed.

It is true that for decades a new intellectual class, in both the Ottoman and Russian sectors of the Armenian people, had challenged the status quo, from the battle against classical Armenian in favor of the vernacular, to the spread of general education, and their disputing the preeminent role of the clergy. Yet, at least in the Ottoman Empire, this was not enough to challenge the church-led millet structure, nor did it call into question the role of the church as the representative of the Armenian people. The rise of the "revolutionary" parties was a confirmation of the failure of the church structure—within the patriarchate and National Assembly in Constantinople—and of the inability of reformist and liberal intellectuals to adequately address issues which they were not equipped to deal with. In fact, the Ottoman sultans never intended the church to perform a political function within the state, serving instead the interests of the state by depoliticizing the Armenians.[5]

During their early years, the parties functioned without any formal contact with the church. One exception was the "Kum Kapu" anti-sultan demonstration in Constantinople in 1890, organized by the nascent Hnchakian Party, which started with a challenge to the leader of the millet and the church. Armed leaders of the local Hnchakian organization rushed into the cathedral where Patriarch Ashekian was officiating. They stopped mass, read their demands on behalf of the poor and oppressed, and demanded that the patriarch join the demonstration. When Ashekian refused, he was forced (some say beaten) to get into his carriage and lead the demonstration until government forces intervened. Alerted by a priest, they surrounded the demonstrators, released the patriarch, and jailed the leaders. Ashekian denounced the actions of the demonstrators and apologized for them. Four years later he would be the target of an assassination attempt.[6]

Within the new community redefined by the parties, differences between Apostolic, Catholic, and Protestant Armenians, for example, became irrelevant, relegated to the realm of personal belief. The parties imposed, at least conceptually, a new distinction: between those who adopted a larger vision for the future and were ready to contribute actively to achieving it, and those who accepted the status quo. The parties consolidated the secular/ethnic understanding of the "Armenian," battling against a definition based on religion. Focusing on the plight of the peasants and craftsmen in historic Western Armenia, they also reterritorialized the concept.[7] The revolutionary shift brought about by these parties was first and foremost within the Armenian world. The radical intelligentsia and guerrilla leaders replaced the church-based and, to a large extent, wealth-based leadership. Thus the rise of the revolutionary parties signaled nothing less than a change of "government" within the Armenian populations of the Ottoman, but also Russian and Persian empires.

EMPOWERMENT OF THE WEAK THROUGH THE POSITIVE LAWS OF HISTORY

The Hnchakian and Dashnaktsoutiun parties were founded by Russian-Armenian radical intellectuals who modeled their organizations after Russian secret associations. They also borrowed elements from the Balkan peoples' struggles for independence. Both recruited adherents among Ottoman Armenians, segments of which seemed ready to find new expressions of resistance, having concluded that armed rebellion against Ottoman oppression was the only option. Paradoxically, the new leaders were self-appointed; there was no other way, it seems, to establish political parties dedicated to the liberation of Ottoman Armenians. Their perspectives combined reliance on the "inexorable" forces of history with the actions of individuals. They had the march of history on their side, they argued, and were convinced that history would prove them right; their claim to legitimacy was the ostensible scientific basis of their ideology. Yet, legitimacy on the ground was to be secured through the self-sacrifice of the fighters who would emerge. The "Armenian Question," with its universal, national, and individual dimensions, was a struggle that was part of the larger struggle for human progress; and, Armenian political aims were seen as integral to the laws and values of progressive humanity as defined by the Western Enlightenment and the French Revolution. This legitimacy had to be earned, rather than inherited, or else transferred from success in other fields.

Party "programs" articulated this new universalism, offering a wholesome and coherent worldview, and claiming a rational alternative to inherited wisdom. A scientific approach to history and its future displaced tradition and reflex as the principles of political discourse. This universalism, linked to the liberation of people with common problems, would eventually open the path for a variety of strategic choices.

The founders of both the Hnchakian and the Dashnaktsoutiun parties framed the "Armenian Question" as part of a universal struggle based on the laws of history. The party organ *Hnchak*, that professed to be closer to the mainstream Marxist views of the time described their "Long Term Goal" thus:

> The current social organization of humanity relies on injustice on the power of the fist, and on slavery. Based on economic slavery, that organization produced in mankind strong fists, strong rulers, who exploit the majority of humankind—the working world—and thus create the injustice of inequality within the relations of mankind. That inequality is expressed in every dimension of human life: economic, political, social as well as material...This complex and unjust state of affairs can be reformed only through the socialist organization [of society] by the respect for [the principle] of direct legislation by the people and [through that means] giving every member of society to participate factually in all decisions of public relevance...

The Hnchak group, being socialists in their fundamental beliefs, accepts the socialist organization of society as its ideal, its ULTIMATE GOAL [capitalized in the original] as it applies to the Armenian people and its fatherlands.[8]

The *Dashnaktsoutiun,* too, saw the Armenian plight in the context of human experience:

> Since the time when mankind set foot on the path to civilization, since the time when it started to have its history, there have been at all times and in all places rulers and subjects, exploiters and the exploited, those who cause suffering and the sufferers...That is how it was in the past, that is how it is today, but that is not how it will be tomorrow, we are convinced of that. We can see very clearly how the ruling classes are falling more and more physically and morally, how labor is increasingly achieving its rights, how the exploited are moving with giant steps toward its complete victory...

But how can that future be achieved?

> There was a time when the reformers of mankind appeared with this or that ideology with their "credo," to cure all mankind's ills, to eliminate all inequalities and to establish brotherhood, liberty and equality... Many centuries passed, one ideology replaced the other, many reformers were martyred; yet, nonetheless, we can see that a segment of humanity refuses to be convinced [of the need for change]—the segment that must be convinced, since it holds the key to injustice—since it is not in its interest to do so. Try to convince the English lord that he has no right to exploit the Irish, try to convince the highly educated factory owner that he is unjustly pocketing the labor of the worker, try to convince our beys and aghas that they should leave peasants alone, try to convince, finally the Kurd that he had no moral right to expropriate the home and the family of the man of Alashkert.[9]

The Dashnaktsoutiun program analyzed the social and economic conditions in the Ottoman Empire and then listed the grievances specific to Armenians and peasants, and those relevant to all subjects of the Ottoman Empire that had to be addressed. These conditions, argued the authors of the program, could not be removed by goodwill and good intentions or Utopian ideologies; change could only come through armed revolution.

The Dashnaktsoutiun had tried in an early stage to include the Hnchakian Party in a federation of revolutionary and oppositional groups. That attempt failed, probably because of the Dashnaktsoutiun leaders' suspicion of the wholly ideologized view of the world adopted by the Hnchakians. The Dashnaktsoutiun's first formal program, formulated over a two-year period and published in 1892, stated:

The sad and cruel lessons of history have demonstrated clearly that to achieve victory it is not sufficient for the suffering segments of humanity to understand its own condition, or even to develop the willingness to see it changed; that it is necessary to obtain real power. But since that power cannot be created overnight, and since that power is the consequence of existing conditions and changes accordingly, it is obvious that any form of social organization, however ideal, cannot be instituted at once, and that such an institution becomes possible only through the reform of existing conditions.

It is for this reason that we do not come forth as proponents of this or that Utopian ideology; it is our purpose that our program be basic. Our attention is focused on the present condition of our land. Our goal is to subject... to an objective critique the causes that have given rise to the present condition... to identify the causes of that condition based on the positive laws of the social sciences; and at the same time to wage a relentless struggle against the factors that have conditioned these causes.[10]

The Dashnaktsoutiun program constituted, in part, a direct critique of the Hnchakian approach. Obviously, the two parties had major differences, even though they both relied on positivist and universal laws governing the development of human history, at least in their respective understanding of the Armenian condition. Initially evident in their conflict on the ideological level, such differences had immediate consequences for their practical goals.

The main goal of the Dashnaktsoutiun was reform in Ottoman Armenia. In fact, the first issue of *Droshak* published the reform plan for this region developed by Patriarch Nerses Varzhabedian in connection with the treaties of San Stefano and Berlin in 1878. The plan called for autonomy for the region, an Armenian governor-general appointed by the sultan in consultation with the Great Powers, equal participation of Armenian and Muslim populations in administrative and legislative bodies, and measures to improve the conditions of all. The explicit endorsement of the patriarchal plan created a problem for the new party, however: If the Varzhabedian plan was acceptable, then what reason was there to create a new revolutionary party? In an editorial note, the second issue of *Droshak* clarified:

In the previous issue of *Droshak* we had written that our current demands are approximately the same as those formulated in the plan presented by Nerses Patriarch. Because these words have given cause to misunderstandings, we deem it important to state, that when writing that we had in mind a circumstance when the Sultan, through his own goodwill, would introduce the reforms in Turkish Armenia proposed by Nerses Patriarch, which is very unlikely. By his behavior, the Sultan is convincing everyone that there is no salvation for Turkish Armenia but through revolt. [11]

The Hnchakians, who had set socialism as their ultimate aim, needed to bridge the "present conditions" and a full-out socialist regime. The problem was solved when the party's founders introduced the intermediate step of independence for Turkish Armenia. The Ottoman system was so backward and decrepit, they argued, that it was impossible to hope for a direct leap into socialism. Independence became the "immediate goal" of the party. In practice, however, the party wavered. In an introductory note to the Hnchakian program, the founders explained that their program was tentative, and that it would be possible that various elements would be revised over time. [12] The objective of Turkish-Armenian independence was finally abandoned after the sixth [congress], the Hnchakian Congress of 1909, following the Young Turk Revolution of 1908 and the establishment of a parliamentary system in the Ottoman Empire. In the public statement relating the decisions of the Congress in Constantinople, the Hnchakians wrote:

> The Congress, in view of all the above factors and in support of class struggle, in accordance with the principles of social democracy, emphasizes one more time the necessity of the actualization of the harmony of nations, recognizing as a condition the necessity of the right of historical-individual existence of nations, rejecting on one hand the idea of secession (separatism) and, on the other, the supremacy and domination of one nation over the other. [13]

For both parties the question of independence was a complicated one. The Hnchakians considered independence to be a necessary tactical step, but following the Young Turk Revolution—which they interpreted as the necessary "bourgeois" transformation of Ottoman society—they decided that socialism was in fact possible in the Ottoman Empire as it stood. For the Dashnaktsoutiun, the goal was a more modest, if less clearly defined, "freedom." This meant liberation from the oppressive political system and an end to Ottoman policies that led to the disintegration of the Ottoman Armenian economic base. Their agenda clearly stopped short of requesting the establishment of an independent state, focusing instead on reform.

In July of 1904, a major confrontation erupted between Armenian guerrilla fighters and the Ottoman army in Sassoun, west of Lake Van. Two of the leaders of the "Sassoun rebellion" sent a letter to the foreign consuls who were interested in the demands of the revolutionaries. The lengthy letter was signed by the then-well-known Dashnak guerrilla leaders Antranig and Kevork, and states:

> Our enemies cry out: "Armenians do not seek reforms, they demand sovereignty and independence!" To this we solemnly declare that the agitation and efforts of the Armenian revolutionists have never aimed at, and do not now aim at any interference with the territorial integrity of the Ottoman Empire, or at any form of political separation. Armenians claim no sovereignty over the races living with them; they simply claim such administrative reforms as will protect their persons and property from the attacks of the local authorities, from Turks and from Kurds.[14]

Independence would not become an official issue for the Dashnaktsoutiun until 1919, when an independent Armenia had already been established in the Russian segment of historic Armenia.

Although both parties shared the vision of a European-style democracy in the future autonomous or independent Armenia, their differences far outweighed their similarities. Disagreement devolved into an antagonism that lasted for many decades, through the years of armed struggle, the constitutional period following the Young Turks Revolution, the genocide, the establishment of independent, then Soviet Armenia, in Eastern Armenia ruled by Russia, and in the Diaspora.

The ideological difference between the two parties was summed up by Kristapor Mikaelian, one of the founders of the Dashnaktsoutiun, during a debate in 1903:

> You are speaking of the surplus labor that the bourgeoisie exploits to its benefit; but we are dealing with surplus blood which is being shed every day because of the Turkish government.[15]

The Hnchakians remained the dominant party among Armenians until the massacres of 1894-1896, when hopes for autonomy evaporated. A fierce debate within the Hnchkian Party regarding the causes of the massacres and the role of socialism led to a schism. Many Western Armenian Hnchakians left the Social Democratic *Hnchak* Party to establish the "*Veragazmial*" or "reconstituted" Hnchakian Party. They regarded socialism as a distraction that may have antagonized the sultan and the Great Powers more than necessary.

The Dashnaktsoutiun, too, had to make adjustments in its party strategy following the wave of massacres. But the more practical ideological perspective it had adopted made it possible to focus more on adjustments: the new strategy included a wider organizational basis and better preparation; exploring more seriously cooperation with Kurdish tribes and groups, an active search for allies among Muslim, including Turkish liberal groups; a European campaign more geared toward intellectuals and the public and not limited to government leaders, and so forth. These adjustments introduced following the massacres allowed the Dashnaktsoutiun to emerge from the crisis as the dominant Armenian party; the Hnchakians never fully recovered from the shock of the massacres and the split that followed.

The antagonism between the parties continued, despite appeals from both parties to work together for the common cause. The Hnchakians criticized the Dashnaktsoutiun for being opportunistic and for exaggerated claims of success and influence, all aimed at securing financial resources. The Hnchakians, true to their professed Marxist position, were also miffed by the insensitivity of the Dashnaktsoutiun toward ideological purity. In their 1910 congress, they berated the Dashnaktsoutiun for their meddling in the affairs of the patriarchate, and their attempts to control it by electing a "political" patriarch: They argued that the church has a religious character that must be respected; that religion is a matter of conscience; and that the church belongs to the faithful and as a socialist party the Hnchakians would not want to disturb the peace of the community of the faithful.[16]

The Dashnaktsoutiun, in turn, had long ago found the Achilles heel of the Hnchakian party. A lead article in the main organ of the party written by one of the founders of the Dashnaktsoutiun, Rostom (Stepan Zorian), conveys the character of the acrimonious relations:

The Hnchak group appeared on the arena as a socialist revolutionary [group]. From the start it stated that it will not be satisfied with a democratic national independence; rather, its goal is socialism. But what was this socialism and how it could be actualized it was impossible to form a clear opinion from the articles in *Hnchak* [the Hnchakian party organ], because the editorial group of the *Hnchak* itself had no specific idea and still does not today. A chaos, a cacophony of ideas and the total absence of specificities: this is what one can see in the views expressed by the *Hnchak*.[17]

Rostom continued his critique of the Hnchakians, accusing them of not having learned from the seven years of their experiment with the future of Armenians. Rostom was the most "Marxist" of the three founders of the Dashnaktsoutiun.

The differences between the parties became more marked after the Young Turk Revolution. The Dashnaktsoutiun embraced the change, while the Hnchakians displayed more caution. The latter considered the Young Turk Revolution a "truncated" one, which is how they had described the Midhatian reforms of the 1870s. The Hnchakians had spurned earlier advances from the Young Turks in Paris, considering them too nationalistic.[18] The Dashnaktsoutiun continued its policy of cooperation with the Young Turk movement by aligning with the *Ittihad ve Terakkı* or Committee of Union and Progress (CUP) Party and trying to work through it to achieve its own goals. That cooperation lasted until 1915.

In view of the events that were to follow, these differences appear fundamental. Should Armenians have concluded soon after the euphoria produced by the Young Turk had dissipated that there was no hope from the Ottoman government for reforms of any kind? Should Armenians have expected the worst and returned to the idea of a defensive war, prepared for an all-out defense, as the *Hnchak* advocated, instead of trying to find a compromise with the ruling CUP, the Turkish party in power? To what extent the differences between the two parties were ideologically inspired and to what extent they reflected practical/political considerations is a question yet to be studied.

This antagonism, essential to Armenian history, and disregarded by most scholars, reached its climax with the Sovietization of Armenia. The First Republic of Armenia, where the Hnchakians had little influence, was established in 1918 under the Dashnaktsoutiun leadership. When the republic was Sovietized at the end of 1920, the Dashnaktsoutiun became a party in exile. The Hnchakians, true to their original beliefs, endorsed it as the realization of their goal, a socialist Armenia.

THE NATION AS A CLASS, WITH A FOCUS ON THE PEASANTRY

The new political parties introduced the concept of class struggle to the discourse about the Armenian situation, having each adopted a form of socialism as the basis of their scientific approach to history and politics. Until their founding, the tensions within the Armenian millet of the Ottoman Empire had been articulated as a conflict between *azkaser* (nation or community lover) and *hayrenaser* (fatherland lover or patriot), loosely corresponding to the Armenians of the urban centers who controlled the millet institutions and the poor Armenians in the provinces. Azkasers were content with the amenities provided by the millet system, and their identity was defined mainly by religion, on which the millet system itself was based.

In essence a diasporan, extraterritorial world of Armenian-ness, the focus on community affairs constituted an adjustment to a new identity away from the historic homeland, an adjustment to an extraterritorial identity centered around the church and ostensibly, faith, which unlike a homeland could not be carried by a emigrants such as their ancestors had been.[19] The azkaser world, as represented by the Armenian millet National Assembly in Constantinople, was consumed by an agenda limited to *azgayin,* national but really community institutions, such as churches, schools, and cemeteries. The provincial Armenian issues—provincial from the point of view of the Constantinople community leaders—were inconveniences at best if not threats to the well-being of the middle- and upper-class Armenians in Constantinople, the segments of Armenian society that defined the *azg,* or the nation.

A hayrenaser's main concern was the worsening situation of Armenians in the provinces. During the second half of the nineteenth century, deterioration due to economic transformation (monetization of taxation, wholesale destruction of home industries due to increased imports from an industrializing Europe) led to increased and often wanton lawlessness, land grabs by resettled Muslim refugees from Russian and Balkan wars in areas inhabited by Armenians had created a situation that reached crisis proportions for Armenians in the eastern provinces or in historic Western Armenia. These Armenians constituted the majority of the Armenian people and lived as they had for centuries, on their ancestral lands in the Ottoman Empire, even if other peoples had come to join them later.

In political terms, the conflict within the Armenian community pitted the "conservatives" and the "liberals" against one another. The azkasers, or conservatives, considered any attempt to use millet structures for the purpose of advancing social and economic grievances a subversion of the system. They viewed such attempts as a threat to the interests of the "nation" and to their own delicate economic standing vis-a-vis the imperial government. The hayrenasers considered the millet structures as a legitimate vehicle for the articulation of grievances most threatening to those living in the historically Armenian provinces.[20]

Once the political parties framed their cause as one of the poor and economically threatened, including the peasantry, they redefined the new political community, or the "people," primarily as a "class." Their opposition to the status quo was not motivated strictly by the non-Armenian-ness of the state but also by its oppressive and exploitative nature. According to their worldview, wealthy Armenian classes constituted part of the problem, unless they actively contributed to the struggle. The parties adopted socialism and the class struggle paradigm as the framework within which to explain existing conditions and alignment of forces inside and outside the Ottoman Empire. According to these parties, the Armenian people could avoid class struggle among themselves if ethnic affinities with their oppressed and exploited brethren—the majority of the "people"— compelled rich Armenians to transform themselves into supporters of the cause by transcending their class interests and supporting the greater cause. Instead of the well-to-do urbanites who were only concerned with their own security, the parties would take the reins, determining Armenian interests, and giving a voice to the poor that constituted the Armenian "nation."

For party activists, the nation stood for more than an ethnic group—or a "minority"—it was an active agent in its history, and did more than simply exist, content with preserving its cultural or religious peculiarities. Yet, in another sense, the parties considered the nation to be less than an ethnic group, since its basis would be an economically defined "people" that could dispense with the privileged elites who did not accept the primacy of the cause of the poverty-stricken majority. In a sense, the "people" represented a "democratized" nation.

The parties' socialist perspective placed the peasantry and the poor front and center. This was no accident. The founders of these parties were Russian-Armenians who had been radicalized and sensitized to the problems of the peasantry by the social struggles within the Russian Empire. The Russo-Turkish war of 1877-78 and its aftermath had brought the plight of Ottoman Armenians close to home.[21]

It was not clear to these intellectuals, however, what role socialism should play in the actual management of the struggle for liberation. Did the parties represent the whole nation or only a segment or a class? Class struggle could be a guide only in its most general sense, placing in opposition "poor" and "rich," "oppressed" and "oppressor," distinctions for which Ottoman Armenians did not need a whole new science. The lack of clarity may have been deliberate, giving the parties room to adjust their tactical thinking.

For the Hnchakians, for example, the strategy to achieve the immediate goal of independent statehood was altogether at variance with socialism; it included the use of existing resources, such as the last remnants of the impoverished Cilician nobility and collaboration with the rebellious Armenians who still kept their arms in that region. Yet, with a few strokes of the pen, the Hnchakian party not only introduced independence and socialism, but reconciled the two, placing them along a continuum in which one led to the other. The idea of an independent Armenian state was not altogether new. Elements in Armenian society, from clergymen to merchants had sporadically pursued independence and devised projects to this effect.[22]

The Hnchakians, however, were the first to introduce the idea of a "modern" nation-state. Except for the analysis of socialist and Marxist writers, including Marx himself, on the "Eastern Question," the transformation of Marxist ideology inspired by the Communist Manifesto into a political program for the Ottoman territories was, to say the least, a genuine innovation. It was a new approach, even if it was really an oversimplification (if not distortion) of what Marx and others had articulated as the positive laws of historical development.

The Hnchakians easily undertook the task of transformation by sequencing but not integrating the national and social projects. If, as Marx claimed, a socialist society could only evolve from a bourgeois society, then it was first necessary to create a bourgeois society; and since a bourgeois society could not be created within an Ottoman administration, it was necessary to create an Armenia where that would be possible.

The Dashnaktsoutiun, less ideological than the Hnchakian party, adapted its discourse to local conditions, and used socialism to color its demands for reforms and a projected transformation of the Ottoman state. Socialism was also useful when the party decided to bring in European public opinion to press their governments on reform in the Ottoman state; it provided the bridge to European socialists critical of imperial designs and protective of oppressed peoples. Yet socialism remained a thorny issue for many, if not most, Ottoman Armenians; it ultimately caused the split within the Hnchakian party in 1896, and brought the Dashnaktsoutiun close to a similar fate in 1907.

The party's focus on and idealization of the Armenian peasantry—those still living on their historic lands in the Ottoman Empire, as opposed to the mostly urbanized diasporas in the Russian and Persian empires, and the relatively secure peasantry in Eastern or Russian Armenia—tended to territorialize an Armenian problem that had initially arisen as a broader social and economic issue. The concept of a *Hayasdan*—which denotes "Armenia" in Armenian—had never disappeared from the political and popular imagination. In fact, it did not disappear from maps of the Ottoman Empire until its waning days. After all, the Empire was proud to name the various lands it had conquered. In the early debates within the millet structure regarding reforms in the Eastern provinces, the Armenians from Constantinople referred to those in the provinces as *"Hayasdantsis,"* or people from or based in Armenia. Their use of the term referred to a geographic location, and not to the place of their forefathers. But in the provinces *"Hayasdantsi"* meant much more. Folklore had kept alive the memory of the kings of Armenia (the last Armenian kingdom in the historical lands had collapsed in 1045), as well as those of Armenian Cilicia, where the last king was taken to Egypt as a prisoner after having been defeated by the Mamluks of Egypt in 1375. For most provincial Armenians, the term "Hayasdan" evoked happier times, before the "yoke of the Turk" had been pressed on their necks.

The Treaty of San Stefano first gave political impetus to the term "Hayasdan" when it referred to the Eastern provinces of the Ottoman Empire as the "Armenian provinces," a term that denotes not only the population to which article 16 referred but also the history of these provinces. The term was revised in article 61 of the Treaty of Berlin to the "Eastern Provinces," and concerned Armenians considered this a major defeat.

Patriarch Varzhabedian's proposal for reform—initially highly praised by the Dashnaktsoutiun—which included the idea that the provinces in question be governed by an Armenian governor-general, constituted the next step in the process of territorialization. The solution offered by Khrimian, that is, reform through the millet system, was no longer viable. With the treaties of San Stefano and Berlin, reforms were to be implemented by integrally merging territory and governance.

The territorialization of the "Armenian Question" had not occurred in an intellectual and historical vacuum. The Armenian cultural revival in the nineteenth century had produced a national history and geography, reviving memories of Armenian dynasties. These scholarly revivals had also been translated into a popular revival with the printing of textbooks along the same lines and the spread of education through an expanding Armenian school system. It was the political parties nonetheless, most of all the Hnchakians in their first program, that took the territorialization of the Armenian Question to a new level: democratic administration by subjects-turned-citizens in a republican Armenia.

The Hnchakians, followed less enthusiastically by the Dashnaktsoutiun, proclaimed the necessity of providing governance to Armenians, by Armenians, in historic Armenia, because that was a political requirement, if not a natural right, since the Ottoman Empire had been incapable of achieving any reforms. Armenians were ready for the "progress" and "civilization" that the Western Enlightenment had ushered in, while the Ottoman state—and by extension the Turkish people—were not. Armenians were different from Turks, the Hnchakians argued, meaning they were capable of understanding the laws of nature, including the nature of history; after all, the Turks had not complained about their regime and had shown no signs of an awakening. Territoriality was integral for the success of the Hnchakian program of change. Historical memory and immediate exigencies had coalesced in an ideological leap.

For both parties, a key component in this step was the establishment of democracy in the Armenian state or autonomous region that was to be created. The point was to turn subjects into citizens. Ottoman and Turkish rulers would not be replaced by Armenian ones; there would be no rulers. If in the popular imagination Armenian kings symbolized happier times, in the imagination of the founders of the political parties, the right to govern of future ethnically Armenian leaders would be contingent on a democratic electoral process, in which all citizens, regardless of ethnicity or religion, would be equal and participate. The problem was governance; the solution was a democratized society of the kind introduced by the French Revolution.

Beyond programmatic pronouncements, changes, and differences, the parties shared one fundamental motivation: the economic base of the majority of the Ottoman Armenian population in the provinces—peasants, farmers, craftsmen, and small merchants—was disintegrating fast; impoverishment and dispossession of land had accelerated; and the "people" were threatened.

The Eastern Armenian background of the party founders presented a problem for some Western Armenians. This background would also create problems for the founders in later historiography. Yet, their personal involvement in Russian *narodnik* (populist) movements, based on the idea of the liberation of the Russian peasantry, had made them sensitive to the problems of the peasantry in Western Armenia, in ways the azkasers and even some of the hayrenasers, with a more urban orientation, were not. The parties' ideological framework, whether the "orthodox" Marxism of the Hnchakian party or the looser "socialistic" one of the Dashnaktsoutiun, had become the intellectual tools with which the founders of these parties transformed the Armenian "people" from object into the subject and agent of history.

Universalistic and positivistic frameworks also mediated between the founders' idealism and the existential threat they sensed to the life of Armenians in the heartland of historic Armenia. They considered the peasantry and their rural economy to be the last bastion of a threatened people, whose urbanized elements had shown signs of embourgeoisement in the capitals and big cities of the Ottoman and Russian empires, and that had turned Armenians into azkasers at best.

The parties, it seems, were responding to two different, at times conflicting, impulses: The historical expectation of salvation from the West, implying a territorial dimension; and the political process that involved change from within: The exhaustion of domestic means for reform, from the *Tanzimat* to the democratization of the millet and the hopelessness that dominated the post-Berlin conference period. The parties moved from one to the other for a dominant framework, in a manner that was often confused between tactic and strategy, and between strategy and purpose.

ARMED STRUGGLE AND "TERROR"

Another dimension of the parties revolutionary nature was their willingness to use arms and shed blood—their own or others—as part of their activities. Non-Muslims being prohibited by law from carrying arms, this decision constituted a daring rejection of the established order. Taking up arms against Ottoman imperial rule was not unheard of; Greeks and other Balkan peoples had provided precedents. But this phenomenon was new in Ottoman Armenian history, especially as a strategic choice to be exercised by the people. Certainly, there had been acts of resistance to encroachments by the Ottoman central government, for example in Zeytoun, which had nominal autonomy, the most celebrated instance being the rebellion of 1860.

Yet such incidents were strictly defensive efforts, even though poets and intellectuals interpreted resistance and revolt as signs of national revival and celebrated them as symbols of a new Armenian fighting spirit. The armed struggle advocated by the parties aimed at changing the status quo, and at acquiring new rights rather than preserving old ones. The parties spent enormous amounts of energy not only preaching their rights to peasants, and inspiring self-confidence in them, but also developing channels to smuggle arms from Russia and Iran. They celebrated new heroes, and composed songs to put in relief their feats against Turkish and Kurdish oppressors and their martyrdom.[23]

Despite all this, it was never clear what the purpose of taking up arms was. On the most basic level, armed resistance was an assertion of the natural right of self-defense against marauders, armed local chieftains, exactions, and kidnappings. If the government was not capable or willing to protect the lives of its subjects, then the subjects had the right to protect themselves.

Beyond self-defense, however, why did the parties arm themselves? Were armed activities and guerrilla warfare tactical means or a strategic choice? At times, operations amounted to raids on gendarmerie stations or punitive actions. On occasion, the parties geared up for rebellions: against the local chieftains, against regional authorities, and against the state.

The parties knew they did not have the numbers to overthrow the regime or even the local rulers through a solely "Armenian" revolution. They realized they would have to enlist the support of other ethnic and religious groups, such as the Kurds, normally considered an enemy. This was part of the new strategy adopted by the *Dashnaktsoutiun* following the 1894-96 massacres. They connected with various Ottoman opposition groups, especially in Europe, where most of them were headquartered. The parties also engaged European public opinion, especially socialist leaders and parties, as a means of compelling the Great Powers to refocus on the Armenian Question. The Dashnaktsoutiun was particularly active and successful in this arena. In their program, the Hnchakians had adopted a policy of cooperation and winning the sympathy of other peoples, such as Assyrians, Yezdis, and Kurds, but there is little evidence that they focused on it in practice.

Until 1908, the two parties continued to entertain hope for external intervention, even if on many occasions, especially at the start of the movement, they insisted that Armenians could not rely on foreign powers to achieve their goals (the Great Powers had been tested in this respect, and had failed). Some large-scale operations were also considered as tactical steps to either ignite a larger uprising or compel the Great Powers to deal with the Armenian Question by intervening in favor of reforms. The parties knew that such activities would invite harsh measures from the government and that blood would flow. They preempted that concern by arguing that the lifelines of the people were being severed anyway, and that there was no salvation without sacrifice. In the end, they believed, the sacrifice would be justified.

The provocation thesis often cited in this respect is correct to the extent that leaders of the parties accepted the consequences of their strategy, although it is unclear if they expected the harshness of the Ottoman reaction, particularly the onslaught of the 1894-96 massacres. The argument that the parties invited repression and massacres, in order to achieve Great Power intervention on their behalf is a false one. It is an argument that takes for granted the existence of Ottoman policies of collective punishment of a whole people through massacres, and thus shifts the responsibility for massacres from the Ottoman government to the victims. Other states have seen rebellions, and have not massacred a whole people. Leaders and states that did massacre were duly held responsible for their actions, or should have been.

The armed struggle continued after the 1894-1896 massacres, albeit with some changes. The Dashnaktsoutiun, now in ascendancy, determined that the struggle required better and more widespread preparation. Meanwhile, the massacres had produced the May 1895 Reforms, proposed by the Great Powers on the basis of the Treaty of Berlin, and accepted by the sultan. True reform was soon forgotten.

One aspect of the armed struggle deserves special attention since it occurred in both parties, and that is the "terror," the assassination of individuals who were held personally responsible for acts considered particularly odious by the revolutionaries. The Hnchakian program devotes a whole section to this dimension:

> The purpose of terror is to protect the people, when it is subject to persecution, to raise its spirit, to inspire and elevate a revolutionary disposition among them, to show daring on behalf of the people protesting against the government, and thus to maintain the faith of the people toward the task on hand, to shake the power of the government, to abase its reputation of being powerful, to create extreme fear [in its ranks]. The means to achieve these goals are: to annihilate the worst Turkish and Armenian personalities within the government, to annihilate the spies and the traitors.[24]

The Dashnaktsoutiun, too, adopted assassination as a defense against external and internal enemies. This tactic continued to be used by both parties throughout their history, although the early abuse of the method against Armenian victims prompted the Dashnaktsoutiun to decree in 1892 that only the central authority of the party had the right to issue a verdict to that effect, and specify that: "The death sentence against Armenians can be applied only in cases of proven treason."[25]

The best-known case of "terror" was the Dashnaktsoutiun attempt in 1906 to assassinate Sultan Abdul Hamid II, the man widely held responsible for the 1894-1896 massacres. The Dashnaktsoutiun had planted a time bomb in a carriage outside the mosque where the sultan prayed every Friday. The attempt would have been successful had the sultan, a dose adherent of his routine, not been delayed when walking out of his Friday prayer.[26] It is useless to speculate what would have happened if the attempt had been successful. That the assassination attempt heightened the sultan's paranoia, there is no doubt.

The "revolution," to the extent that it involved the use of violence, assumed many forms. Assassination attempts against the worst enemies of the revolution became a critical component of the Armenian struggle for liberation. In many cases there were practical consequences, such as the elimination of spies and traitors, who, nonetheless, were replaced easily by the Ottoman authorities. The assertion of the right to armed violence seems, in the end, more an act of desperation than a strategy that would bring about the changes sought by the parties. Such use of violence represented, possibly, an assertion of the right to resist. A nation cannot be forced to die, without resisting, without hoping for the best, and doing its best to survive. In the end, the confusion the parties showed in their tactics and strategies did not stem from their ideologies. Rather, it stemmed from the existential choices they were confronted with, once they decided that the people should resist.

ONE NATION CONCEPT

Both parties imagined all three segments of the Armenian people, then living under the Ottoman, Russian, and Persian empires, to be part of one nation. They considered the international borders separating them to be artificial and of secondary importance. The parties focused on Ottoman Armenians because of the urgency of their social and economic situation. According to these parties, the Ottoman Armenian plight ought to have been of concern to all Armenians. The Hnchakians were the clearest formulators of what might be called a "trans-state" nation, when they articulated as their ultimate goal the liberation of the three Armenian segments from imperial rule and their unification in one federative state. In support of their operations in Turkish Armenia, both parties created organizational bases in Russia and Iran.

From the start the Dashnaktsoutiun had focused on Turkish Armenia. And yet, when the tsarist government initiated a policy of Russification and attempted to confiscate Armenian Church properties and shut down Armenian schools during 1903-1905, the *Dashnaktsoutiun* used its organization in Russian Armenia and the Caucasus to mount a resistance to the move. It was not difficult for the "socialistic" Dashnaktsoutiun to join forces with the left wing in Russia during the first Russian Revolution against the tsarist regime in 1905. More importantly, when civil war broke out between the "Tatars" and Armenians in many parts of the Trans-Caucasus, the Dashnaktsoutiun was mostly responsible for the organization of fighting units. That shift included the redeployment of experienced Western Armenian guerrilla leaders from the Ottoman to the Russian sector. In addition, both parties provided support to the Constitutional movement in Iran in 1907.[27]

That year was critical for the Dashnaktsoutiun, not only because the party was now involved in Russia and Iran, but the Young Turks had become active themselves, providing hope for change in the Ottoman Empire as well. The fourth World Congress of the Dashnaktsoutiun met in Vienna in 1907, under these difficult, yet promising circumstances. Western Armenian representatives, especially some of the guerrilla leaders, were critical of the party's engagement in Russian and Iranian politics; they accused Russian Armenian leaders and intellectuals of forgetting why the party was founded. Some young socialist Russian Armenian participants proposed that the party be split along Turkish-Armenian and Russian-Armenian lines. The party could not ignore the struggle for social and political rights of Russian Armenians, they argued, but this battle had a different character than the one in Turkish Armenia, which was largely a national liberation struggle.

The leadership managed to preserve the integrity of the party, arguing that the unity of the nation was necessary for the success of the movement, whatever their particular character in each case. The party also clarified its goals by amending for the first time the program of 1892: now the Dashnaktsoutiun aimed at the establishment of federated Ottoman and Russian states, an Armenian component being part of each.[28]

Eventually, the two parties, and especially the Dashnaktsoutiun, would also be involved in the Constitutional movement in Persia. This extension of the struggle to the Russian and Persian sectors was also a challenge to the extraterritorial nature of the millet system, within which an Armenian living in the Balkans or Constantinople had the same standing as the one in Van or Erzurum. In fact, Armenians in Constantinople had dominated the politics of the millet, which made it easier for the Ottoman government to control its direction and activities. The concept of nation had changed, and so had its leadership.

The involvement of the parties in the revolutions of the three empires where Armenians lived constitutes as much a manifestation of the seriousness of their devotion to constitutionalism as an indication of their national character.

STRUGGLE FOR THE PEOPLE BY THE PEOPLE

Finally, these parties worked toward making grassroots participation—both in politics and in a fighting force—a part of the transformation process. The role assigned the people in the strategy of achieving freedom was unlike that in earlier efforts at "liberation," where the "people" were seen at best as a tactical means. Having proclaimed the welfare of the people as the goal of the movement, the parties realized that their participation was integral to the process of bringing about change. The parties measured other values—from loyalty to the territorial dimensions that the transformation might imply—by the degree to which the people could be part of a solution to the problem.

Under section 4 of its program, the founders of the Hnchakian Party proposed four separate components to the struggle. Other than the first, "terror," these were (a) widespread revolutionary organizations among the peasantry, (b) widespread revolutionary organizations among the workers, and (c) revolutionary war organizations among both the peasantry and the workers. These people-based organizations were considered essential not only for the upcoming struggle but also for the creation of social and political institutions after the successful war and defense of independence.[29]

Criticizing those who relied on demonstrations by the few to advance their cause, the Dashnaktsoutiun argued that such measures had only limited impact:

> Demonstrations alone, in distant centers at that, have never liberated and will never liberate a people. [Liberation] requires a steady disposition and a battle that has potent force which can occur only with the direct participation of the majority of the Armenian people.[30]

Whatever role they assigned to the Great Powers in their sometimes confused and confusing strategies, the revolutionary parties could not conceive of liberation without the full participation of the "people." It was *their* liberation, after all, and not simply a matter of changing rulers. Both parties went to great lengths in their programs to detail the nature of that future society, that future Armenia, imagining it to be as fully democratic as the constitutions of most states today. For the most part, the parties considered using ethnicity as a basis of that future society a questionable element, seeing that it was forced on Armenians by the discrimination of an Ottoman state that refused to reform and accept principles of governance to provide equality, fairness, and justice with a view of allowing citizens and society to develop to their fullest potential.

This is not to say that the parties were not also inspired by the precedents of the Balkan peoples' struggles for independence or, as in the case of the Hnchakians, of the Lebanese struggle, won in 1863, all with the support of the Great Powers. Nonetheless, in the programs of both parties the nature of a future society was at least as important as the "vessel" within which the society would evolve. And both programs were sufficiently flexible that they could accommodate a reformed Ottoman state. This flexibility was as much a product of the ideological roots of the founders as of their realization that their strategic options were limited.

Where Armenians were most vulnerable were areas that were no longer homogeneous in population. The party leaders argued that, although the democratic nature of a future society would protect non-Armenians and non-Christians, an Armenian-based society was necessary because the

Turkish or Muslim peoples had manifested no drive toward the highest ideals of a progressive society, whether socialist or socialistic, and certainly no impulse toward democracy.

In the parties' view, the Armenian people constituted a beacon of enlightenment and human progress. Did they need to wait for all their neighbors to wake up, while their existence was being destroyed by the policies of a despotic sultan who made sure the fundamentals of the relationship between state and subject would not change?

The sultan considered Armenians to be a Christian conquered people who should be satisfied with their status as a "People of the Book," a distant memory of the Prophet's tolerant view of non-Muslims. According to him, Armenians should be satisfied with the generosity of Ottoman rulers, who had allowed them to be constituted as a millet and to run their internal affairs. Affairs of state were not, and could not possibly be the business of Christian communities. The Armenian revolutionary political parties saw the nation as following an ideological trajectory that was closer to the modem understanding of a nation than that assumed by the Balkan peoples in their liberation struggles. In fact the Armenian trajectory foreshadowed the national liberation ideologies of a century later, with their strong social and economic components, in addition to their anticolonial foundation. With their insistence on democratic governance, the Armenian parties were threatening to the Ottoman and Russian empires.

Even between the two parties there were certainly differences in the political imagination of the "nation." The Hnchakians imagined an ideal humanity and decided the nation was the "vessel," or the means to achieve it (a convenient metaphor for reconciling inherent contradictions in their ideology). The Dashnaktsoutiun defined the nation as the peasantry and the downtrodden who were in need of and worthy of salvation. They felt the nation should be allowed to develop to its fullest potential, and thus become part of humanity.

A QUESTION OF LOYALTY

The activities and very existence of the revolutionary parties raise the question of "loyalty." It was a concern for the Ottoman leaders of the late empire, and remains one for official Turkish historians today. Yet, such a question is problematic. Applying today's values to a historical period when the imperial mindset was dominant is a grave error. In addition, those who accuse Armenians of disloyalty never make it clear what the charge consists of: Were they supposed to be loyal to the empire, its territorial integrity, the sultan, or the CUP?

The fusion of progressive ideologies and the worsening conditions of the majority of the Armenian population, especially in the provinces, had produced programs aimed at creating a better society. That is where, nonetheless, the parties' priorities rested ultimately. These parties sought to change the nature of the state and its relations with its subjects; in short, to transform subjects into citizens that had a contractual agreement with the state. The Ottoman state would be acceptable if it were based on the equality of its citizens, and if its purpose were their welfare, not merely its self-perpetuation. The Ottoman government could claim the loyalty of its subjects only if and when it changed the basis of its legitimacy.

Loyalty to the state could have been possible. All their programmatic goals notwithstanding, the parties were ready to endorse the state, and did so after 1908. But such loyalty could no longer be taken for granted or offered unconditionally. The Ottoman state and its system were concrete realities for its subjects, not abstractions defined by the sultan and, later, the CUP. Within such a context, "Armenians" could have been part of the solution, if the men in charge had cared as much for their subjects as they did about the regime. Instead, having permitted, if not encouraged, the situation to deteriorate, and having created an environment where armed resistance, rebellion, and appeals to the Great Powers remained the only options, the sultan and the CUP deemed the "Armenians" as a threat.

That demands for such political and economic reforms came under the rubric of a "revolution" may be misleading to some extent. That this revolution was supported by a segment of Ottoman society that happened to be ethnically Armenian is the actual conundrum. Were the land and economic crises less significant because they were felt most by Armenians who were able to articulate and, at some point, try to act on them? Who was responsible, ultimately, for the "Armenianization" of the economic and political crises? What should Armenians have done in order not to be seen as a threat or as "disloyal" subjects that they did not try to do?

When the parties challenged the state, they empowered society; and they ended up collaborating with others who had apparently similar aims but who ultimately ended up hurting their cause. The Young Turks initially empowered themselves in the name of the Turkish people, but ended up placing a higher premium on the survival of the state. When the Dashnaktsoutiun was cooperating with the CUP during the Constitutional period, the Armenian leaders urged the CUP to spread the ideas of equality and democracy among the Turkish Muslim peoples of the region, to ensure that the Constitution would have grassroots support, and thus solidify its hold on the general population. The CUP did reach out to the "people," but only to solidify its rule, and make sure that they would follow the dictates and designs of the CUP. The empowerment of the latter excluded the participation of the "people."[31] It is not a coincidence that the state which the CUP imagined, and which eventually came into being, was anything but democratic, and remained a one-party system for a long time.

No analysis today can illustrate so poignantly the problem of loyalty as the exchange that took place in May 1915—during the last session of the trial of the Hnchakian leaders—between Khurshid (Hurşit) Bey, the presiding judge of the Ottoman court, and Paramaz, the main Hnchakian spokesman. It is worth quoting extensively. The Hnchakians had been accused of incitement to insurrection and secessionism and were awaiting their sentence. Before condemning the group to death, Khurshid (Hurşit) Bey reflected:

> The attributes of history in our reality are arranged in such a way that what constitutes "patriotism" for one is viewed as destructive treason by the other. And thus the mutual relations between nations living together amount to the negation of international law and social concepts. Today is the last session of these trials and it is with great pain in our heart that we are visualizing in our inflamed memory these few days that we spent here with you. There was something unusual and unqualifiable in these trials. Unqualifiable because neither you nor us had enough wisdom to penetrate each others [worlds]...
>
> You cannot imagine, effendis, that it is with such grief that I will pronounce the depth of my conviction regarding the patriotism accumulated in you. What can be more heartbreaking that warm blooded beings like you full of life have sacrificed logic to sentiments; your false beliefs have placed you on a path that leads to an impasse...What great deeds vigorous individuals like you could have accomplished, if the ideal of a common welfare had been pursued under one banner...What

benefits could have been borne from a mutual understanding that eluded [us], the other end of which is sad and dark. You languished with the idea that you are struggling against injustice; while have felt, every minute, that the rules of the world are abasing higher tendencies under the weight of cruel necessities.[32]

Paramaz was visibly moved when he took the stand:

A while ago Khurshid Bey made some statements here and I, who has never cried in my life—I who was unmoved when, after many years of absence from home returned and realized when my child did not recognize me—I am not ashamed to say that I was deeply moved by the sincerity of Khurshid Bey's speech...and I cried, I, Paramaz, because Khurshid Bey put his finger on the wound when he stated "What good deed could have been accomplished..." I cried because in those words I found the brilliance of truth.

[Yet] We would be asking that same question, and add, "What was left that we did not do for the welfare of this country?" We accepted such sacrifices, we spilled so much blood and spent such energy to bring about the brotherhood of Armenians and Turks; we lived through such suffering to elevate each other through trust. And what did we see? Not only did you condemn our gigantic efforts to sterility but also consciously pursued our annihilation...You encouraged crime and oppression and tried to silence every expression of protest...You started massacring us when one day we decided to do something to defend our dignity...You left us outside the protection of the law when we tried to benefit from the rights granted us by the truncated Mithatian Constitution...

Gentlemen, judge people by their work, by their traditions, within the realm of their ideas. I am not a separatist from this country. On the contrary, it is [this country] that is separating itself from me, being incapable of coming to terms with the ideas that inspire me.[33]

HOW REVOLUTIONARY?

The ideologies and strategies of these two revolutionary parties were made complex by the social, economic, and political dimensions of the struggle for liberation; they also required a degree of flexibility that bordered on the uncertain. They rejected the status quo, both among the Armenian people and within the Ottoman state; they rejected the idea of a politics whose purpose was the perpetuation of the state at the expense of its citizens. On one level, at least, these parties were far from revolutionary: both parties assigned Great Power intervention a large, though shifting role. There is no question that the founding of both parties was related to the Armenian frustration at the non-implementation of reforms promised first in the Treaty of San Stefano, then revised in the Treaty of Berlin in 1878.[34]

In their founding documents, the revolutionary parties explicitly refer to the reforms mandated by the Treaty of Berlin. Yet, their subsequent behavior manifested a distinct lack of clarity on whether they regarded the provisions of that treaty as the main goal or looked on the failure of that strategy as a basis for the legitimation of a new kind of struggle. In the end, it was the realities on the ground that dictated the parties increasing reliance on Great Power intervention. The Ottoman state proved to be more resilient than the revolutionaries expected, ready to use the harshest measures of repression. Guerrilla warfare, however heroic the actions of the fighters, however large the support from many segments of Armenian society, failed to topple the state. In addition, by the end of the nineteenth century, following losses in the Balkans, Anatolia's significance for the Ottoman Empire and for the British-Russian rivalry had increased. However, the Armenia of 1900 was not the Greece of 1830, and it was certainly not the Serbia of 1880.

"Objective analysis," ideological coherence, the adoption of universal values, and thus partaking in the logic of human progress may have been sufficient to "shake the Sultans throne," as revolutionaries had hoped, but it was not enough to bring about the outcome for which they ultimately hoped. And shifting the focus of lobbying by the revolutionaries in Europe from unreliable statesmen to "principled" socialist and liberal leaders in order to gain support for reforms did not change the game the Great Powers were playing; after all, they had become "great" by playing with smaller nations, exploiting their weaknesses, and benefiting from their woes.

Among the innovations revolutionary parties introduced to the Armenian subjects was the use of arms, a tactic familiar to the Greeks. But the fact that some Armenians had adopted the use of arms certainly represented a threat to those who placed the state above society as well as to the more conservative Armenians in the capital. Similarly, the idea of one nation—identified through a common history and predicated on the negation of borders—constituted a recognizable and threatening aspect of the struggle unleashed by the parties; but it is also one that would have been equally threatening to Russia and Persia.

Yet, given the threat that the Ottoman state presented to the individual and collective well-being of Armenians in the empire, the parties considered armed struggle as a legitimate course. The internal Armenian revolution, the concept of class struggle, the primacy of the interests of the peasant and craftsmen classes, and the strategizing of grassroots participation in politics, were new and revolutionary not only for the Armenian community but also for the Ottoman state.

The socialist dimension of the Armenian movement was dangerous to the Turkish elites, especially to the ultimate winner of the rivalry within the Young Turk movement—the CUP. Integral to the CUP vision was the kind of state that could resist Great Power intervention in its internal affairs, and allay, if not reverse, the disintegration of that empire. It was not sufficient that the eventual state be Turkish; it was also necessary that it be a "strong" state, free of the burdens of democracy and parliamentarianism. By the early twentieth century, peoples and otherwise distinct elements inhabiting the empire would be assessed by Turkish elites in terms of their potential contribution to—or detraction from—the creation of such a state. Thus, in addition to religious and ethnic differences, "Armenians" had become a political liability; the Hnchakian and Dashnaktsoutiun parties had come to be seen as representatives of a people that generated a different logic than that of the state.

The Armenian political parties constituted a threat, but it was a threat to the regime of Sultan Abdul Hamid II, against which "Turks" themselves ultimately acted. Most "revolutionary" or otherwise threatening dimensions of the Hnchakian and Dashnaktsoutiun party programs disappeared with the reinstatement of the Ottoman Constitution in 1908, including the Hnchakian goal of Armenian independence, the use of arms, and appeals to the Great Powers. What remained were the demands for a participatory parliamentary system and for economic, especially agrarian reforms.

Partly due to their ideological concern for the lower classes and awareness of the need to be pragmatic, the parties had shown their willingness to accommodate the state, but they were not ready to accommodate any regime that failed to deliver on its promise of reform. It was the CUP's failure at reform that compelled the parties to return to their earlier strategy of appealing to the Great Powers some time after the 1908 Young Turk Revolution.

Another way to answer the question I raise in this chapter is to address what was "negotiable" in the ideology, program, strategy, and tactics of these parties and what was not. In the end, it was their opposition to a repressive and regressive regime that was consistent. On a practical level, agrarian and administrative reforms in the empire remained nonnegotiable as far as the Armenian "revolution" was concerned. If the rulers of the Ottoman state were unwilling to introduce such reforms throughout the empire, these parties, as well as the patriarchate, demanded that reforms be introduced in the "Armenian" provinces. But even that was too much for the CUP. That says as much about the CUP regime—its concerns, its visualization of the future, the framework within which they perceived the world and themselves—as it does about the Armenians.

The CUP and the dominant "majority" had a choice to change the character of the state in ways that accommodated its various "minorities," by making the state serve society. Instead, by making the state a self-serving entity, they chose to change its demography. Their failure to implement reforms promised under the Tanzimat, Abdul Hamid II, and the CUP, had led to the internationalization, territorialization, as well as the radicalization, of the "Armenian" problem. This, in turn, assured that Armenians would be considered incompatible with the CUP vision. It is paradoxical that the Armenian revolutionary parties, which came to be seen, and are still viewed by some, as a threat to the Ottoman state, came closest to offering a solution that may have assured the survival of the Ottoman state. This raises the question of the elites' own loyalty toward the Ottoman state. It is possible that, consciously or not, they were already imagining a different kind of state, one within which reforms—economic or political—did not figure as the most important component of change.

The Ottoman state lacked an integrative component or program for non-Muslims particularly, except on rare occasions, when Armenians supported it fully. It was an empire, created through conquest; as such, it was keen to preserve the politics of rulers and the ruled and maintain ethnic, religious, and other divisions, making an exception only for selected individuals from all backgrounds who did not need to be reminded of their place in government.

The system's components, including the millet system, ensured that Armenian subjects would cling to their past, and at some point transform these differences into assets. If the legal and social system of segregation and discrimination made certain that Armenians felt inferior, the Armenian past and collective memory ensured that, when these subjects were forced into a corner and ready to become citizens, they would emerge as a force that was not only conscious of its ethnic identity but that it would be that dimension of their identity that would be invested with the new ideas, energy, and program.

Yet the primacy of economic, domestic, political, and social issues, and the ideological underpinnings of party programs provided an avenue for the newly defined Armenian nation to reach out to the Ottoman state, a significant act of Armenian "nationalism." Obviously, this move took on a different character than that of the millet, where subservience was assumed. The parties constituted the link between universal principles and the ever-worsening economic crisis inflicted on the majority of Ottoman Armenians. Armed with the "laws" of history, energized by universal rights, and pressed by conditions on the ground, the parties could reach out more easily to Turks and Kurds who might have shared their principles, ideals, and concerns, than Armenians who felt secure in their millet-based identity and politics could.

In the final analysis, however, one cannot properly assess the politics adopted by the Armenian parties by looking only at the Ottoman state and society. For the dynamics of this period were propelled by three factors: the state, society—including its Armenian component—and the Great Powers.[35] We must understand the dual nature of each of the three elements to assess their consequences: the Ottoman state, repressive and regressive—technical and technological modernization notwithstanding—was vulnerable to the Great Powers; the Armenians, victimized by the state, but reaching out to the Great Powers; and the "West," with the liberating influence of its ideals of freedom, equality, and human progress, and the debilitating impact of its imperialism on the Ottoman state, and indirectly on the subjects of that state. Both Armenians and Turks suffered the consequences of these tensions, but the price Armenians paid was far more dear.

By all accounts, the Young Turk Revolution of 1908 represented the best opportunity for the "Armenian" and "Turkish" movements to find common ground and continue cohabitating as part of one state. There is not yet a consensus as to whether a multiethnic empire was still possible as a parliamentary democracy in 1908, but it is possible that the answer will differ for Balkan and Arab peoples and for Armenians, whose home was in Anatolia, a more sensitive and contested region, with a mixed population. The Young Turks envisioned a liberal state, and were willing to try parliamentarianism; on the other hand, the Armenian parties were willing to compromise and adopt a similarly liberal position, as long as the state ensured reforms. Yet, absent on the Young Turk side, was any social dimension; by and large, society and social concerns remained tangential to their ideology. Theirs was a revolution from above, concerned mostly with the preservation of the state, gradually imagined as a Turkish one.

While Armenian revolutionary parties were not representative of all Armenians, they primarily articulated the concerns of its majority. The addition of the *Ramgavar* Party, in 1908—antisocialist, antirevolutionary in the sense of rejecting violent means, and liberal bourgeois, in the classical sense—meant that most segments of the Armenian people were now represented through the three political parties. All three endorsed the 1908 revolution and committed themselves to its success. The *Dashnaktsoutiun* partnered with the CUP and vested its whole political capital on that relationship. One question that may be asked is, why was there no Turkish equivalent to the Armenian revolutionary parties concerned with their social and economic interests? For Muslims, a primarily religious and increasingly ethnic self-identification with the leaders of the state provided them with a false sense of sharing in the power of that state.

In a sense, the separation of the two histories, "Turkish" and "Armenian," started from the time the Ottoman Empire added Armenian populated regions to its territory. Armenians were never fully integrated into Ottoman society, although some elements took part in the economy. Their status as second-class subjects ensured that separation. The economic and social woes of the empire during its waning decades affected all subjects, however, especially non-Muslim peoples in Anatolia; the state provided support to Kurdish tribal leaders and resettled Balkan *muhajirs,* Muslim deportees from the Balkans, in the region.

There is no question that the two Balkan wars preceding World War I and the imperialistic machinations of the Great Powers, including the use of the Armenian pleas for intervention to their benefit, pushed the CUP leadership in a more dictatorial, nationalist, and state-based direction, away from any concerns for social and economic reforms that might benefit the Armenian element.[36]

Inherent in the Armenian parties' position was a paradox. Reform being the "non-negotiable" component of their programs, often at the expense of ideology, they were able to make compromises and reach out to the Young Turks. That same logic led them to ask for assistance from the Great Powers when the state was unwilling to deliver on such reforms, promised many times. Yet, the Great Powers were the same instruments that threatened the Ottoman state and the "survival of Turkey" as imagined by the leaders of the state. In brief, the problems collided but the solutions did not meet. The exchange between Khurshid (Hurşit) Bey and Paramaz cited above constitutes a most telling testimony to two phenomena: the historical depth of the two histories ensconced in the current debates, as well as the missed opportunities.

---

1.   See Gerard Libaridian, *Modern Armenia: People, Nation, State* (New Brunswick, N.J.: Transaction, 2004), pp. 89-124. A third party, the Liberal Democratic [Ramgavar] Party (ADL), was established in Cairo in 1908 and reorganized in 1921; it was heir to the Armenagan group founded in 1885 in the city of Van. The Ramgavar Party differed markedly from the first two since it rejected political or economic radicalism. Although its founding, following the Young Turk Revolution, and its liberal ideology constitute an important part of the larger historical picture, I chose not to discuss the Ramgavar Party in the present paper, since they were neither "revolutionary" nor a determinant of the character of the conflict.

I will also put aside, for the time being, the analysis of the Armenian Marxist groups that emerged early in the twentieth century, because they had no direct participation in the political life of the Ottoman Empire before the war, even though their approach to the "Armenian Question" remains important for the understanding of post-war Armenian political thought and Armenian history. There are also a number of small parties that will not feature in my article, such as the Armenian Socialist Party founded in Europe, in 1900, whose approach was quite original from the point of view of intellectual history but who did not have a particular impact on the course of events

2. For a general overview of the rise and development of Armenian political parties, see J. M. Hagopian, "Hyphenated Nationalism: The Spirit of the Revolutionary Movement in Asia Minor, 1896-1910" (PhD diss., Harvard University, 1943); Richard Hovannisian, *Armenia on the Road to Independence* (Berkeley and Los Angeles: University of California Press, 1968); Libaridian, *Modern Armenia*; Louise Nalbandian, *The Armenian Revolutionary Movement* (Berkeley and Los Angeles: University of California Press, 1967); Louise Nalbandian, "The Origins and Development of Socialism in Armenia: The Social Democratic Hnchak Party, 1887-1949" (MA thesis, Stanford University, 1949); Anaide Ter Minassian, *Nationalism and Socialism in the Armenian Revolutionary Movement, 1887-1912* (Cambridge, Mass.: Zoryan Institute, 1984).

3. *"Tsragir"* [Program (of the Hnchakian Party)], in *Hnchak*, no. 11/12, 1888; reproduced in Arsen Kitur, *Badmoutiun S. T. Hnchakyan gousagtsoutian* [History of the S(ocial). D(emocratic) Hnchakian Party] (Beirut, 1962), 1, pp. 32-37; *Droshak*, no. 2, 1891.

4. *Droshak*, no. 2, 1891.

5. For developments in the nineteenth century, see Gerard Libaridian, "The Ideology of Armenian Liberation: Armenian Political Thought before the Revolutionary Movement (1639-1885)" (PhD diss., UCLA, 1987).

6. Arsen Kitur, 1, pp. 53-62.

7. *Droshak*, no. 1, 1890.

8. *Tsragir* [program of the HSDP.]

9. *Tsragir* [Program of the Dashnaktsoutiun], 1892.

10. *Ibid*.

11. *Droshak*, no. 2 (September) 1890.

12. Kitur, p. 32.

13. *Ibid*, pp. 327-28.

14. "Letter from Antranig and Kevork, Chiefs of the Insurgents Near Moush," July 1904. This letter is part of dispatches numbered 131-136 sent from August 3 through 13, 1904, by the US Consul in Harput, Thomas Herbert Norton to the US State Department, US National Archives, Department of State, Recond Group 59. Norton was the US

consul in Harput but had been sent to Moush and Van during this period to report on the rebellion and the massacres.

This important "letter," in English translation, is composed of three segments. (There is no indication regarding the author of the translation; the style of the translation indicates that it might have been an Armenian; possible Kegham Der-Garabedian, the secretary of the Armenian Prelacy in Moush.) The first part of the document consists of a list of 85 grievances Armenians held against the Ottoman authorities and their Kurdish allies, followed by a presentation of the reasons why Armenians resorted to revolution and 16 concrete demands for reforms in the Armenian provinces. The third segment is a short "cover letter" signed by Antranig and Kevork and addressed personally to the US Consul.

The second segment, the listing of the demands, but not the others, appeared in the original Armenian on the front page of *Droshak* (No. 8, August 1904). The caption by the editors of the journal states that the document was presented by Dashnaktsoutiun's Central Committees of Daron and Sassoun to the consuls of the three Great Powers (Great Britain, Russia and France) and signed by "Antranig, Sarhad, Daronetsi, on behalf of the Daron-Sassoun Central Committees."

15. Gabriel Lazian, *Heghapokhagan temker*, [Revolutionary figures] (Cairo: Housaper, 1945), p. 17.

16. *Ibid*, p. 338.

17. *Droshak*, no. 7, 1894.

18. Undated meeting between *Hnchak* representative S. Sapah-Gulian, and Ahmed Riza and Doctor Nazim, at the Cafe Voltaire in Paris, prior to the Young Turk Revolution but after 1906. Ahmed Riza asked that the Hnchakian Party desist from appeals to the Great Powers and accept the Midhatian Constitution as the basis of co-operation. Sapah-Gulian insisted on the autonomy of the Armenia provinces and the May 1895 reforms as proposed by the Great Powers following the 1894-95 massacres of Armenians. The Hnchakians, according to Kitur, were very concerned with the Pan-Turanic designs of the Young Turks, which would have spelled disaster for the Armenians.

19. The Armenian diaspora existed even before the word was invented or used for Armenians, just as genocide would occur before a word was coined for the phenomenon. One can argue that an Armenian diaspora was formed during the collapse of the last Armenian kingdom in historic Armenia at the end of the tenth century.

20. See Libaridian, *Modern Armenia*, pp. 51-71.

21. For a thorough discussion of the rise of populist thought among Eastern Armenian intellectuals, see Ronald Grigor Suny, *Looking Toward Ararat* (Bloomington: Indiana University Press, 1993), pp. 63-93.

22. These projects were for the most part seeking the reestablishment of the lost Armenian medieval kingdoms, which would be achieved with the help of "Christian" kings of the West. Shahamir Shahamirian, of the Madras community of merchants, promoted the vision of a republic, a most revolutionary idea for the eighteenth-century Armenian world, which, unfortunately, did not survive the prevarications of the serf-owning class, who dominated the imperial Russian occupation of Eastern Armenia and the Caucasus. The initial territorialization of the Armenian problem by the Patriarchate, in the Treaty of San Stefano—"reforms in the Armenian provinces"—was diluted in the Treaty of Berlin, under the form of "reforms in the Eastern provinces" of the Ottoman Empire.

23. Libaridian, *Modern Armenia*, pp. 73-85.

24. Kitur, p. 35.

25. *Droshak*, no. 3, 1892.

26. Kristapor Mikaelian, one of the three founders of the Dashnaktsoutiun, and its leading figure, had proposed the idea in 1904 to the Third World Congress of the party, and had been assigned the task. He died in 1905 while testing the time bomb, in Bulgaria.

27. See Houri Berberian, *Armenians and the Iranian Constitutional Revolution of 1905-1911* (Boulder, Colo.; Westview Press, 2001).

28. Libaridian, *Modern Armenia*, ch. 5.

29. *Tsragir of the HSDP.*

30. *Droshak*, no. 4,1893.

31. Libaridian, *Modern Armenia*, ch. 8, and Dikran Kaligian, *The Armenian Revolutionary Federation under Constitutional Rule, 1908-1914* (New Brunswick, N.J.: Transaction Books, 2008).

32. As reported in Kitur, pp. 386-87.

33. *Ibid*, pp. 387-388.

34. Inviting the intervention of the Great Powers was not a new strategy; Patriarch Nerses Varzhabedian first adopted it, with the support of some of his National Council, in anticipation of Russian victory in the 1877-78 war with the Ottoman Empire.

35. The value of the internationalization of the Armenian Question is still debated in Armenian political literature.

36. Much has been written, with justification, regarding the role of the rivalry between Great Britain and Russia, in the determination of positions regarding the "Armenian Question." Russian interference has often been pointed out as a possible cause for the rise of the Armenian revolutionary

movement. Two points need to be made here. Russian interest in territorial expansion did play an indirect role in promoting the interest of Eastern Armenians in the fate of their brethren in the Ottoman Empire. But that does not diminish the significance of the social and economic factors in the rise of the movement. Second, Russian authorities were equally concerned about the revolutionary aspects of the Armenian movement. After all, Russia was an empire, too, opposed to popular and socialistic movements.

7

CHURCH AND POLITICAL PARTIES
IN ARMENIAN HISTORY
Notes

2006/2019

Each of the organizations under consideration have acquired, since the Genocide, a kind of legitimacy reserved for ancient and venerable institutions worthy of preservation and preferably beyond criticism as institutions. Their relationship is even less scrutinized. This essay explores the relationship between religious and political institutions over time but concentrating during the more recent period, since the rise of Armenian political parties; a relationship which has been wavering between competition and complementarity. The essay highlights the political nature of the Church and the spiritual dimensions the political parties acquired, without which it is difficult to understand the resulting confusion, assessing the role played by these organizations and responsibilities they bear in the making of modern Armenian political culture.

This article should be viewed as a brief overview and not as an attempt to write a history. A first, shorter version of this article was presented as a paper at the 2006 conference at the University of Michigan, Ann Arbor, marking the 1700th anniversary of the adoption of the Christian religion in Armenia.

The history of relations between the Armenian Church and political parties is complex and elusive. In a sense, it is a story that is older than the institutions themselves; it is also one that is still continuing. That story covers most of the modern and contemporary periods, engaging some of the most fateful events in Armenian history, and still suffering their consequences.[1]

The story of their relations began with the founding of two revolutionary parties, both focusing on the plight of Western or Ottoman Armenians: The Social Democratic Hnchakian Party (founded in Geneva in late 1887, Hnchakian Party or Hnchakians for short) and the Armenian Revolutionary Federation (founded in Tbilisi in 1890, Dashnaktsoutiun or Dashnaktsakans for short). The two parties challenged the role of the Church in three important respects.

The political parties aimed to replace the Church as the primary institution that determined the identity of the Armenian individual, and which represented the Armenian people. They intended to become the institutions that articulated the Armenian people's collective goals, and which outlined the policies necessary to achieve them. Certainly, there had been Armenian groups and organizations other than the ancient Church following the loss of Armenian statehood in the 14th century, long before the rise of these parties. But such groups—remnants of the feudal order in Armenia and Cilicia, merchants, and 19th century intellectuals—had not attempted to supplant the Church. Even when claimed as a separate identity, for the most part, such groups perceived themselves as partners of the dominant institution.

The establishment of the parties raised an important question: "Which of these institutions, the Church or the parties, embodies the Armenian people, and on what basis of legitimacy?" In other words, when early in their histories the parties challenged the Church, the confrontation entailed a struggle for a redefinition of Armenian identity. Wars that involve identity are deadlier than wars on policies. To begin with, they are deadlier for the institutions themselves. Yet they are also deadly for the "nation" they represent.

Secondly, the parties challenged the role the Church assigned the "people" in whose name it spoke. Since the 16th century the Church had occasionally acted, in some cases bravely, on behalf of the downtrodden Armenians who constituted majorities in historic Western and Eastern Armenia, under Ottoman Turkish and Safavid Persian rule. Yet in the clerical imagination, the "people" were the object of history, passive and on the receiving end, waiting to be delivered from the heathens by Christian rulers elsewhere. For the political parties, in contrast, the people were agents of history. They were participants in the changes sought on their behalf, and actors in the making of their future.

The third challenge was on a more basic, even philosophical level. The Church functioned within a fatalistic framework that saw what had befallen the Armenians as God's will, possibly as a punishment for past collective sins. Their "salvation" would be sought as a favor from rulers, without questioning the status quo. The parties sought to bring the Armenian people into the fold of the "modern" world, defined by a scientific analysis of history which, in the case of these two parties, meant the socialist interpretation of change and progress. Christian fatalism and transcendentalism leading to bliss in the life to come would be replaced by the idea of innate rights and scientifically proven progress in this life, leading to a change in the political status quo. To the Hnchakians, for example, this meant Armenian statehood.

These challenges by the parties were not direct, in the sense that the parties did not declare war on the Church and rarely engaged in direct confrontation. The genesis of the parties can be traced, at least partially, to the frustration of a young generation of activists with the non-application of reforms in Ottoman Armenia. These reforms, promoted by the Armenian Patriarchate of Constantinople, culminated in Article 61 of the Treaty of Berlin in 1878. The parties thought they would succeed where the Church had failed by compelling the Sultan and the Great Powers of Europe to implement the promised reforms in the Armenian provinces. Yet the worldview the parties adopted to undergird their actions, combined with continued failure to achieve reforms, inevitably led them in more radical directions. Even then, none of the parties were able to maintain a direct opposition to the Church, whatever their ideologies, not even the Armenian Bolsheviks who appeared later in history. One may explain such resilience on the part of the Church by recalling the powerful symbolism the Church developed to define the nation, and the paradigms of political thought it perpetuated as main transmitters of written culture and historical memory.

It is also possible to argue that the position of the Church was not a product of its strength as much as the defeats and weaknesses of Armenians that so compelled otherwise antagonistic institutions to coexist and cooperate. Even at their most radical, political parties eventually adopted the symbols, paradigms, and even the terminology of the Church. In the end, when the parties discovered they could not fully supplant the Church, they instead joined or tried to control it. By doing so, they also gave up much of their radicalism.

Ultimately, what determined the behavior and relations of these two institutions were not their philosophies or worldviews, but rather their weaknesses in relation to the power of the Sultan and policies of the Great Powers. Patterns of behavior far older than the two institutions, and events larger than their capacity to control, determined the character and story of their relationship.

PROBLEMS OF WRITING A HISTORY

It is not the purpose of this essay to write that story. Rather, it offers a framework for the understanding of the relations between these institutions by placing events in perspective and sketching major issues as best known to date through periodization. This attempt will have served its purpose if it invites others to look more closely at the issues raised here. The author would be even more grateful if some of the conclusions in this essay, admittedly non-laudatory, were refuted by more detailed research and further analysis. For to write that story, the historian requires much more material than is available at this point.

The task of the researcher in these subjects—to the extent that they are to be found—is made difficult by either the absence of archives or the limited and arbitrary access to what is potentially available. Most leaders of the Church and of political parties passed away without leaving us a full picture of what went into the making of their decisions. Churchmen and political party leaders who did write memoirs rarely divulged contacts between themselves and their counterparts at critical times, and we have no oral histories to offer relief. Circumstances surrounding events fifty years ago are treated in the same way as today's states protect national security secrets. The Armenian world functions in a securitized state of mind: any revelation outside official lines is interpreted as a threat to the image of the given institution and, therefore, to Armenian identity and Armenian interests, since each institution claims to embody that identity and the interests that flow naturally from that source.

It may appear paradoxical that despite the age of these institutions, or perhaps even because of it, both the Church and the political parties are constantly on the defensive. In the literature published on their behalf, it is as if every article, pamphlet and book is written to justify their existence. This is as much, if not more evident in their decisions and policies.[2] Rare are the cases where introspection and critical analysis facilitate our understanding of complexities; rarer even are those that admit to errors and misjudgments. While betraying a sense of vulnerability in the face of history, the ideology of survival seems to function as a plea for readers to suspend disbelief and relegate what otherwise may be construed as questionable decisions and behavior to oblivion, and expect continued belief in these institutions just because they have survived so long and made it so far. It should be sufficient enough, as they are the reason why Armenians are Armenians today. Maybe it is.

The continuing secretiveness of these institutions is reinforced by the sensitivity which most scholars feel toward them. The liability of these institutions to probing questions has often become the vulnerability of researchers reluctant to probe. Thus, the second paradox we encounter in this investigation is the participation of a relatively large number of people in the decision-making processes of both Church centers and the political parties. Much more is known by the people at large than scholars and researchers are willing to reveal or explore, unlike events that deal with the outside world. Admittedly such mundane knowledge is sometimes just gossip. But even when what is known is factually true, these truths turn out to be only part of the picture. Each preserves or chooses to remember what reinforces a preconceived notion of what the narrative is, and what it should be.

But if we are to overcome the elusiveness of that story, there is one premise that one must accept: That it is possible to subject that story to analysis, even some perceive that such an analysis might demystify these institutions, especially if mystification lies at the foundation of their legitimation at this time. We must accept the premise that whoever speaks and acts on behalf of Armenians—whatever they say and do or not say and not act upon in their name—makes them part of history, and part of events that made the history of Armenians and the peoples around them. With the right of representation comes responsibility, and with the battles that such entails also comes the right of subsequent generations to know that history—and analyze it.

It should not surprise us, then, that when churchmen and political party historians have written about their institutions, with rare exceptions, they have been defensive and partisan, if not altogether silent on important issues. And despite the significance of these institutions, and their relationship to modern Armenian history, we do not have, as yet, critical histories of either the Church or of political parties, with the possible exception of Ormanian's *Azkabadoum*.[3] Each of these institutions has had a complex history in terms of their internal battles, their relations with other institutions, and their role in larger events. And in each case, we are analyzing an institution with more than one body. Having more than one political party goes with the terrain. The Armenian Church has many centers. Yet even so, it is still possible to speak of one Armenian Church, as during the period under consideration, the history of the Church was not defined, nor characterized by spiritual or theological battles. Even so, we must note that just as within each political party, amazing battles have been fought between centers of the Church.

A HISTORICAL LOOK AT CHURCH AND POLITICS

The intimate relationship between Armenian political and religious institutions is as old as the organizations themselves, probably more so than is the case in many other societies. We know that in Urartian times, the temple represented economic and political power as much as spiritual and religious authority, and that kings appointed members of their own family as *krmapets*, or chief priests. Christianity was imposed as the state religion of Armenia early in the 4th century AD by an edict of the king. The Church subsequently inherited the wealth and properties of pagan institutions, and continued to have economic independence. It sought the protection of the state and political leaders, while kings, princes, and the privileged classes tried, at least, to control the Church. When needed, as in the Bagratuni period, kings and princes created their own catholicosates, and churchmen acquiesced.

One can argue, in fact, that the Church—albeit in an extraterritorial capacity—historically behaved very much like a feudal *nakharar*, or lord. After the initial period following the adoption of Christianity, however, succession to the throne of the catholicosate was no longer a matter of heredity. As such, since its inception, the Church had an interest in state matters, though church and state on occasion found themselves in conflict with each other as institutions. The Church, more often than not, also internalized the various conflicts and policy divisions that plagued the Armenian ruling classes, and often found itself divided from within. In this way, intra-Church conflicts were rarely spiritual or theological in nature. By and large they were political, the term political referring to personal animosities and conflicts on domestic policies, internal power struggles over resources, and the nature of relations with foreign dominant powers. Within both political and Church leaderships we have seen moments of rebellion and rejection of policies of foreign rule, as well accommodation and submission.

The long period of Armenian statelessness changed the character of the relationship between political and religious institutions. In fact, the migration and decimation of the Armenian *nakharar* elites, as well as the policies of foreign powers beginning with the Seljuks and Mongols, made the Church not only the only surviving national institution, but also a preferred instrument of management of Armenians in their empires. The Ottoman and Safavid, then Russian empires institutionalized their relations with the Church, and formalized their overall control of Church affairs. The Islamic foundation of the Ottoman state, where most Armenians lived, defined Armenians as a religious community within the elaborate *millet* system. With the creation of the Armenian Patriarchate of Constantinople in the 15ᵗʰ century, the Ottoman state formally assigned the Church to be the intermediary between the state and the Armenian Christian "community," with the patriarch as its leader.[4] By default and/or design, the Church constituted the political leadership of the Armenian people, or at least the only one with a national scope. In policy decisions, and to mitigate differences, emerging elites—both of the merchant and intellectual classes—either sought the support of the Church or operated within Church structures.

Beyond Constantinople, the Armenian Church was "national" in a number of ways:

1. It was national in its organizational independence from other churches, in accordance with its adherence to the Orthodox Christian creed;

2. It was national in its history, i.e., in its continuity, as opposed to the *nakharar* system that had ensured political continuity for almost two millennia but had mostly disintegrated by the fifteenth century; the surviving elements—the *meliks* of Karabakh or *ishkhans* [nobility] of Zeytoun or Sassoun—did not preserve their old power and could not claim national leadership;

3. It was national in scope, in the sense that it encompassed the absolute majority of Armenians;

4. It was national also in the sense that in the three of the four centers of the Church—the Catholicosates of Etchmiadzin and Cilicia and the Patriarchate in Constantinople—laymen participated to varying degrees in the election of their ecclesiastical leader, the management of the institution, and in the formulation of policy with regard to the dominant powers.

5. Finally, it was national because the dominant states said so, especially in the case of the Ottomans, since the millet system was extra-territorial and encompassed Armenians anywhere in the empire.

These are important dimensions and significant distinctions, since each entails a different form of politicization of the Church, even if they are intertwined. The Church was politicized long before the parties were born. Its financial needs and state sponsorship also ensured that it was essentially a conservative institution: it was inclined to preserve what it had, and it was cautious in its methods. It was not uncommon for parish priests to invoke God's will to curb the anger of common people over the deteriorating circumstances of their existence. Yet the Church could not manage not to be influenced by the changes within and around the community. It is interesting to note that the Armenian term used to designate political parties, *gousagtsoutiun*, was in use within the Patriarchate of Constantinople, which had jurisdiction over the majority of the Armenian people—and its most problematic part, by the 19th century, long before the known political parties were founded. This term described groups with opposing views over the degree to which the Patriarchate should represent the Armenians at the Sublime Porte, as opposed to representing the Sultan to the Armenian millet.

Throughout its history, the Church nonetheless remained a conservative institution, as it depended on wealthy Armenians for financial support.

While local priests could live on the contributions of parishioners, administrative centers needed the support of major contributors—and the permission of the state—to build or maintain churches, monasteries, and seminaries. The Church also on occasion required the help of influential Armenians to get out of political or other difficulties.

The treaties of San Stefano and Berlin, ratified in 1878, exemplify the extent to which the deteriorating conditions of Western Armenians and the opportunities offered by Great Power interference in Ottoman affairs pushed the Patriarchate to the limit of its political and representative functions. (The efforts of liberation initiated in earlier centuries by some Catholicoses of Etchmiadzin and other clergymen ended when Russia occupied Eastern Armenia in 1828.) Also in 1878, the Church appealed to Russia and, subsequently, to the Great Powers to achieve reforms in the Armenian provinces of the Ottoman Empire. This was due in part to the willingness of these powers to use Armenians and their plight in pursuit of their imperialistic interests, and to the opportunity presented by the Russian defeat of the Ottomans in the war of 1877-1878. But it was also a response to the evolving democratization of the structures of the Patriarchate, the failure of Ottoman reforms, and the refusal of the Sultan to accept ultimately the political role of the Patriarchate. The failure of Article 61 of the Treaty of Berlin exposed the contradictions inherent in the multiple natures of the Church, leading the Church to end its forays into foreign policy, if only for a while.

POLITICAL PARTIES: CONFRONTATION OR CONTINUATION

The rise of two Armenian revolutionary parties a decade or so after the signing of the Treaty of Berlin, the Hnchakians and the Dashnaktsoutiun, first and foremost constituted a rejection of the millet system. Therefore, it was a rejection of the Church as a political institution, and as the national structure that defined the Armenian individual and Armenian interests. In the view of the founders of these parties, the limits inherent to defining Armenians as a religious community had to be transcended. Rather, Armenians had to be redefined in terms of "modern" national institutions. Although initially inspired by the promise the Church had secured through Article 61, in essence, the parties were challenging the political role of the Church by offering themselves as alternative leadership. They considered their organizations the ultimate form of a democratization process that had reached its limit within the Church. One was born an Armenian and being part of the Church came with the territory. Yet being a member of a party was a matter of choice. In addition to the organizational and institutional factors that distinguished the newcomers from the Church, the quasi-Marxist or socialist beliefs of the parties—which the parties viewed as the ultimate expression of modernity and enlightenment—left no room for religion, and thus questioned the essential legitimizing power of the Church itself.

Yet in the early years both revolutionary parties were unsure of a number of issues regarding their agenda. Debate raged within, and between parties, over whether their missions consisted of employing means the Church could not use to pursue reforms—violence and bloodshed, which would attract attention and force the Great Powers to act—or if they were engaging now in revolution as a strategic goal. Did revolution aim at rising against the Ottoman state to change it or to establish an Armenian state? Finally, did either of these strategic goals require first a revolution within the Armenian people? The parties were never clear on which of the two—Great Power intervention or a popular liberation movement—was the main strategic approach, and which had a supporting role. They were also unclear about the extent to which they could, or should revolutionize Armenian society.

The Ramgavars, who would appear in 1908 as the Armenian Constitutional Democratic Party and consolidate in 1921 in Constantinople as the Liberal Democratic Party, were the only major Armenian political party to have seen the Church and religion as an integral part of the national "character" and structures.[5] Anti-revolutionary and anti-socialist, the Ramgavars remained true to their program by accepting the Church as an equal partner in the determination of the Armenian character and goals. The Ramgavars replaced the Hnchakians as the second most important party after the First World War, while the Dashnaktsoutiun retained in the Diaspora the dominant position it had achieved by 1896.

The only party to be anti-Church by definition and seeing the Church as a major nuisance was the Armenian Communist Party, heirs to the early 20th century Armenian Bolsheviks. After Armenia was Sovietized in 1920, the Church in Armenia was reduced to a skeletal existence and persecuted. But even the Soviets adjusted their policies beginning in the 1950s, seeing some legitimizing value in the old institution.[6]

PERIODIZATION

A. 1887 to 1908

The paradoxes in the relationships between the Church and political parties were evident from the first action in the field the first Armenian party ever took. The Hnchakian Center, or central executive body, sent one of their members to establish organizational branches among Ottoman Armenians, beginning with Trabizon and Constantinople. In June 1890, Ottoman police decided to raid the Armenian Church in Trabizon on the basis of rumors, which Armenians knew were false, that Armenian revolutionaries had stockpiled weapons in the building. The Hnchakians of Trabizon organized a defense of the Church. Police did not normally enter churches. But Marxists also would not have normally made the defense of a church their first act of resistance. The encounter ended with a couple of dead Armenians, and few more imprisoned.

A month later, frustrated by the lack of a proper response from the Great Powers to the Trabizon incident, the Hnchakians moved their show to Constantinople and organized a demonstration against the Sultan, most likely the first such political manifestation by a non-Muslim, non-Turkic group. To maximize the impact and increase participation, one of them read a statement of grievances in the Patriarchal Church, interrupting the Divine Liturgy. Then others forced the Patriarch, Archbishop Khoren Ashekian (1888-1894), to lead the demonstration, some say after he was actually beaten. As far as reforms were concerned, this event too produced little practical result. But it did increase the Sultan's paranoia and heightened the fears of the privileged Armenians in Constantinople, in turn attracting attention to the Hnchakians. It might also have shocked many ordinary Armenians out of their lethargy. It appeared possible to act against the state, and also the leader of the Church.

Regardless, the parties tried to ignore the Church during their early years, especially in their theoretical writings. But in the field, they instinctively realized its omnipresence, as well as its value as a tool to reach the people. Their larger framework and sources of ideology for liberation notwithstanding, both the Hnchakians and Dashnaktsakans had defined their immediate concerns in "national," even if not nationalistic terms. And it was impossible to imagine the nation without its Church. The parties considered their national struggle as a form of class struggle, since the nation, by and large, was being treated by the Ottoman system as a disenfranchised class. But the revolution could not start with an internal "class" struggle when so much more of Armenian life was threatened, even as the new political leaders pointed out that the Armenian privileged classes had aligned themselves with the oppressor.

In 1890, when the two socialist and revolutionary parties were negotiating the joining of their forces, they released a statement inviting all Armenians, regardless of age, class, gender, or station, to join the struggle under one banner. Their words best express the problem of the parties early in their historical development:

> ...Therefore, brothers, let us unite in the name of the Holy Task, against the common enemy. You, the young, the defenders everywhere of noble ideas, join the people.
> And you, the white-haired elderly, exhort your sons and help them with your many years of experience.
> And you, the rich, open your purses to provide arms to the people so that it is able to defend its breast that it has now opened against the enemy.
> And you, Armenian Woman, you inspired soul to the Holy Task.
> And you, Armenian Clergyman, bless the soldiers of freedom...[7]

The assignments were clear enough. The declaration also made it clear that the rich and the clergymen were not regarded, by definition, as the "enemy." Or not initially, anyway, unless they did not perform according to the new, rearranged hierarchy. At the top of that hierarchy were "the people," as imagined by the intellectuals who founded the parties, who imagined that they too best represented it. The ambiguity toward the clergy and the rich, just as toward the meaning of revolution, would remain integral to the story of the relations between the Church and the political parties. There was no ambiguity, however, in the imagery and symbolism used intended to embed the new struggle—and the new hierarchy—in religious and historical contexts.

Many churchmen, usually of the lower ranks, joined the struggle. Some monasteries played a crucial role in the communications and arms transport system of the guerrilla fighters. Many guerrilla fighters, the fedayees, asked for and received the blessings of priests before going on missions, just as Ghevond Yerets had done for Vartan Mamigonian and his army before the paradigmatic 5th century battle against the Persians to preserve their Christian religion.[8]

Though some priests and even bishops encouraged, or even cooperated with the armed struggle, the cautious and conservative Church hierarchy was, understandably, not supportive of the movement. The movement clearly indicated loss of the Church's control over the flock and, therefore, its value to the Ottoman government. It also created fears of reprisal against the civilian Armenian population.

The parties tried to influence the Patriarchate, with only limited and sporadic success. For all practical purposes, even as Ottoman Armenians regarded the Catholicos of Etchmiadzin as their Supreme religious authority, they afforded the Patriarchate more importance. The parties, especially the Hnchakians, were more successful in their influence on Patriarch Mateos Izmirlian (1894-1896), who harbored no illusions regarding the Ottoman government's ability to implement reforms, and who showed more understanding of revolutionary party tactics than any other clerical leader of Ottoman Armenians. Known as the "Iron Patriarch," Izmirlian showed his contempt toward the politics of accommodation to the Sultan by once refusing to meet Abdulhamid II, whom he considered personally responsible for the 1894-1896 massacres. Patriarch Maghakia Ormanian (1896-1908) was far less accommodating toward the parties, aware of why Izmirlian's tenure was so short, and harboring a dislike of revolutions and parties. "During tenure in office and in activities, it is not abstract ideologies that justify [conduct of] the person," he argued, "but it is realities that must determine the path."[9] Or, as he stated it to the party representatives, "In my position, it is not the personal preferences that will dominate [the course of action] but the imperatives of the office and the calling of the position."[10] He insisted that the physical survival of the nation was the highest priority, and that bloodshed should be avoided at all costs. "A captain cannot stop a storm," he explained, "but must keep calm and lead the ship to port, even if that is done by detours."[11] From the point of view of the parties, to use the Patriarch's metaphor, the storms were man made, specifically by the Ottoman Government, and conditions should be changed before it turned into a hurricane. A strong, almost authoritarian leader of his Church, Ormanian survived an assassination attempt in 1903. The Dashnaktsoutiun, suspected of the act, denied any involvement in the attempt.[12]

This uneasy relationship became even more difficult following the massacres of 1894-1896, which both ended the primacy of the Hnchakian Party and provided the Dashnaktsoutiun an opportunity to ascend to first position. The Church had no strategic options to respond to the tragedy. It either accepted quietly Ottoman state policies or, at best, lodged protests, some louder than others. Having engaged in open and antagonistic diplomacy with the Russians in 1878, the Church no longer saw such initiatives as advisable, considering the policy the Sultan had opted for in response to revolutionary activities. But the political parties did not have such limitations. The Hnchakians responded to the tragedy with internal dissension and mutual recrimination, leading to a debilitating split. In contrast, the Dashnaktsoutiun honed its strategy and organization. Intense contacts with Western socialists and liberals, as well as cooperation with Turkish and other Ottoman liberal parties, became part of its adjustment process. This wider net, supported by more intense grassroots organizational efforts and bolstered by the paralysis of the Patriarchate, gave the party prominence that still undergirds its historical capital. For the rest of this period, the parties and Church continued their uneasy coexistence.

But while "Ottomanizing" its politics and Europeanizing its outlook and propaganda, the Dashnaktsoutiun also expanded its agenda by taking up the cause of Eastern or Russian Armenians in 1903. Until then Armenians on the other side of the border had been considered as part of the supporting mechanism for the struggle in Western (Ottoman) Armenia, where the conditions were considered untenable, and the threat to Armenian communal existence thought imminent. When the tsarist government decided on a policy of Russification and attempted to confiscate Armenian Church properties in its realm, the Dashnaktsoutiun and other parties rose to the defense of the Church, acting in the name of the nation and national rights, and in view of the Church's national, rather than religious significance.

The opposition to the confiscation of Church properties, on which the Russian government eventually yielded, was a prelude to the decision of the Dashnaktsoutiun and other Armenian leftist groups to join in the First Russian Revolution in 1905 against the tsar for the defense of political and economic rights of Russian Armenians. This came to the dismay of many Western Armenian leaders of the party, who considered it downright dangerous to fight on two fronts, as it would consolidate the Russians' distrust of Armenians except when they could be manipulated for their purposes in the Ottoman Empire. 1905 also marked the start of a three-year civil war throughout the Caucasus between Armenians and Tatars (Caucasus Turks or, later, Azeris). In a war probably fomented by tsarist agents, the Dashnaktsoutiun took the lead in organizing self-defense in towns and villages, accentuating the national, rather than class character of the party.

More importantly, for our story, having become the champions of Armenians on both sides of the border, the Dashnaktsoutiun took the initiative to compel the Catholicos of Etchmiadzin, Mgrdich Khrimian (1893-1907), to convene a National Assembly. Khrimian had been the champion of the poor in the Ottoman Armenian provinces. As Patriarch of Constantinople (1869-1873), he had tried to use the institution of the Patriarchate to press the Ottoman government for reforms in the Armenian provinces. Yet he lost the battle, in part because of the conservatism of the Constantinople based privileged Armenian elite. The latter feared that hoisting the situation of provincial peasants and craftsmen to the top of the political agenda would result in the Ottoman government considering the Armenian millet a "problem." In 1878, Khrimian was the head of the Armenian delegation to the Congress of Berlin, where he tried to lobby for the preservation of the more stringent Article 16 of the earlier Treaty of San Stefano regarding Armenian reforms. He lost that battle too, for the new Article 61 on the subject was too vague to be effective. The speeches Khrimian delivered upon his return at least indirectly advocated the use of arms and became a source of inspiration for many of the early revolutionaries, who considered him a natural ally. When Hnchakian representatives met him early in the history of the party to secure his support for the revolution, Khrimian was extremely cautious. He clarified his famous post-Berlin speeches, interpreted in 1878 as calls for arms, by pointing out that his was not a call for a couple of youths to battle the Ottoman state with a few hunting guns. Revered by most Armenians as an icon, deeply patriotic and paternal, Khrimian was otherwise profoundly conservative in his worldview. He also was too old and powerless to resist the Dashnaktsoutiun, even though they would give him crucial support in 1903 when, as Catholicos of All Armenians, he resisted the confiscation of Church properties by the Russian Government.

The purpose of the National Assembly that convened in Etchmiadzin in August 1905 was to democratize and modernize the Church. That is, to bring it under popular (i.e., party) control with a constitution that would give control of the Catholicosate to laymen, as was the case in the Patriarchate of Constantinople. According to Ormanian, Khrimian was not averse to seeing some change in the management of Etchmiadzin.[13] But the gathering was dominated by members who looked forward to a more radical transformation. Presided over by Simon Zavarian, one of the founders of the Dashnaktsoutiun, many participants labeled the Church a nuisance that had exceeded its mandate. The Assembly was dispersed by the Russian police at the invitation of Church leaders who did not wish to see their institution revolutionized in such a manner as to invite the wrath of the tsarist regime and diminish their autonomy.

B. 1908-1923

The Young Turk Revolution of 1908 changed the landscape in a manner that even the most radicals could not hope. And that may be the reason why many revolutionary leaders became blind to the shortcomings of some of their Turkish partners, especially those among the Dashnaktsoutiun who thought their "Ottomanization of the Revolution" policy had borne fruit. During this period, they hoped against all hope that Young Turk leaders would remain faithful to the principles that led them to de-claw the Sultan and reinstate the 1878 Ottoman Constitution.

The Dashnaktsoutiun and others celebrated their moment of triumph in the euphoria of the new era of equality and brotherhood of peoples and religions declared by the new leaders of the Ottoman Empire. One of the first acts undertaken by the revolutionary parties and their associates was the change at the helm of the Patriarchate. Realizing the meaning of the revolution, Ormanian, the anti-party clergyman, resigned and was replaced by Izmirlian (1908-1909), who had been deposed in 1896 for being too close to the parties. Izmirlian's second tenure, now dominated by the Dashnaktsoutiun, was cut short by his election to the Catholicosate of All Armenians in Etchmiadzin. Interestingly, the two major candidates for the position in Etchmiadzin were Ormanian and Izmirlian. The Dashnaktsoutiun was able to control the majority of candidates, ensuring Ormanian would not win.

Otherwise, this was a period in which the strategies and framework of the Church would avert major confrontations: guerrilla activities had ended; change from within, reform through a liberal Ottoman government, legislation through an elected Parliament where there was Armenian representation, including some who were members of the revolutionary parties had become possible. Constantinople, now seen as a beacon of democracy, became the center of activities for all Armenian parties, except for the Bolsheviks.

Even the culture of the period, the literature and the arts reflected a critical mood toward the Church and Christianity. Pagan gods and goddesses were recovered from oblivion in literature. Atheism became fashionable among the youth. One group in Van advocated free love.

The revolutionary organizations were now joined by the newly formed Democratic Liberal party, the Ramgavars. Despite their recent emergence, they reflected the interests and worldview of middle and upper middle-class Armenians. They also benefited from the prominence of Boghos Nubar Pasha, once the prime minister of Egypt under British rule. As indicated above, the Ramgavars explicitly endorsed the Church as an integral part of Armenian life and any decision-making process. During their first convention in Constantinople the founders of the new party promised to participate in every election, everywhere, to "supervise over the affairs" of the Church, especially in Constantinople, and ensure that the schools were safe from "extremist social views."[14]

This was when, in fact, the parties established their ascendancy in the eyes of the Government. It was also when the people marked their dominance over the Church, even though the Patriarch insisted that his office was the equivalent to that of a head of state, and the Patriarchate remained a structure through which formal business was conducted.[15] For some party members in the National Assembly, their presence was to ensure that the Church did not disrupt the work of the parties. Sarkis Atamian would later reinforce this view by arguing that the National Assembly, and therefore the Church, had no legitimate business getting involved in politics. He maintained that those who tried to keep the Church in politics, such as the Ramgavars, were the representatives of the Armenian bourgeoisie who had for years done nothing for the Armenian peasantry and the poor. In fact, Atamian recast the initial conflict between Church and revolutionary parties and the later Ramgavar antagonism with the Dashnaktsoutiun in terms of a class conflict: The Ramgavar-Church alliance represented the clerical-bourgeois class, in his view, as opposed to his party that represented the poor and the peasants.[16]

With the failure of the Young Turk Government to address the reforms issue, the political parties and the Patriarchate in tow returned to the Great Powers for help beginning in 1912. Patriarch Hovannes Arsharouni (1911-1913) kept his contacts with the Turkish Government but also met separately with the Russian Ambassador. At some point he argued that "Russia was the only hope" while disparaging Boghos Nubar Pasha for his lack of a specific plan.[17] His successor, Zaven Der Yeghiayan (1913-1922) tried to resist. He urged all to "leave aside the Great Powers, as such a course could only bring a disaster," he argued.[18] But the Dashnaktsoutiun, supported by the Hnchakians and others, controlled all institutions, and were able to impose their own policies on the Patriarch through the Patriarchate's National Assembly.

The dominance of the parties was not in doubt for the remainder of this period leading to the First World War and the Genocide in the Ottoman Empire. On the eve of the war, Patriarch Zaven continued to urge Armenians to comply fully with the law on the conscription of Armenians into the Ottoman Army, as did the Dashnaktsoutiun. But the Patriarch disagreed with the activities of the party and others in the Caucasus who, while formally supporting the Ottoman war effort against Russia in the Ottoman Empire, sought the volunteer mobilization of Russian Armenians against the Ottoman Empire, as the latter was suspected of sinister plans. The organization of volunteer units was achieved with Russian support, under the patronage of the then Catholicos of All Armenians, Gevorg V Sourenyants. Patriarch Zaven failed in that effort too.[19] The results were a Church divided in its policies and the dominant party with conflicting ones.

The rest is history. Genocide became the great equalizer in Armenian life, making all differences, conflicts and battles immaterial. Both the Church and the parties lost leaders on the national and local levels. Neither would ever be the same again. It is true that for a brief period following the occupation of Constantinople by the Allied Forces, the Patriarch and the parties each returned with renewed hope and fervor. But that too ended abruptly with the rise of Mustafa Kemal's movement. The Patriarchate survived with no remaining political field of action, with its patriarch the leader of a religious community far smaller in numbers. The Armenian parties were no longer tolerated in Republican Turkey; there were no political parties that might try to challenge, nor dominate the Church. And in historic Armenia, there were no Armenians left to speak of, people whose cause the parties might otherwise have championed.

In Eastern Armenia, where an independent republic dominated by the Dashnaktsoutiun was proclaimed in 1918, relations between Church and state did not represent a problem. The Catholicos continued to enjoy a prestige the leaders of the republic did not challenge. On the contrary, as was the case during the war, the position of the Catholicos was used for humanitarian and diplomatic purposes. The Republic did not have time to write a constitution that might have provided a framework and basic principles determining a long-term relationship.

C. 1920-1990 Soviet Armenia

During the Soviet period, relations in Armenia between the Church and the parties was much simpler, though much more difficult for the Church. There was one Church with one administrative center, Etchmiadzin, although it happened to be the Mother See of the Armenian Apostolic Church, of historical and spiritual significance to all Armenians. More importantly, there also was one party, the Communist Party. Particularly during the first decade after Sovietization in 1920, the Bolshevik apparatus was zealously anti-Church and anti-religion. A 1922 Soviet decree abolished any remnant of the principle of separation of Church and state. The Party established complete control over the Church, impoverished the institution, and led campaigns against religion. One element in the state's campaign against religion and church was the establishment of "*Azat Yekeghetsi*" or free church, for those Armenians who, while ostensibly harboring religious beliefs, were let loose to propagandize against the established church, assailing it as reactionary, and impugning its clergymen as lecherous and corrupt.[20]

Alexander Myasnikyan, one of the early and cautious leaders of Soviet Armenia, argued:

> What is Soviet Armenia doing against the Church? Of course, it does not accept the Church, it is not religious, it is not feeding the freeloading clergy, but it also knows that there are believers, that there are people who recognize the church, who worship religion with all their consciences. To make these people understand the harmfulness of religion, we do not feel the need at all to close down churches, to shut down places of worship, to ban funerals or forbid by decree weddings and christenings. We know that literacy and education, and real life will eliminate these things. We see that the church is being destroyed by forces from within; and we will contribute to that destruction with our sermons, with our schools, with electricity and dams.[21]

Initially, the leaders of Soviet Armenia did not care much about the extraterritorial value of the Mother See. In fact, they did not much care about the Diaspora, except as a vehicle for spreading revolution throughout the world as a cure that would eliminate all human problems. For all practical purposes, Myasnikyan advocated the dissolution of all Armenian political parties in the Diaspora as well.[22] Soviet Armenian authorities kept the seat of the Catholicos of All Armenians vacant after the death of Gevorg V Sourenyants. They allowed a new election only in 1932. The new catholicos, Khoren I Mouradbekyan, is thought to have been murdered by Soviet authorities in 1938.

In the general atmosphere of tolerance and needs during and in the aftermath of the Second World War, Gevorg VI Chorekyan was elected Catholicos in 1945. His tenure seems to have coincided with the Soviet reappraisal of the value of the Church and the Catholicos of All Armenians for Soviet policy beyond the Soviet borders. Gevorg VI was allowed to establish closer contacts with the Diaspora. During the brief moment when Soviet leaders made noise regarding territorial demands from Turkey toward the end of the Second World War, the Catholicos made a statement supporting the Soviet claim, implying that the territories in question, Kars and Artahan would be returned to Soviet Armenia.

Although both Khoren I and Gevorg VI kept contact with communities and dioceses abroad, it was Vazgen I Baljian (1955-1994) who was able to actually visit diasporan communities as Catholicos. The Cold War was in full throttle by then. Moscow had rediscovered the benefits of a visible Catholicos to promote its interests abroad, while the Catholicos himself used the new opening to strengthen the position of the Church in regards to the Soviet state. The Church appeared as a historically legitimized institution as opposed to the Soviet state, whose legitimacy was mere ideology, and to the Communist Party.

But as the two sides needed each other, neither carried their inherent antagonism to its logical conclusion. Vazgen I was dispatched to Lebanon in 1956 to prevent the Dashnaktsoutiun from taking control of the Catholicosate of Cilicia, when that party had clearly aligned itself with Western, or more specifically American interests. The failure of his mission initiated a rivalry in the Diaspora between the two sees, with dire consequences that are still relevant today.

When Soviet Armenians pushed for the relative re-nationalization of Armenian history beginning in the 1960s, Moscow acquiesced, allowing Vazgen I to reestablish the Church in Armenia as one of the guardians of its history and culture. Many of the changes occurred in the context of a Soviet need for new sources of legitimation and the state policy to deflate the strength of the Dashnaktsoutiun in the Diaspora, the party which until the late 1960s was ideologically and politically opposed to Communism and the USSR as antagonistic to Armenian national interests. By the 1970s, however, the Dashnaktsoutiun itself was changing its priorities and targets, remembering its socialist heritage, considering the Soviet Union as the ultimate guarantor of what was left of Armenia, while focusing on Turkey as the main enemy of the Armenian nation.

The gradual accommodation between Church and state in Soviet Armenia continued until the end of the Soviet period.[23] Vazgen I lived long enough to see Armenia's independence and give his blessing to its first President.

D. 1920-1990: Diaspora

Outlining issues in the history of relations between Church and parties in the Diaspora is far more complex. The Diaspora is not a homogeneous entity. Some communities predate the Genocide, while others are largely post-Genocide. Middle Eastern states that became heirs to the dissolved Ottoman Empire, such as Lebanon, Syria, Egypt, Iraq and Jordan, initially absorbed the largest numbers of Genocide survivors. In these states, regardless of the political regimes, the millet system continued in one form or another. A definition of Armenians above all as members of a religious community also dominated the community in Iran. In these cases, the Church continued to enjoy state recognition which other institutions could neither bypass, nor match. The Church was on its own in Western countries, although it was perceived as the institution which most Armenians considered as the most natural and traditional as well as least partisan affiliation. The parties had more influence in some communities than others.

The Church functioned in most pre-Genocide Armenian communities abroad, such as in the Middle East, Europe and the United States. In most cases, the Hnchakians and the Dashnaktsoutiun in the Diaspora had shown little inclination to get involved in Church affairs at the time, unlike the Ramgavars. The indifference continued to some extent even after the Genocide in many of these communities, including the US. Only the Ramgavars had a program-based affiliation with the Church.

But the Genocide had made exiles of both the Church and the parties. The main reason for the existence of the parties and the object of their struggles, the situation of Armenians in Ottoman or Western Armenia, no longer existed, though the Wilsonian solution to Armenia's boundaries still inspired and motivated many. On a practical level, however, communities were preoccupied with recovering from the Genocide, the worst national tragedy in Armenian history. They were regrouping, reorganizing and recapturing a communal identity as the least they could do to reassert their existence and respect the memory of the dead and a lost homeland. For most Western Armenians, now refugees, gone were the grand battles, the antagonistic positions on political or social philosophies, and the debates over land reforms or on the choice of strategic partners to achieve them in the homeland.

Much was gone indeed that changed the dynamics of communities. But not the bitterness, the need to blame, the internalized aggression. It seems small, victimized nations cannot live without battles on grand issues. The survivors of the Genocide, including the parties and the Church, did not lack choices in fields of battle.

In political parties, the Diaspora communities had ready-made structures that could constitute the sides. The parties, whose programs were territorially defined, could not compete with the long history of extraterritorial history, legitimacy and authority of the Church. The parties needed to reassert and project their organizational power, as well as protect their history from blame in the Genocide. Control of community institutions became a simple necessity. This was particularly true of the Dashnaktsoutiun, which had not only been the leading party negotiating with the Young Turks on behalf of Western Armenians, but also the founder of the Republic of Armenia in 1918. The story with the Young Turks had ended in Genocide, and the Republic of Armenia with Soviet Armenia. This was too much of a burden for any organization that had, at least in its view, achieved and sacrificed so much.

This burden—and the internal debates—resulted in a reexamination of the party's past and future in a conference in Vienna in 1923, where some prominent members argued that the party should dissolve itself, having accomplished its historic mission, with dubious results at that.[24] They lost. The party decided to entrench itself in the communities and continue to struggle, in whatever form possible, for an independent Armenia.

The year 1923 also coincided with the resurgence of defeated Turkey, and also the signing of the Treaty of Lausanne, which discarded, albeit in the absence of an Armenian voice, the 1920 Treaty of Sèvres that awarded the First Republic parts of the Ottoman Empire or Western Armenia with access to the Black Sea. For all practical purposes, the Treaty of Lausanne closed the chapter on what was known since 1878 as the Armenian Question, with only a vague reference to the rights of non-Muslim communities in Turkey.

In trying to reconstruct community life, it was impossible to leave out the Church. It is true that even up to the early 1930s the Dashnaktsoutiun flirted with the idea of an Armenian nationalism without the Church and without Christianity. Garegin Nzhdeh, a Dashnak hero from the days of the

First Republic, considered Christianity a negative factor in Armenian history, one that weakened the resolve of the nation to use whatever means needed to attain national goals. After an initial tour of communities in the United States, in 1933, Nzhdeh founded the "tseghakron" or "race-based religion" movement. Akin to, and in part inspired by European fascist movements, Nzhdeh extolled the virtues of the Armenian "race," and brought forth the pre-Christian deities that were considered more virile and invigorating.[25] This movement would eventually become the Armenian Youth Federation, a wing of the Dashnaktsoutiun that has no quarrels with the Christian religion or with the Church.

What mattered most, though, even for the "tseghakrons," was anti-Communism. By the end of the 1920s, the parties had agreed on what to disagree about: what to think of Soviet Armenia. The battle lines were clearly drawn. The Hnchakians and the Progressives[26] argued that Soviet Armenia was the realization of a socialist Armenia they dreamed of since their birth, even if on a smaller scale. The Ramgavars, who had adopted an essentially middle-class liberal program, maintained a visceral distaste of socialism in any form, and scorned the First Republic of Armenia as not the real homeland, decided they should support Soviet Armenia, because it was an Armenia. And it was an Armenia that might be safer in the hands of the Russians than, probably, the Dashnaktsoutiun.[27] One of the main ideologues and leaders of the Ramgavars argued in 1927 that liberal democracy disagreed with Soviet ideology, but his Party would act as a "friendly opposition" and "provide constructive criticism" even as it supported Soviet Armenia. For the Dashnaktsoutiun, battling Communism and the Soviets appeared as a task holier than the one against a Republican Turkey that had completed the work of the Young Turks by deporting most Armenians remaining in their territory. The once socialist Dashnaktsoutiun considered Communism worse than capitalism, and the Soviets usurpers who should return the government to its rightful owner. In this battle, the Church for the Dashnaktsoutiun was transformed, as one protagonist indicated, into "a sort of fatherland for all, whether believers or non-believers."[28] Of all Armenian institutions, the Church was, after all, the one with the widest membership and affiliation.[29] A battle as titanic as anti-communism could not be won without controlling the Church, as the anti-

Dashnak side would argue, or saving it from Communists, as the Dashnak side would.

The battle for or against Communism was one the outcome of which, obviously, could not have been determined by any of the Armenian political parties, nor by all of them combined. Yet it was a fierce discussion that continued through the 1960s. Incessant and poisonous debates and mutual accusations covered the inability of the parties, and the communities, to digest what had happened to the nation. It was only a matter of time before that battle spilled over to the Church, an institution which commanded the loyalty of most Armenians for reasons of faith, habit, history and identity. This did not prove to be a difficult task, since the Church was an integral part of communities. Many churchmen had their own political views, and were ready to take sides. The question was the control of the Church as an institution through its National Assembly, modeled for the most part after the Patriarchate's structure. In this system, laymen dominated, while a clergyman acted as the chief executive accountable to the National Assembly of each diocese.

The pre-Genocide antagonisms had now been transferred to the Diaspora, with an almost incomprehensible vehemence and enmity. The earliest skirmishes took place in Romania, Greece and Egypt. The most important, however, occurred in the United States in 1933, concerning the reelection of Archbishop Ghevond Tourian, an energetic, politically opinionated clergyman who had long sided with the Hnchakian-Ramgavar-Progressive position on the question of Soviet Armenia. The Dashnaktsoutiun opposed his reelection. The result was that the 1933 Diocesan Assembly in New York split into two opposing meetings, with each claiming sole legitimacy. Tourian was reelected in one of the assemblies and the Catholicos of Etchmiadzin recognized him as the Prelate of North America; his opponents did not recognize his reelection.[30] The anti-Tourians eventually organized as a separate Church in 1956 and adhered to the Dashnak dominated Cilician Catholicosate seated in Antilias, Lebanon. Hence the "two churches."

Even if the new division could have been ascertained as an administrative question, the assassination of Archbishop Tourian later in the year in the Church of the Holy Cross, in Manhattan (New York) sealed the division in the community. Two members of the Dashnaktsoutiun were apprehended, charged, and found guilty of the assassination of the archbishop, although the Dashnaktsoutiun denied party involvement. The immediate cause of the assassination was Archbishop Tourian's refusal to participate in the Armenian Day events at the 1933 Chicago World's Fair if the tricolor of the First Armenian Republic remained on display. The assassination cemented the positions of the sides, turned a political struggle into a moral one, sealed the division, forced almost every Armenian to decide his or her position on the subject, and deepened a cleavage reaching into family and personal relationships which has yet to be fully overcome. Armenians at this time were not only caught up with the way they dealt with the losses of 1915 and of the First Republic, but also in US politics. Years after trying the accused assassins, prosecutor Thomas Dewey touted his clean-up of the "ethnic Mafiosi" during his successful campaign to become the Governor of New York.

One of the lesser appreciated consequences of these destructive events was the alienation of an undetermined, but sizable segment of the community, particularly its youth. They had a different idea of ethnic identity, considered the hatred unacceptable, and were alienated from the Church, parties and the community. Severing their ties with these elements of the Armenian community, many joined Catholic or Protestant churches.

Like several others in Armenian history, the Tourian assassination and its aftermath suspended the sense of time, as well as defined collective memory. Every event before and after is interpreted in light of this one event. The identity of most Armenians was reduced to what they felt and thought about this event, the distinction between parties and Church—just as between parties and nation or nation and Church—having disappeared.[31]

For those engaged in this stormy battle, it seems that identification with a partisan position was an easier way to find and exude ethnicity, and to feel passion. As far as the Dashnaktsoutiun were concerned, this was afforded a transcendental, quasi-religious value. For their opponents, the Ramgavars, it was pragmatic super-patriotism. More at ease with the Church and religion, and considering themselves to be the "only nationalist Armenian party," untainted by notions of class struggle, the Ramgavars considered the "nation" most absolute. As the Ramgavar leader Hrach Yervant theorized in 1927,

Only an idea [nationalism] that defies examination and analysis could have conquered and subjected to its awesome power the whole of humanity; and the infinite sacrifices which men have willingly made for the defense of that idea more than any other is evidence of the gratitude that nations feel toward the benefits and rewards that have been derived from it.[32]

It seems that such a characterization was more commonly and appropriately used to describe a deity. Vahan Navasartian, an ideologue of the Dashnaktsoutiun who was to become the authoritarian leader of the party for a couple of decades, addressed party followers in the US during a visit prior to World War II. He compared the position of the Dashnaktsoutiun under attack, and its readiness to be sacrificed, to that of Christ during the Last Supper: "Arek, gerek, zays e marmin im," he proclaimed, or "Take, eat; this is My body" (Matthew 26:26).[33] American Dashnaktsoutiun activist Sarkis Atamian would argue later that the party constituted "the formally organized aspect of Armenian nationalism," thus comparing it to the role of the Church in relation to religion.[34]

The archbishop's assassination became the fulcrum of an intensified anti-Dashnak and, indirectly, pro-Soviet Armenia campaign. The anti-Dashnak side organized a "Tourian Committee" that published a series of five pamphlets under the general title "For History" that presented the slain clergyman as a martyr to Church, faith and nation, a trinity that had become one in the minds of the combatants. The pamphlets repeatedly charged the Dashnaktsoutiun with failures at critical moments in Armenian history.

With fifty years of revolutionary activities and with incalculable victims, they were unsuccessful in liberating an inch of territory from "The Sick Man of Europe" or to compel the implementation of Reform plans sanctified by the European Powers. This is a fact that cannot be denied.[35]

Who was responsible for the fact that the tricolor [of the First Republic] ceased to be a living flag? The Dashnaktsoutiun, the sole master of the Armenian Republic, prepared the tragedy of Kars with senseless adventurism, the natural consequence of which was the fall of the Republic and the succession of the Soviet regime. The tricolor now belonged in history and took its place in the national museum.[36]

The otherwise anonymous pamphlets considered the assassination as a symptom of the Dashnaktsoutiun's sense of its own historical failures:

> Following the failed attempt at the February Revolution, left without the prospect of recapturing its lost position by the use of force, the Dashnaktsoutiun conceived the devilish plan to achieve its monopoly of power over the Diaspora. The growing sympathy toward contemporary Armenia was an obstacle to its success; it was necessary to make [Soviet] Armenia unlikable, and for that purpose unabashedly declared it unauthentic and alien.[37]

The anti-Dashnak camp was not loathe to remind its opponent that the Dashnaktsoutiun had collaborated with the Young Turks, who then committed the Genocide.[38]

The last of the Tourian pamphlets and by far the thickest (392 pages) was titled *Azkatav Yeghernu yev Tadabardoutiunu*, or "The Holocaust that was a Plot against the Nation and its Condemnation." *Yeghern*, or holocaust, was the term used at the time to describe the Genocide. In this case, it referred to the assassination of Archbishop Tourian.[39]

From the start, argued Armen Partizian on the other side, the Armenian Church has never been an exclusively religious institution.

> The Armenian Church, as such, has never considered itself a separate entity from the Armenia people. Truly it has itself been the Armenian people, organized through a religious framework and spiritually...
>
> As is known to all, the Mother See of the Armenian Apostolic Church is located within the boundaries of the Soviet Union of which Armenia is part. In 1922 the Interior Affairs Commissar of the Soviet government of Armenia issued a decree annulling the unified character of the Church in Armenia and instead recognizing the individual rights of religious communities, without an organic link between them...
>
> The Soviet Union had enough cunning not to revoke the "Catholicosal" rights of the Catholicos of All Armenians on Armenians abroad. It granted this much freedom with the future in mind... By doing it [the Soviet Union] hid from Armenians abroad not only the realities in which the Church existed in Armenia but also its ultimate plans and win over many naïve believers. Moreover, by keeping in its hands a Catholicos and a Mother See that had authority

over Armenians abroad, [the Soviet Union] hoped to use Churches in the diaspora to pursue its own goals within the masses of Armenians abroad and thus win their support for the international proletarian revolution...[40]

The "two church" system also survived a brief period of cooperation between the sides that followed the Soviet suggestions that may demand Kars and Ardahan from Turkey as Western/US cooperation with the USSR during the Second World War was replaced by the Cold War.[41]

The 1956 battle for the Catholicosate of Cilicia crystallized the new divisions. When Cilicia, in the northeast corner of the Mediterranean Sea, outside of historic Armenia, had turned into an Armenian kingdom and Armenia itself was deprived of sovereignty, the Catholicosate of Etchmiadzin had also moved there. The institution was in the Cilician capital and Sis continued its existence even when the kingdom collapsed in 1375. Etchmiadzin resumed its own line of Catholicoses beginning in the 15th century as the hope of a revived kingdom in Cilicia waned. With the rise of the power of the Patriarchate in Constantinople, the Catholicosate of Cilicia was reduced to a bishopric with authority within Cilicia and, later, parts of Greater Syria, though its prelate retained the title of Catholicos. During the final expulsion of Armenians from Cilicia in 1921, Catholicos Sahak II Khabaian (1902-1939) moved with his flock to the south and settled in Antilias, a village near Beirut. His jurisdiction continued to be recognized over areas where most of Cilician Armenians resettled: Lebanon, Syria and Cyprus.[42] His successor, Karekin I Hovsepian (1945-1952), who attended the election of the Catholicos of All Armenians in Etchmiadzin in 1945, recognized the "spiritual and moral supremacy of Etchmiadzin," but reasserted the administrative independence of the Cilician See.[43]

The advent of the Cold War had deepened the cleavages in the Diaspora and the Armenian political parties internalized the arguments of the two sides. The Dashnaktsoutiun, already driven toward control of community institutions, and most probably encouraged by the United States, strove to control the Catholicosate of Cilicia by having a bishop who sympathized with its policies elected Catholicos. The opposing side, supported by the USSR, sent the newly elected Catholicos of Etchmiadzin, Vazgen I, to forestall such a possibility. The victory of the Dashnaktsoutiun followed a bruising battle that also turned violent at times. Archbishop Zareh I

Payaslian, prelate of Aleppo, was elected Catholicos of Cilicia, but at the cost of divisions in the Diaspora that are yet to heal. The Dashnaktsoutiun now had its own Catholicos.

The "two church" system that evolved, one "Dashnak" and the other "anti-Dashnak," combines the worst features of Armenian feudal behavior: political institutions controlling religious ones; and when political power is divided, so also is the Church. Each prince or petty king is his own Church and Catholicos.

The election of Zareh I was followed immediately by a campaign by the Dashnaktsoutiun and its supporters to extend his jurisdiction into dioceses that had traditionally been under the authority of the Catholicosate of All Armenians in Etchmiadzin. The party argued that Etchmiadzin could not be trusted to lead the Church or have control over Diasporan communities, charging that it was a tool of the Soviets and lacked independence. Based on requests from local Church executive councils, dioceses in Iran, Greece and Cyprus—countries where American influence was predominant—shifted their allegiance from the See of Etchmiadzin to that of Cilicia, inviting charges of usurpation and theft from the other side. An attempt to wrest the Marseille diocese failed.

One of the dire consequences of the now institutionalized enmity followed in the summer of 1958 when Lebanon plunged into a civil war in the midst of Arab nationalist fervor supported by the USSR and opposed by the US. The Dashnaktsoutiun and an anti-Dashnak alliance of Hnchakians, Ramgavars and Progressives managed to mount their own little civil war against one other. Fortunately, the community had matured enough to stay out of the fray when a second, more disastrous, and longer-lasting civil war broke out in 1975.

Equally important, perhaps, the control of the Cilician See by the Dashnaktsoutiun solved the problem of Dashnak oriented parishes in North America, which had remained in limbo since 1933. These parishes, acting as the Prelacy—to distinguish from the Diocese, which represented those loyal to Etchmiadzin—declared their allegiance to the Catholicosate of Cilicia. After these segments of the original North American diocese fractured, the anomaly of having two prelates of the same church, claiming the same territory, was later extended to California and Canada. The division of the Church was institutionalized.

Defending itself against the charges of Dashnak control, the pro-Dashnak Church argued:

> That members of the great Armenian Revolutionary Federation, the Dashnaktsoutiun (Federation), support our Church is never to be denied. We proclaim it proudly, and cannot understand the fascination of the dissident [Etchmiadzin affiliated] Church in trying to prove this fact—*which has never been denied* [italics in original].
>
> We feel that it is an honor to give spiritual sustenance [sic] to the members of an organization which has throughout the many years done so much to protect the sanctity and purity of the Armenian national institutions, and which established the independence of the Armenian state (1918-1920) after 543 years of tyrannization [sic] by foreign forces.
>
> We feel that the members of the Armenian Revolutionary Federation are true Christians, and are worthy of the great glory of the Christian Church.
>
> What we cannot understand is how the dissident church dares to make an issue of providing spiritual sustenance [sic] to members of a great patriotic anti-Communist organization—when it represents the spiritual home of Communists, pro-Communists, pro-Soviets, Marxist "Progressives", leftists and all other brands of Armenian fellow-travelers who support the Soviet Union, founded on the dogma of Karl Marx.
>
> *It is absurd to say that Armenian Communists and fellow-travelers are deserving of the Kingdom of God, and not Armenian Anti-Communists.* [Italics in original][44]

The Dashnak side hid behind the argument of the godlessness of a Church supported by and supporting Communism. In contrast, the anti-Dashnak Church aligned behind political realism and devotion to the security of Armenia.[45]

The Soviet Armenian historian and ideologue Lendrush Khurshutyan, among others, joined the fray by lambasting the "socialist" Dashnaktsoutiun as an American, specifically CIA-affiliated organization.[46] He also thought that the Dashnaktsoutiun was wrong when it considered all members of the Ramgavar Party as Soviet sympathizers; some were pro-Soviet, he said, others were anti-Soviet but pro-Armenian.[47] Nonetheless, he praised the "bourgeois" Ramgavar Party for its correct understanding of national interests.[48]

Nonetheless, passions cooled down with time, with the thawing of the Cold War and the change in the external agenda of the Dashnaktsoutiun. From ideological and political foe of the USSR, the dominant party transformed itself into the implacable enemy of Turkey, and made Genocide recognition and territorial reparation its main goals. This was one issue on which Armenian parties, as well as the Church, were more likely to agree. Beginning in the 1970s, the Dashnaktsoutiun moved closer to the position the Ramgavars had taken earlier: All seemed to agree that the USSR provided a security system for what was left of Armenia, and it was likely to be the world power that could wrest territory from Turkey on behalf of Soviet Armenia. Independence and freedom could wait, argued the Dashnaktsoutiun. A *united* Armenia was now considered the more important, and the more feasible aspect of the party's goal, declared in 1919, of a "Free, Independent and United Armenia."

Change of external agenda allowed for Dashnaktsoutiun cooperation with the other parties, as well as the Churches, which true to their national character, were not ready to be left out of the achievement of the international recognition of the Genocide, what among Armenians had emerged as a most basic need.

The change of priorities for the Dashnaktsoutiun without much questioning by the rank and file was facilitated by the support given to it by Soviet Armenia, and the USSR in general. It was better that all Armenians focus their attention on Turks and Turkey, rather than for some to hate the Communists and the USSR. While nurturing false hopes of territorial recuperation, even if indirectly, the USSR of course continued its normal relations with Turkey, and reaffirmed in treaties that it had no such demands from its neighbor.[49]

More immediately, the change of agenda was placed squarely within one of the dominant paradigms of Armenian history. An eight-year campaign of violence against Turkish diplomats and institutions mainly in Europe and North America (1975-1983), intended to avenge the Genocide, produced heroes and martyrs. One of the groups that claimed responsibility for assassinations and bombings was the Justice Commandos for the Armenian Genocide, generally seen as affiliated with the Dashnaktsoutiun.

The more interesting group, however, was the Armenian Secret Army for the Liberation of Armenia (ASALA). It claimed to be a new political party, the first significant such organization to be established in the Diaspora.[50] ASALA considered other parties "traditional," parties that had been co-opted by the comfortable conditions of the Diaspora, lost their fervor or revolutionary zeal, and accepted the rules of the game set by imperialist powers antagonistic to Armenian interests. Armed with a Third World liberation ideology, ASALA claimed to be the true revolutionary party, ready to move from propaganda tactics to actual liberation activities, including military cooperation with other struggles for liberation, such as the Kurds in southeast Turkey and far left Palestinian organizations. One important aspect of ASALA's ideology was its disinterest in Church affairs, although some clergymen seem to have been sympathizers. As all genuine revolutionaries, their understanding of the struggle also involved a change in community values and structures. The fate of ASALA was no different from what occurred to the Hnchakians after the 1894-1896 massacres almost a century earlier. After a 1983 bombing at Orly Airport, near Paris, hard core ideology came face to face with realities for ASALA. The party split into its radical and moderate wings and, for all practical purposes, disintegrated. The field was once again left open to the "traditionals" and the Church, although elements of its moderate wing continued to sponsor publications and very traditional activities.

The changes in the international climate and in generational leadership, gradually supported by the spirit of cooperation created by the change of the external agenda, brought out the anomaly of the two Church system. This was especially true in the United States, fast becoming the most important Armenian community outside the USSR. The traditional parties and the Church began unity talks in 1971. After 11 years of negotiations the talks produced the Memorandum of 1982, which expressed good intentions on all sides.[51] But no practical consequences have ensued and the talks have stalled since Armenia's independence in 1990. The parties were not ready to cede turf. A change in the agenda of the Dashnaktsoutiun did not include shifts in its position regarding community control.[52] Besides, the parties and the Church had learned to live with one another. Each had its "territory," so to speak, within the community. The Dashnak side had its Catholicos in Antilias, Lebanon; the anti-Dashnak forces had theirs, in Etchmiadzin.

They had made their peace on the basis of the division of Diasporan communities as well as the nation. After listing the advantages of Church unity, the late Archbishop Mesrop Ashjian, once Prelate of the Eastern US, Cilician See, argued that, "If antagonisms are in our makeup, and if conditions are not propitious, then unity is neither desirable nor possible."[53]

By this time, it was also difficult to distinguish between the parties and the Church in the Diaspora, which had reached a mutually advantageous, albeit tacit arrangement. The Church preached national identity and endorsed nationalist goals, in fact playing politics. Yet it shirked responsibility for the salvation of Armenian souls because it was too preoccupied with what was ailing the nation and it was, after all, responsible for religion and not politics. The parties preached spiritual values—hope, dreams, ultimate salvation, even if in the form of an ostensibly political agenda—but could not be held accountable for their failures, because they were taking care of the spiritual, i.e., identity needs of the nation.[54]

E. 1990-present

The Karabakh Movement erupted in Soviet Armenia in February 1988. Uniting Armenians there as much as they ever had been, or were to be, Karabakh turned into a movement of national renewal, democracy and independence. The Movement posed a new and more potent challenge to the *modus vivendi* that had recently evolved within the Diasporan communities. It also strained Diasporan organizations' relations with the USSR and Soviet Armenia. Just as the Dashnaktsoutiun had joined the others in accepting the Soviet state as an almost desirable partner, the people of Soviet Armenia decided, to the dismay of entrenched Diasporan organizations, that a democratic and independent state was preferable. The Diaspora was supportive of the movement in its early stages, when it was limited to the demand of the people of Nagorno Karabakh that their Autonomous Region, then part of Soviet Azerbaijan, be attached to Soviet Armenia. But when Moscow demurred and the Movement changed character—by May of 1988 the signs were there—Diasporan institutions were confused, threatened by or opposed to the direction the Movement had taken. The people of Armenia, an entity the Diasporan organizations had long dismissed as politically irrelevant, were in the streets. In doing so, they were challenging the powers in the USSR and Soviet Armenia with whom the Diaspora as a whole had made accommodations. The confusion deepened when it also became clear that the Movement leadership, commanding hundreds of thousands of street demonstrators, did not regard the Genocide as the focal point of national identity, nor international Genocide recognition as central to their agenda of change.[55]

In determining their positions regarding the Movement, Catholicos Vazgen I responded in Etchmiadzin with the usual cautiousness of the Church and, following the Armenian Communist Party, withheld his support.[56] Catholicos Karekin II Sarkissian in Antilias too remained aloof, given the Dashnaktsoutiun's vehement opposition to the Movement and to its leadership from the start. The power and position of the Church did not depend on Armenia's status. Nor, it seemed, did the Diaspora's.

The three parties in the Diaspora, the Hnchakians, Ramgavars and Dashnaktsoutiun, signed a joint Declaration in November 1988 admonishing the Movement leaders for disrupting Armenia's economy with strikes and demonstrations. The economy was more important, they argued, than Karabakh. They also charged that the Movement endangered the security of Armenia by antagonizing its protector, Moscow, which had consistently rejected the demands of the Armenian people in Karabakh and Armenia. While, by agreeing to sign the declaration, the parties showed their concern for the unforeseeable consequences of destabilization in Soviet Armenia, they also expressed their mistrust of, if not disdain for the judgment of the people of Soviet Armenia, and an underlying concern for their own destabilization.

The Movement had attracted worldwide attention, fired the imagination of many in the world, Armenian and non-Armenian alike. It was a bigger story, as far as the world was concerned, than any generated by the campaign for Genocide recognition.[57] International media were certainly also more positive toward the Movement than the Genocide issue, despite the support Western governments gave the new leader of the USSR, Mikhail Gorbachev. The main problem was, of course, that Diasporan Armenians had learned to define themselves, their political aspirations, their value systems, and their relations with the rest of the world in terms of the Genocide—subsuming the religious identity over which the parties and the Church were guardians. The Movement had no particular position on the role of religion in society but appreciated the role of the Church in its drive to reestablish a state with a national character. But it had no room for Genocide-based identity in its drive toward democracy and independence. Additionally, not only had the parties and the Church not been participants in the rise and management of the Movement, they also did not possess the tools—both in programming and in terms of values—to inject themselves into it. Major changes were happening and big stories were being written. Institutions that had delineated the parameters of Armenian history for a century, such as the parties, and for centuries, such as the Church, had little to do with them. It was, indeed, destabilizing for both. That was the price they paid for seeing in Armenia an "open air museum" rather than the home of a real people, the price for abstracting the homeland in their quest to accommodate being Diasporan institutions concerned primarily with ethnic identity and community control. The reaction of Diasporans did not necessarily follow the instincts of those directing the institutions. There has been no quantification of this distinction, but large numbers of Diasporan Armenians who had supported the Diasporan agenda as presented by the parties and the Church, but were not inspired by it, were fascinated by the alternative offered by the people of Armenia. Theirs was an alternative that was not only of larger significance, but was also based on real politics. This too was a threat to institutions concerned that the loyalty their national program had commanded would lose out to a value system that did not necessarily reject theirs, but certainly was more fascinating, less staid, less depressing and paralyzing, and less reliant on a national defeat than was an agenda related to the Genocide. The specter of an Armenian nation in Armenia acting as a sovereign entity provided an alternative that had a liberating effect on many Diasporans, liberation even from the depressing position of Genocide survivors who had no choice until then than being beggars from the international community for the recognition of the Genocide whether by propaganda, lobbying or violence. The parties had joined the Church in becoming conservative institutions in the etymological sense of the term, institutions whose community support could erode speedily unless they fought back.

From a political point of view, the position of the Ramgavars and Hnchakians still made sense. They had always maintained that regardless of ideology or practical concerns such as democracy and human rights, an

Armenia that was Soviet was also secure. The experience of the Genocide, and then its politicization, had conditioned Ramgavars and Hnchakians to think that a Turkey that does not recognize the Genocide was not only the greatest threat to the survival of the Armenian state, but also an imminent threat without a guaranteed system of Soviet security. But the Dashnaktsoutiun was a newcomer to this viewpoint. Generations of members and sympathizers of the party had grown up thinking of independence as the ideal for which to strive. Ostensibly, the party leadership had reached that conclusion on pragmatic considerations. Considering the strength of the USSR, its role in the international community as one of the two superpowers, and Armenia's membership in the Soviet Federation as a constituent republic, a territorially united Armenia was a more realizable goal than a free and independent one. Yet even when independence and freedom seemed more likely and closer to the hearts of the people in the homeland, the Dashnaktsoutiun opposed the Movement's aims and leadership to the last minute, arguing that it knew better what was best for the "nation." In a parallel reversal, the Hnchakians and Ramgavars acquiesced more easily to what was clearly inevitable by 1990, finally supporting the Movement and its drive for independence.

Under popular pressure, the Supreme Soviet of Armenia changed election laws and allowed parties other than the Communists to participate in the legislative elections in the spring of 1990. The Armenian National Movement, the party formed by the Karabakh Committee, won nearly half of the seats and had enough support from young Communists to elect one of the leaders of the Movement, Levon Ter-Petrossian, President of the Presidium of the Supreme Soviet of a still-Soviet Armenia. Among other principles, Armenia's Declaration on Independence (August 23, 1990), which laid the groundwork for the Declaration of Independence that was to follow in September 1991, adopted the principle of "freedom of conscience" for all its citizens.[58] One of the first Basic Laws adopted by the revived legislative body was a law on the freedom of conscience and religion and the separation of church and state. The Republic adopted its Constitution in 1995. By then, the state had returned to the Catholicosate of Etchmiadzin all Church properties that had been confiscated following Sovietization.

The Constitution reaffirmed the freedom of conscience and religion first guaranteed in 1991 (Article 23). The Basic Law secured the separation of Church and State while recognizing the "special position" held by the Church in Armenian history and culture, without declaring it a state religion. The Catholicos attended the major ceremonies symbolic of statehood as well as of nationhood.

Yet this was often not enough for the Armenian Church. Freedom of conscience and religion had opened the door not only for Armenian denominations other than the Apostolic Church, such as the Armenian Protestant and Catholic Churches, but also for a variety of other denominations and sects who sent their missionaries and advocates to Armenia. Following the devastating earthquake of December 1988, humanitarian relief had opened the door to many charities affiliated with such religious groups. There were no practical obstacles to their activities, although proselytizing was proscribed by law. Clergymen and others from the Apostolic Church complained about the inroads other denominations and sects were making in Armenia. They expected the state to use its resources to prevent further erosion of the hold of an Apostolic Church that had been too political/national to focus on the spiritual and daily needs of the citizens, and too complacent about its position in the nation. By and large, the state rejected further sponsorship of a single church or religion. Yet when the country was still on a war footing, some officials did take extra-legal action against sects whose members refused to serve in the army as conscientious objectors. But such actions were ended quickly, and subsequently a law on conscientious objectors was adopted.

The main test for Armenia's liberal position on Church and state came in 1994 when Vazgen I, Catholicos of All Armenians for four decades, passed away. For the first time, a new catholicos was to be elected in independent Armenia. President Ter-Petrossian was reluctant at first to involve the state in the election of the new catholicos, despite the urging of many of his associates. He based his objection on the principle of the separation of church and state as well as on practical grounds. Ter-Petrossian felt the state had enough problems to resolve, and that the Church should take responsibility to solve its own and elect a leader who can do so, and be held accountable to his flock. He did not think the state should return to the old days of tsarist and Soviet rule. But such a position was hard to maintain, considering the campaigns for one or another candidate being led by other states and by influential members of the Diaspora. In the end, the Armenian state would be held responsible for the consequences of a bad and divisive choice.

Ter-Petrossian was compelled to intervene. He did so by mentioning in an interview his personal preference for the clergyman he considered "the best qualified," Catholicos Karekin II Sarkissian of the House of Cilicia, an erudite, energetic, reformist and charismatic leader. But he was the Catholicos of the See that had been in conflict with the Mother See, a conflict that had internalized and reflected the divisions within the Diaspora along party lines. In addition, technically speaking, Karekin II was not a member of the Etchmiadzin brotherhood. As such, he could not even vote for himself, although the Catholicoses of Cilicia just as the Patriarchs of Constantinople and Jerusalem were always invited to attend the election of the Catholicos of the Mother See. Informal campaigning and probably some arm twisting resolved these problems. In the second round of balloting, Karekin II Sarkissian of Cilicia was elected to the highest post in the Mother See as Karekin I, Catholicos of All Armenians in Etchmiadzin.

But any hopes that the selection of the holder of the rival seat might have encouraged the unification of the Church when the Mother See was no longer controlled by Communists were dashed by the hardening of the position of the Dashnaktsoutiun. The latter argued that the Cilician See and its jurisdictions were necessary for the health of the Diaspora.

The tenure of Karekin I was relatively short, as he succumbed to cancer in 1999. His impact was less remarkable than he and others expected. It required a few years for him to command the environment in which he found himself in Etchmiadzin, one of the leftovers of the Soviet period. It was also not easy for him to generate enthusiasm among Etchmiadzin clergymen, now his subordinates, who had grown up looking at the House of Cilicia in pejorative terms, and who now saw him as the inheritor of usurpers and a stooge of the Dashnaktsoutiun. There were also differences in the administrative systems of the two Sees. The Cilician See was quite centralized and closer to the 1863 Constitution adopted by the Church in the Ottoman Empire. Long decades of Soviet rule and limitations on the actions of the Catholicos of Etchmiadzin had provided more of a leeway for prelates subject to the jurisdiction of Etchmiadzin, giving them more authority and power within governing lay councils than was the case with those subject to Antilias.

The election of the successor to Karekin I was an easier affair. Archbishop Karekin Nersessian, a native of Armenia and closest rival to Karekin I in the previous election, won easily. Karekin I Sarkisian remained aloof of domestic conflicts and in his relations with international entities and leaders, he displayed respect for the state's policies and interests as defined by the government. Karekin II Nersisyan aligned completely with the government in domestic conflicts and behaved as a political leader who favored oligarchs and repression of the opposition, seriously damaging the moral authority of the Church and the position of the Catholicos.

With independence, the significance of relations in Armenia between the Church and the parties are not a matter of controversy. Parties in Armenia have not shown much fervor to interfere in the affairs of the Church, nor to control it. For three reasons, in Armenia, as in Karabakh, it is relations with state authorities, and not political parties, that matter most. First, there are no legal bases for these relations. Secondly, because there is no jurisdictional dispute or rivalry. There are no ecclesiastical disputes between the Sees in Armenia and Karabakh, or any of the other communities within the former Soviet space, which have always been under the jurisdiction of the Etchmiadzin Catholicosate. Finally, the parties function as normal political forces vying for a share of government power, unlike in the Diaspora, where most of the struggle is for control of non-state ethnic institutions. Only in a few countries electioneering takes place for the one or two seats allotted to Armenians in the legislatures of the host countries.

Since independence, most Diasporan institutions have faced the challenge of the emergence of Armenia and Karabakh as vibrant, even if at times faltering realities. For the Church there was no problem of projecting itself as active in Armenia, since the Church was always in Armenia. It was a different story for the political parties, which were at best mere outside observers in the major events that brought independence to the homeland. Members and sympathizers of Diasporans parties, imbued with visions of Armenia and quarreling on its abstracted present and future, could not be indifferent to real events—and real politics—in Armenia.

There were three solutions to the problem faced by the Diasporan parties. First, they might assist the new state by limiting their activities to organizational matters in Diasporan communities, leaving the definition of external and national political goals and diplomacy to the Republic of

Armenia. But they did not follow this path because there would be no justification left for the self-appellation as political parties and every dubious advantage that went with it. In addition, the president and administration of the newly independent state did not claim to be a representative of the whole Armenian nation, just of the people of Armenia. As such, the Movement and the new state had not adopted the cherished external agenda of the Diasporan parties. The parties also argued that they, being products of the free world, still had the mission to teach democracy to the Sovietized citizens of Armenia, and bolster the value of their Diasporan political agenda. And so, they opted for a second course: to establish party branches in Armenia and inject themselves into Armenia's politics.

A third option, to dissolve themselves as superfluous, did not occur to anyone. The parties had considered themselves as the embodiment of the historical wisdom, traditions, and vital interests of the nation for too long to consider such a possibility. Despite the injection of Diasporan funds in self-promotion, membership drives, the establishment of a press, and sponsoring activities, the contribution of the Diasporan parties to the development of Armenia's political institutions has been of dubious value. Their experience in participatory politics on a state level in the Diaspora was limited, and their press in the Diaspora has not emulated the standards, policies and practices common to European and American media.[59]

Nonetheless, the Karabakh Movement, the 1988 earthquake, independence, and the subsequent conflict with Azerbaijan over Karabakh diverted attention from inter-party and Church conflicts. The travails of Armenia and Karabakh are now the focus of the nation.

PRELIMINARY CONCLUSIONS

Armenian political parties arose as the response of a modernizing society to failed reforms in the Ottoman Empire. Revolutionary in their ideology, methods and goals, they were never secure enough to supplant the Church, or religion completely, for any duration of time. Neither ideology nor heroic acts were sufficient to allow them the luxury of dismissing, nor ignoring the Church. They could not control developments affecting the Armenian people in the face of determined Ottoman and Turkish authorities and shifting Great power politics. Events were larger than either the Church or the political parties, or both combined. The Dashnaktsoutiun and

Hnchakian parties were able to consider the idea of separation of state and church only when they felt the nation was safe, which was not that often. The Ramgavars had adopted the Church from the start. It was only the Communists who followed through their program under a Sovietized Armenia, but even they, at the end, relinquished. The Armenian National Movement learned from history: it recognized the Church, but strove to keep it separate from the state.

The history of the relations of the political parties with the Church is, in a sense, the history of Armenians since 1878, alternating between confrontation and cooptation, manipulation and control. The Church, always attuned to shifts within its flock and the outside world, internalized the divisions within both and, in its effort to remain relevant beyond the spiritual sphere, allowed itself to be part of the personal, partisan, political and international conflicts and dilemmas that characterize the tortuous history of the Armenian people. If the Church had become a kind of "homeland" for all Armenians, nationalism and the "survival" of the nation ideology, it had to become a kind of safe haven for the Church. The Church could survive because an Armenian could be an Armenian anywhere as long as there was a Church. The parties might play the same role for Armenians outside Armenia as long they propagated the idea of a homeland to strive for, one that was too historical, too abstract, too idealized, and so great as to never be achieved. In fact, this Armenia had become a spiritual home one could dream about in the distant future. Meanwhile the parties survived by not only co-opting and being co-opted by the Church, but also by imitating it. They would act as temporary caretakers of Armenian souls on this earth through community control. There is little difference in the discourses, or even personalities of the Church and political party elites. More often than not, and with minor adjustments, they are interchangeable in the Diaspora.

The parties survived, then, by not only co-opting the Church, but also by imitating it. At the least, the parties remained part of the Armenian social fabric in the diaspora by relinquishing any claim to being the enlighteners and modernizers. Rather, they preferred to bear the historical burden of expressing grievances from the past, and increasingly abstract demands for the future. Thus, the parties, having lost their initial base and purpose of operations, as well as their fervor to modernize, survived by increasingly adopting the language of the Church and the politics of symbolism. To the extent that the recognition of the Genocide has become the main item of their agenda in the Diaspora, there are hardly any differences in their approaches that might justify them being called political parties. By and large, this goal is universally accepted by Armenians, and a large number of organizations and groups pursue the same agenda effectively without assuming the label and character of political parties.

It is also possible to argue further that the history of the relations between Church and state, and subsequently Church and political parties, is the intersection of two stories. In the first story, foreign powers attempt to use the Church to control Armenians. In the second, Armenian organizations try to control the Church in order to lay claim to sole representation of the Armenian people, corner access to community resources, and garner legitimacy wider than their own following. That intersection is the point at which Armenian parties try to control the Church while both are trying to represent Armenians to the outside world, in contexts defined by the outside world. In their attempt to be relevant to that world, the parties framed their understanding of vital national interest in some universal value, and in circumstantial but "irrefutable" strategies, later easily discarded. By doing so, knowingly or unwittingly, they ended up on occasion serving the interests of foreign rival powers. The Church, always more resilient and in less need to prove itself, became part of this process, even as it claimed to be above it. But as long as "survival" and "preservation of identity" were at stake, it became difficult to clearly differentiate between the two. In survival and identity battles, critical discourse is difficult to maintain against patterns of behavior that seem to be easier to repeat than to question.

Yet if the issue is framed as a contest to represent identity and defend survival, there is no equal for the Church. For the Church, institutional survival has been the most consistent value since Armenia adopted Christianity in the 4th century, and especially so following the demise of Armenian kingdoms in Armenia in the 11th and Cilicia in the 14th centuries. Its legitimacy came from the importance afforded the self-identification of most Armenians, framed in the religious terms imposed by the Muslim states under whose rule they lived for a long period of time. That identity and the role of the Church—imposed by the foreign rulers—were taken for granted. The political parties that challenged the church's rather staid agenda had the onus of proving themselves with every generation, after every momentous event, or with every change of policy—whether evolved internally, or imposed externally. And the revolution they started—the one to change Armenian identity and make it part of modernity—did not have an opportunity to be completed.

In more ways than they might imagine, the Church and the political parties in the modern period have repeated the patterns of behavior characteristic of ancient and medieval Armenian institutions. This point is particularly relevant for the parties, which explicitly claimed to be part of the modern world. The Church need not prove that it is part of the modern world. In fact, its charm is its perceived embodiment of the old, traditional, and abstracted past that fuels Diasporan identity. Rare is the Armenian who understands classical Armenian, but rare is also the one who demands that services in the Apostolic Church be conducted in modern Armenian.[60] For Diasporans in the process of assimilation or integration in host societies, it is important to know that the real thing is being preserved somewhere, and that he or she is part of the effort to preserve it.

Frameworks of "preservation" and "survival" (whether physical or cultural) seem to have transcended reflexive and involved collective behavior, along with their attendant dangers. When acting with a sense of exclusive legitimacy as the guardians of an identity rather than of policies, or when confusing policy with an identity that is presented as non-negotiable, the parties and the Church would rather rule over a segment of the nation, but do so completely rather than have a share of power over the whole. In significant ways, the behavior of the Church and the parties, especially since the Genocide, is no different from that of the Church and feudal lords during the decisive 4th century, and certainly close to how the Bagratuni kingdom and the See of Etchmiadzin were divided up among super-nakharars and Catholicoses. The wresting of control in 1956 of the Catholicosate of Cilicia by the Dashnaktsoutiun, while its opposition controlled or was identified with the Mother See of Etchmiadzin, was merely a repetition of a pattern long engrained in Armenian political culture.

The Genocide has blurred the collective Armenian memory of their inter-institutional relations before World War I, and compelled coexistence, if not cooperation, in its aftermath between the Church and parties for continued mutual legitimation. But the search for legitimacy and control has also moved each to trespass into the domain of the other. For parties representing rival policies and interests, that meant more direct control of the Church, even at the cost of dividing it or keeping it divided. The parties have not only lost their intellectual vigor, but also their different visions of Armenian society. The Armenian Church had long stopped asking fundamental questions on the nature of man, society and God. The parties lost whatever enthusiasm they had for such critical thinking after the Genocide. To ask such questions may encourage others to question values they would like Armenians to take for granted.

The starting point of this project was to identify the differences in two institutions that have been so relevant to Armenian history, the Church and the political parties, and to explore their relations as such. It has been difficult to avoid the conclusion that they in fact represent slightly different articulations of an unfulfilled and damaged national identity, and a stunted effort at modernity. Sometimes they are in competition, often they complement each other, and certainly they are using each other. Clear distinctions and accountability for each are possible only in a sovereign state that is responsible for the welfare and security of the nation. Then the Church can be held accountable for the salvation of souls and the parties for earthly endeavors. But even statehood is not sufficient, since there is a Diaspora beyond its borders.

In fact, the fundamentally different and often opposing realities of the state and the Diaspora are creating more challenges within the parties than between the parties and the Church. One of the consequences of the migration of the three Diasporan parties to Armenia has been the clash of political cultures between Armenia and the Diaspora. In one way or another the three parties faced internal conflict after some years of functioning in both realities. The Hnchakian and Ramgavars underwent open splits and disunity; the Dashnaktsoutiun has faced a number of moments of heightened internal conflicts that resulted in periodic resignations and group expulsions.

In the end, neither Church nor parties have won the battle on how the nation should be defined. Diasporization pushed the parties toward an extra-territorial existence, just as the Church had been, and an almost otherworldly definition of the homeland. It also deepened the national character of the Church, raising its significance as a community institution.

The distinction between the two institutions had been blurred. That was also true of Soviet Armenia, though for different reasons. For the most part, the distinction has been reestablished in independent Armenia. But Diasporan identity and psychology rely too much on the confusion between the two to yet imitate the homeland example.

---

1. By Church, this article refers to the Apostolic Church, the predominant denomination among Armenians. The Armenian Catholic and Protestant denominations have been left out of the discussion because by and large they have not been associated with political parties and the parties have not displayed the need to control them. This article will leave out one of the four centers of the Armenian Church, the Jerusalem Patriarchate, relevant in other ways and beset by its own problems, but largely immune to political party influences because of its autonomous administrative status that gives full control to the ordained members of the St. James Monastery brotherhood.

2. See, for example, Arsen Katter, *Badmoutiun S. D. Hnchakyan gousagtsoutyan, 1887-1962* [History of the Social Democratic Hnchakian Party, 1887-1962], 2 v. Beirut, 1962-1962; Mikayel Varantian, *H. H. Tashnagtsoutyan Batmoutiun*, [History of the Armenian Revolutionary Federation], 2 v. Paris, 1932 and Cairo, 1950; and Sarkis Atamian, *The Armenian Community*, New York, 1955. For a less idealized view of the history and ideology of the revolutionary movement, see Leo, *Tourkahay heghapokhoutyan gaghabarakhosoutyounu* [The Ideology of the Turkish-Armenian Revolution], 2 v., Yerevan, 1934; Anaide Ter Minassian, *Nationalism and Socialism in the Armenian Revolutionary Movement, 1887-1912*, Cambridge, Zoryan Institute, 1984, and Gerard J. Libaridian, *Modern Armenia: People, Nation, State*, Transaction Books, Rutgers/ New Jersey, 2004, esp. chapters 4-6. Levon Chormissian's *Gousagtsoutiunneru* [The Political Parties], published in Beirut in 1965 is a little-known volume whose lack of sources do not diminish its value as one of the most insightful works on the subject.

3. Maghakia Ormanian's *Azkabadoum*, a history of the Armenian Church from its origins to the early 20th century is a monumental work of three volumes published in Constantinople, 1912-1927. The work was continued by Fr. Zaven Arzoumanian in the same style, structure and format bringing the story to more recent times (New York, 1995-2003), so far in another three volumes. Here too, Levon Chormissian's

Hayastanyayts Yegeghetsin, [The Armenian Church], published in Beirut, 1966, presents itself as a rare example of critical analysis.

4. The 1863 Constitution of the Armenian millet democratized, to some extent, the functioning of the Patriarchate. See Vartan Artinian, *The Armenian Constitutional System in the Ottoman Empire, 1839-1863.* Istanbul, [1988].

5. For a sympathetic history of the Ramgavar Party, see Vache Ghazarian, *Hamarod Badmoutiun RAGi*, [Brief History of the ADL], Beirut. 1978, and Karlen Dallakian, *Ramgavar Azatakan Kousaktsoutyan patmoutyoun*, [History of the ADL], vol. 1, National Academy of Sciences, Republic of Armenia, Institute of History. Yerevan, 1999. The Ramgavars trace their ideological and organizational origins to the Armenakan Party established in Van in 1885 and thus claim to be the first party in Armenian history but also the only one established on Armenian soil. They thus argue that their ideology was closer to the needs of Armenians as opposed to the revolutionary and adventurous character of the Dashnaktsoutiun and Hnchakian parties. See, for example, Ghazarian, pp. 7-13.

6. For practical purposes, this article will not deal with one important dimension in Armenian history. Part of many conflicts and antagonisms has been the mutual dislike and mistrust between Ottoman or Western Armenians and Russian or Eastern Armenians, antagonisms that often surfaced and to some extent can still be seen today between Diasporans and Armenians in Armenia, Karabakh and the former Soviet space.

7. Kitur, v. I, p. 44-45.

8. See Libaridian, Modern Armenia, esp. chapters 2 and 3.

9. Ormanian, v. III, Part 3, p. 5061.

10. Ibid., p. 5082.

11. Ibid., p. 5083.

12. Ibid, pp. 5152-5156. Ormanian considered Ashekian too compliant and Izmirlian too defiant. He considered his course the middle road and the wise one with regard to relations with the Sultan and his Government.

13. Ormanian, v. III, Part 3, pp. 5321-5326.

14. Dallakian, p. 53.

15. Patriarch Zaven Der Yeghiayan, *My Patriarchal Memoirs*, Mayreni Publishing, 2002, pp. 29-30. The original Armenian of the Patriarch's memoirs were published in 1947 in Cairo.

16, Atamian, p. 164 and passim. While such an analysis has relevance for the pre-Genocide and to a lesser extent a decade or two after, it has lost all significance since World War II.

17. Arzumanian, *Azkabadoum*, v. IV, Part 1, pp. 95-97.

18. Ibid., pp. 101-102, 114-115.

19. Der Yeghiayan, p. 33.

20. The Free Church had supporters in the Diaspora. According to one source, they included at some point Archbishop Ghevond Tourian, then prelate of the Armenian Church in Manchester (Armen Partizian, *Hay yekeghetsvo taknabu yev anor badaskhanadouneru* [The Crisis of the Armenian Church and Those Responsible for It], Boston, 1936, p. 9).

21. Al. Martouni (Alexander Myasnikyan), *Kousaktsoutiunneru gaghoutahayoutyan mech*, [The political parties in the Diaspora], Soviet Socialist Republic of Armenia, (Berlin, 1925), p. 55.

22. Ibid, pp. 84-95 and, generally throughout the work.

23. For the shifting attitudes toward nationalism and national institutions in the Soviet Union, see Ronald, G. Suny, *The Revenge of the Past*, Stanford, Stanford University Press, 1993.

24. Hovannes Kachaznouni, *Dashnaktsoutiunu anelik chouni aylevs*, [The Dashnaktsoutiun has nothing left to do], Vienna, 1923.

25. See, for example, A. Barseghian, *Tseghagron Sharzhoumu*, [The Tzeghakron Movement], Boston, 1935.

26. In essence Armenian Diaspora Communists.

27. Hrach Yervant, *Ramgavar Azadagan gousagtsoutiunu. Ir aysoru yev vaghu* [Democratic Liberal Party. Its Today and Tomorrow], Boston, 1927, p. 27.

28. Armen Partizian, p. 143.

29. It is important to note that the number of members of political parties were a relatively small percentage of the total Armenian population, counting in the thousands at best. The influence of the parties was disproportionate to their numbers since a) the parties were centrally organized, usually with members with a strong sense of loyalty to their parties and discipline; and, b) parties had created, gained the support of, or controlled various cultural, social, and athletic community organizations and the press.

30. Each side found procedural faults in the behavior of the other. While with more detailed research it may be possible to ascertain which assembly had legitimacy—without leaving out the possibility that both may have been in contravention of one or more assembly rules—it is clear that the overwhelming issue was the political one, in which case who was right or wrong from a technical point of view would not have mattered.

31. The aim of this article is not to make a final determination as to whether the assassins, members of the Dashnaktsoutiun, acted on orders from the party, although there is circumstantial evidence that they may have been. Rather, it is to indicate the state of mind of a whole community. The

vehemence and violence can be explained to some extent by the use of these conflicts to consolidate and extend control over the loyalties and resources of a community that has yet to overcome the damage caused by the Genocide. But this may not be a wholly adequate or sufficient explanation.

32. Yervant, pp. 3-4. Discussing the role of faith in the context of his discussion of the Armenian Church, Chormissian argues: "[Having faith] is to harbor a deep consciousness of the inadequacy of human power and the conviction of the existence of a supreme creator of all phenomena in nature that are inexplicable and un-understandable... Thus, it is useless and senseless to exert any mental effort to find real and palpable causes for these phenomena. All is explained by divine creation... All was created by God and is done by Him... There is not even the need to find why and how God had done and does all of that. He defies examination and understanding and man [it added] does not have the power and the right to understand and judge Him." (*Hayasdanyayts Yegeghetsin*, p. 93.)

33. Literal translation of the Armenian equivalent of "This is my body, which is for you; do this in remembrance of me." In Chormissian, *Gousagtsoutiounneru...*, p. 164.

34. Atamian, p. 338.

35. Tourian Committee Series, No. 4, *Gazmagerbyal ahapegchoutiunu*, [The organized terrorism], New York, 1934, p. 7.

36. Tourian Committee Series, No. 3, *Tourian Srpazan anmegh zohu yerakouyn troshin*, [Archbishop Tourian, the Innocent Victim of the Tricolor Flag], New York, 1934. "Kars" refers to the Treaty of Kars signed in 1921 between five states, including Armenia and Turkey, just as power in Yerevan was being transferred from the Dashnaktsoutiun to the Soviets.

37. Ibid, p. 5. "February Revolution" refers to an uprising in 1921 led by the Dashnaktsoutiun against the newly established Soviet Armenian authorities that was followed by a short-lived return to power of the Dashnaktsoutiun.

38. The response to this charge is best summarized by Atamian, who argued that the party had made sufficient sacrifices and was strong enough to be able to deal and negotiate with Turks (p. 266).

39. New York, 1935.

40. Partizian, pp. 8-11. See also Atamian, pp. 430-440.

41. The Dashnaktsoutiun later considered this incident as another ploy by the Soviets to endear the Soviet Union to the Armenian Diaspora and diminish opposition toward it. See, for example, *Crisis in the Armenian*

Church. A Memorandum to the National Council of Churches, Armenian Prelacy, Boston, 1958, pp. 67-73.

42. For an overview of the history of the Catholicosate of Cilicia, see Papgen Catholicos Gulesserian, *Badmoutiun gatoghigosats Giligio* [History of the Catholicosal of Cilicia]; the 20th century history of the See is the subject of Piuzant Yeghiayan's, *Zhamanagagits badmoutiun gatoghigosoutyan hayots Giligio, 1914-1972,* [Contemporary History of the Catholicosate of Armenians of Cilicia, 1914-1972], which covers also the critical years discussed below.

43. Chormissian, *Hayasdanyayts Yegeghetsin*, pp. 179-180.

44. *Crisis in the Armenian Church*, pp. 165-166.

45. In addition to some partisan works published on this subject already mentioned, see *Documents on the Schism in the Armenian Church of America*, Diocese of the Armenian Church of America, New York, 1993.

46. Lendrush Khurshutyan, *Spourkahay kousaktsoutiounneru zhamanakakits edapoum,* [Diasporan political parties in their present phase], Yerevan, 1964.

47. Ibid, p. 186.

48. Ibid, pp. 185-186. Khurshutyan would later join the Dashnaktsoutiun and not the Ramgavars when that party, along with the others in the Diaspora, were allowed to function in Armenia following the establishment of the multi-party system in 1990.

49. The change in the external agenda of the Dashnaktsoutiun coincided with the election to the head of the Party of Mr. Hrayr Maroukhian, who remained in control of the party through the 1990s. No serious study or accounting has been undertaken for the reason(s) of this most important transformation.

50. The impact of others, such as the "Mardgotsagan" organization or movement that originated in Paris in the 1930s, was of shorter duration and limited largely to intellectual circles.

51. Archbishop Mesrop Ashjian, *The Armenian Church in America*, NY Prelacy, 1995, p. 52. The prelacy seems to have conceded on the unification but changed its mind after Armenia's independence, given the opposition of the Dashnaktsoutiun to independence and the first administration under President Levon Ter-Petrossian.

52. These negotiations, between the Diocese and the Prelacy, as the two churches are known, remind one of the "harmony" negotiations with the participation of representatives of the parties and the Church that began in 1914 in Boston, all concerned with expected cataclysmic events in the homeland. Despite their concerns for the need to be prepared through joint action and fundraising, the negotiations were still continuing when

the Genocide was already in full progress in 1916. They were never concluded. See *Hamerashkhagan panagtsoutiunner* [harmony negotiations], Boston, 1916.

53. Ashjian, p. 86. The author makes no mention of political parties in his book and rarely mentions the causes for the division in the Church or antagonisms underlying it in this or other publications.

54. Sermons and statements by Armenian clergymen will refer to the Armenian identity dimension more often than the spiritual one. See also Hrayr Maroukhian, "Dream of Independence," *Droshak*, June 1988, where he argues that independence is a nice dream that is useful for the purpose of inspiring the young to be attached to the community and the party, but is neither a practical nor even a desirable goal at this time. His view was imposed on the party when the Dashnaktsoutiun opposed Armenia's drive for independence in 1990 and supported the candidacy of the Armenian Communist Party Secretary against that of the Armenian National Movement for the Presidency of the Presidium of Soviet Armenia in the summer of 1990.

55. For a detailed look at Diaspora-Armenia relations, see Gerard J. Libaridian, *The Challenge of Statehood* (Blue Crane Books, Watertown, Mass., 1999), esp. ch. 5.

56. Vazgen I fired the scholar Levon Ter-Petrossian, one of the emerging leaders of the Movement, from his teaching position at the Etchmiadzin Gevorgian Seminary. Three years later, he was to give Ter-Petrossian the oath of office as the first president of independent Armenia.

57. The three parties and other groups had much difficulty getting stories on the Genocide in international media. The Movement's actions were often front page or main story in press, radio and television beginning in 1988.

58. Gerard J. Libaridian, *Armenia at the Crossroads* (Crane Books, Watertown, 1991), p. 109.

59. The experience of these parties on a state has been mostly in Lebanon, Syria, and Iran where "managed" sectarian politics dominate. Parties involved in the politics of these countries and legislators elected to seats assigned to Armenians have never felt responsibility for the basic policies of their countries, being always viewed as tolerated religious communities and rarely seeing themselves as full fledged partners in policy making. The stronger of the parties, the Dashnaktsoutiun, has not been able to receive more than 10% of popular votes in any election in Armenia, despite the huge financial and human resources it has poured in and despite the aura it had for large segments during the Soviet period for its heroic past and the campaign which the Communist Party carried against it for decades. The party media in the Diaspora are not known for separating fact from

opinion or for publishing articles that might be critical of the positions and policies of the given party.

60. The Armenian Catholic Church, following the rest of the Catholic world, has changed the language of its Mass. Protestant Armenian Churches have always used Modern Armenian in their proceedings.

8

THE PAST AS A PRISON, THE PAST AS A DIFFERENT FUTURE

2005

This essay explores some of the socio-political realities underlying one of the most difficult historiographical problems of the twentieth century, the opposing views on the treatment of Armenians by the Ittihad ve Terakkı government in the waning years of the Ottoman Empire. The essay considers the politics of Genocide recognition and denial in relation to entrenched social and political structures, tracing it to a battle of identities. The essay argues that identities are dynamic phenomena; changes in circumstances may also change the dynamics of the relations between Armenia and Turkey, and Armenians and Turks.

The essay was first published in the Winter 2005 issue of Turkish Policy Quarterly.

The past dominates the general perception of Turkish-Armenian relations. Or at least it appears so. The past dominates that perception because these relations ended tragically in the Ottoman Empire and because each side has so much invested in its own perception of that past. Some questions suggest themselves: Can we take responsibility for how we have recreated that past, just as it has created us? What have the two sides invested in the battle for the recognition of their version of the past? And what is to be done with these two different, disparate, and (more often than not) conflicting perceptions of the past, if and when there is a willingness to transcend it?

By and large, for the Armenian side, differences can be resolved if and when the Turkish side acknowledges the Genocide perpetrated by the Young Turk government during World War I. This expectation of the victim has been countered by the official Turkish view, which places its own victimization by the Great Powers at the center of its own perception of history, a perception that makes what happened to Armenians an almost irrelevant detail, a nuisance at best, a past that should be denied, trivialized, or explained away. For decades, the official Turkish position has been to assume all of this at the same time.

Clearly, we are not dealing with a mere academic disagreement between scholars of different persuasions or schools. The entrenched position of each side is now part of their respective identities, identities which not only define the boundaries of ethno-cultural self-definitions, but also the socio-political context through which they see their present and project the future. We have learned that conflicts that deeply engage identities often produce the bloodiest wars and are the most difficult to resolve, especially when the parties to the conflict seek the affirmation of their identities by the rest of the world as an integral component of their strategy.

To understand what has been a stalemate for some time, to change gears, so to speak, and in fact to make the best use of history, each side must understand some basic realities about the other.

The Turkish side, and especially officials and policy makers, must realize that no matter how the events of 1915-1917 are characterized, there is no doubt that they brought the collective existence of the Armenian people on their ancestral homeland to an end. The violent, abrupt, and permanent break in the long history of a nation, the sheer finality of it, was enough to make survivors feel death for generations. The passage of time has only deepened the sense of collective death, even if the survivors themselves were paralyzed by the personal tragedies they endured, and were unable to sense and articulate adequately the full extent of the tragedy. For less-traumatized descendants of the survivors in lands near and far, the past is the present. Denial of the genocide is a denial of not only their past, but also their present.

Furthermore, the sustained policy of denial of that past by successive Turkish governments only infuriates new generations of Armenians. It makes it more difficult for them to focus on the historical context in which these events took place, or to generate a desire to understand the position within which Turkish society finds itself. This is true even for those Armenians who would like to transcend the limitations imposed by self-defining as a victim nation. Attempts by Turkish officials and official historians to equate Armenian actions against the Ottoman regime before the war, or the Turkish state since the policies of the *İttihad ve Terakkı* during the war, only leads new generations to think of the Turkish state as an unreformed and hopeless entity. The more the Turkish state denies the past, the more adamant new generations are in asserting it. That part of the collective memory tends to take over as the determinant of their identity, more difficult to transcend, more important to have others recognize it. There are good reasons why the use of the term "genocide" has become so important for the Armenian side.

Those are some of the immovable realities worth a moment of reflection on the Turkish side, setting aside the defensive wall that is best characterized as a fear of knowledge. Almost twenty years ago, a promising young scholar– now a well-known and respected historian in Turkey–related to me a story about his dying father, who asked him not to become a historian. When he realized his son was set on his course and did not wish to become a doctor or an engineer, the father begged him at least to not engage himself in the "Armenian issue."

There are many ways to deal with conflicting perceptions of history. Ignoring history is not one of them. Not in a healthy society.

What the Armenian side must realize is that, first, the Turkish position is based on willful ignorance, one that is promoted by the state for reasons that must also be understood. There is an ideology of statehood and nationhood that is at the foundation of the central value of the Turkish War of Independence to Turkish collective memory. That ideology relies on a well-known theological model: No sins were committed during the process, and the purpose of the newborn was to save the world, in this case the world of Turks. This is a most comfortable past, a most blissful birth.

Ideologies have a coherence, and are therefore fragile. Removing one stone in that foundation threatens the collapse of the whole system. Under the circumstances, to integrate a sin as serious as genocide in that theology is asking too much from a state, as well as from a people.

Second, the Armenian side must recognize that the Great Powers did in fact prey upon the Ottoman Empire. Until the rise of the Kemalist Movement, the rivalry between Great Britain and Russia was probably the main reason why Anatolia did not suffer the same fate as Africa in their hands. The importance of the centrality of Great Power threat to the Ottoman state cannot be underestimated. Nor can one underestimate the role of that threat in the rise of the modern Turkish state and in Turkish perceptions of the past.

That such historical facts are also used to justify a security-oriented state, the role of the military in Turkish politics, and the use of force to settle political conflicts are very much part of the ideology, just as for some Armenian political parties the Genocide is at the basis of territorial demands from Turkey. Such territorial demands feed into the logic of denial. Turkish officials argue that recognition of the Genocide will result in demands for reparations, including territorial claims. Whether Turkey will face a real threat in this area is immaterial. What matters are that such fears find a receptive audience, are embedded in the political psyche, and are easily manipulated in a society educated in the historical threat of dismemberment.

When taking a longer view of what Turks and most of the world takes for granted today and considering Turkish statecraft within its present borders, and given that generations of Turks have been taught to accept the primacy of the state over society as the foundation of that statehood, one should not be surprised at the resistance to injecting a series of horrors into one's pristine history.

The Armenian side should take a moment and look at these realities. There are many ways to deal with conflicting perceptions of history. Force feeding is not one of them, not if there is to be genuine recognition and reconciliation, especially now when Armenia, a neighbor of Turkey, is a sovereign state.

This long running conflict has its own history, politics, and sociology. Until the rebirth of independent Armenia in 1991, the battle was between Turkey on the one hand, a well-defined nation-state with boundaries and policy-making institutions, and an Armenian Diaspora outside Turkey on the other, a transnational entity made up of communities defined extra-territorially and endowed with many structures, but none that could speak and act on its behalf with a singular voice. The battle was asymmetric; it allowed for little direct interaction. Not only were the Turkish state and Armenian Diaspora totally alienated from one another, but the logic of their respective positions evolved almost independently from the other, neither having to account for the failures or successes of their policies against the other's means and resources. After all, beyond the stated goals of compelling or rejecting recognition, the battles were their own justification, since they served to affirm the battlers' identities.

The arena for the battle was the international community to which each addressed itself. Rare encounters between Turkish and Armenian scholars were not meant to promote understanding of each other's position, but to state positions and satisfy their own audiences. The one known meeting between Turkish Foreign Ministry officials and representatives of the *Dashnaktsoutiun* (Armenian Revolutionary Federation), occurring in the late 1970s and still shrouded in mystery, does not seem to have served any other purpose. And the series of terrorist acts by secret Armenian groups against Turkish diplomats and institutions could hardly have been construed as encounters of mutual understanding.

Most Armenians in the Diaspora had never met a Turk. The "Turk" had instead become an abstraction in the Armenian mind, easier to hate than to know. Any and each Turk in this context represented all at once the invader of a thousand years ago, the killer of a hundred years ago and the denier of today. Turks had no other characteristics. For Turks, the "Armenian" was the friendly and harmless baker in the neighborhood at best, a discomfiting thought from the past pushed to the recesses of the mind, a troublemaker, slanderer, and terrorist at worst. For each, the other was "the other."

This skewed process had serious consequences for both.

Part of the legitimacies of historical Armenian institutions in the Diaspora, such as the church and political parties, are based in their pre-genocide existences. They are part of the patrimony that has survived, and must be kept alive. This is a powerful argument in the Diaspora, where the fear of assimilation pushed Diasporans to find anchors that reconfirm their identity. Thus, the battle for genocide recognition has become an organizing concern and unifying principle. It connects the past and the future. The future consists of the recognition of the past. The present is just the moment where the struggle occurs.

Yet identities are not frozen. They evolve and adapt as a result of internal dynamics and external stimuli. They also change as a result of conscious choices, whether cultural or political. While the name of the ethnos remains the same, history shows that in fact some attributes of ethnicity become less important, while others grow more poignant over time. Even collective memory undergoes mutations to project new sensibilities. Contemporary needs seek different dimensions of the past. New research and more critical history seep into the domain of the general public. Sensibilities change with regard to perceptions of the past and of the future. In an anecdote ascribed to the ubiquitous Radio Yerevan, a listener asks the radio commentator if he knows what the future will look like. The commentator's answer is telling indeed: "The future is not a problem; we know what it will look like. Our problem is with the past. They keep changing it."

The advent of Armenia's independence created another level of interaction in Turkish-Armenian relations: state-to-state. Neither the Ter-Petrossian nor Kocharyan administrations in Armenia made recognition of the Genocide by Turkey a precondition for the establishment of diplomatic relations with its neighbor, although the latter administration did raise the issue. Soviet Armenians knew their history as well, many of them progenies of Genocide survivors. This included a number of the founders of the Republic who in the 1960s had organized street demonstrations in Yerevan against Turkey. The difference is that state-to-state relations require a different logic, particularly with neighbors, since leaders of states, especially those just born, must take into consideration a host of overwhelming issues. The Armenian National Movement, which led the country to independence, also considered the genocide-led national agenda and the psychology behind it as factors that had justified Armenia's subservience to the Soviet Union and oppressive Communist rule. Now citizens of a sovereign republic, Armenians in Armenia did not resist this change away from the primacy of the genocide issue, a change in strategic thinking which was nothing less revolutionary in Armenian political thought. Besides, as citizens of a state, they did not need an organizing principle. The state is that principle. The present forces its own agenda and priorities. The future must resolve other problems for the citizens of Armenia, who nonetheless are keenly interested in the recognition issue.

The normalcy, if not normalization, of relations between Turkey and Armenia lifted the taboo in the Diaspora as well. For Diasporans, sovereign Armenia without barriers represents a new reference of identity, one able to absorb as much energy from the Diaspora as it can emit.

For the Turkish governing elite, control of the past is a justification for the present form of government and an insurance policy for its perpetuation. The future, indeed, would look different if the past was tampered with. If the Soviet Union changed the past to justify shifts in policy, the Turkish state held a firm grip on it to guarantee that the future does not change. Here the denial of parts of history is the affirmation of that future. A Turkey that has matured enough to recognize that history would have to be a very different Turkey than the one they know and cherish, the one they present as the indispensable form without which Turkish identity would be denied and Turkish security threatened.

But here too there have been changes. An expanding civil society and a more inquisitive and critical intellectual class feel secure enough in their identities to question the hegemonic ideology of the state and its hold on history. They can imagine a different, and better future for Turkey. Therefore, they can also imagine a different past. This development constitutes a tribute to Turkish society.

The coming to power of an AK Party not so much beholden in its ideology and legitimacy to the nationalist past has also offered new responsibilities. Prime Minister Erdoğan's offer to leave history to historians is a valiant recognition of the possibility of a history differently conceived, to say the least, as he too imagines a Turkey differently construed.

The dynamics of confrontation have changed as a result. Turkish and Armenian societies have now come to interact in more ways than one. More Armenians now travel to Turkey and visit their ancestral towns and villages. While not influential enough, the Turkish Armenian Business Council is a reflection of newly-emerging interests. Turkish journalists have visited Armenia and developed contacts in the Diaspora. Armenian journalists from Armenia and the Diaspora have visited Turkey and established contacts there.

But two undertakings deserve special attention. The well intentioned, but badly conceived Turkish Armenian Reconciliation Commission (TARC) provided a forum to discuss the issue of whether the past would determine the future. Even in its failure, that forum contributed to the acceptance of dialogue.

The more successful enterprise has been the less ambitious, let more fruitful Workshop for Armenian and Turkish Scholarship (WATS), initiated in 2000 by a small group of scholars of Armenian and Turkish origin at the University of Michigan, Ann Arbor. WATS aims at developing the historical context within which Turkish-Armenian relations evolved. The scholars involved did not feel the need to start with terminology and focused on the necessity to understand the context, offering perspectives on events, processes, policies, and causation. The four sessions of WATS have involved over a hundred scholars from various disciplines and countries. The Workshop is based on the principle of respect for the intellectual integrity of its participants, whose scholarship is recognized by universal standards. WATS has already had a major impact on both the quantity of scholarship produced and the quality of the dialogue. A larger picture of the period in question is emerging, a picture that recognizes the calamities that the *İttihad ve Terakkı* policies produced, the ideologies and mechanisms involved, the engagement of Armenian political parties and the church as actors in Ottoman politics, and the role of the Great Powers. The number of conferences and colloquia addressing the issue have multiplied, the prominent being the Istanbul conference in September 2005, organized by, and with the exclusive participation of Turkish scholars, despite vehement opposition from some quarters in Turkey.

Genuine scholarship freed from the burdens of legitimation of power, political leadership freed from the need to preserve the status quo, and a re-humanization effort of the "other" all are making it possible to redefine identities and challenge identity politics as we know it. Turkish-Armenian relations may yet have a future.

9

HISTORICAL AGENCY AND ETERNAL VICTIMHOOD: DO ARMENIA AND ARMENIANS MATTER IN HISTORY?

2015

Armenian historiography and, more generally Armenian political culture, display certain patterns that are at times dominant. One such pattern is the articulation of Armenians' role in history as victims rather than as agents who participated in the making of their history. The theme of eternal victimhood is both a cause of paralyzed political thinking and a necessity ingredient for that paralysis. Eternal victimhood also offers a model within which the victims, being only victims, bear no responsibility for their past and present words and actions.

This is the full text of a paper presented at the April 2015 conference held at the University of California, Los Angeles, on the occasion of the 100th anniversary of the Armenian Genocide.

The perpetrator/victim paradigm dominates at least the memory, and often the discourse on Turkish/Armenian relations, just as it has dominated Armenian political thinking for some time. This paradigm is generally disturbed only by the occasional rise of an Armenian hero.

The Genocide that began in 1915 has almost obviated the need to look at these relations critically—whether as policy options or as possible frameworks for the interpretation of past policies.

This paradigm, based on essentialist understandings of Turks and Armenians, challenges what we understand history to consist of. Here we have a problem of historical agency that is implied directly from that paradigm. If Armenians' relationship with Turks is one of victimhood, or Armenia's relationship with Turkey is one of victimhood, past and future, we can be assured that we do not have a history to write. What we have is a series of stories on martyrdom. At best, a hagiography.

The question is do Armenians have agency in their history, especially in their relations with Turks? Has it mattered at all what Armenians have said or done, what they have said and done that they should not have said or done? Has it mattered that there may be things that they have not said and things that have not done that they could or should have said or done? These questions become critical in the case of relations between Armenia and Turkey, two internationally recognized states. I will leave aside, for the purposes of this presentation, a discussion of the relevance of these questions to the pre-World War I history of relations between the Ottoman state and the Ottoman Armenian leadership.

The experience of the Third Republic of Armenia is as close as we can come to an experiment on alternative perceptions and approaches to Turkey.

One simple way to begin the discussion is to ask two seemingly unrelated questions: What role was the Genocide assigned in independent Armenia's conception of its security and foreign policy in general, and specifically as referring to relations with the Republic of Turkey, one of Armenia's four immediate neighbors? And can Armenia be an independent state?

Just to help to set the stage, let's remember that the recognition of the Genocide emerged as the dominant item on the agenda of Diaspora communities beginning in the 1960s, and only then. And it has remained so since then. In the Diaspora, the Genocide has become an essential marker of ethnic identity, a principle of community organization, and a source of power legitimation within the community. By the 1980s, leaving behind the big battles between pro- and anti-Soviet forces, Armenian institutional and political forces had discovered in the Genocide recognition campaigns a basis for a *modus vivendi*: Whether for ideological or pragmatic reasons, all forces had now reached agreement (a) that Soviet Armenia was a good thing to have and to keep, (b) that good relations with the Soviet Union were essential, and (c) that recognition of the Genocide and demands from Turkey, however formulated, should constitute the substance of Diasporan Armenian concerns, beyond the building of community institutions and the preservation of culture.

The problem with this quasi-idyllic, if not unprecedented harmony was that it gave little consideration to what the Armenian people in Soviet Armenia and immediately around it—Nagorno Karabakh, Javakhk— thought about their state of affairs. And it so happened that the Karabakh issue erupted in February 1988. The movement was powerful and supported by the people in NK as well as in Armenia; it also spawned a new leadership and very quickly evolved into a national movement of renaissance and independence.

The question was, could Armenia become independent? That issue was one of the most thoroughly and universally debated in Armenian history. It was carried from 1989 through 1991 in public, in the press, and eventually in the Supreme Soviet of Armenia, which drafted the "Declaration on Independence" in the summer of 1990, nearly a year before the Declaration of Independence. There were two approaches.

1. Those who endorsed the first approach argued that Armenia could not become independent because it had no way to resist the inevitable assault from Turkey. And Turkey would necessarily attack and destroy Armenians in Armenia because it was (a) the inheritor of the Ottoman empire, responsible for the Genocide, (b) Turks by nature are violent and genocidal, (c) Turkey had not recognized the Genocide of 1915, and (d) the only reason why it had not done so was because Armenia was part of the Soviet Union; should Armenia leave the USSR, Turkey was certain to attack and exterminate its population in order to complete the task begun in 1915. This position was maintained by the Communist Party and the ARF, and to some extent by other Armenian political parties in the Diaspora. Anyone

who thinks differently, argued this side, was either naïve, ignorant of the lessons of history, or treasonous, or all of the above.

2. For those who had offered the second and novel approach, the Genocide of 1915 was a historically defined catastrophe. Armenia can and should be independent, argued the leaders of what is known as the Karabakh Movement. The conventional view had been promoted in order to legitimize Russian/Soviet domination of Armenia, and in general, reliance on a third force, thus making independence undesirable and, they argued, seemingly impossible. Armenians can manage their affairs as an independent state, insisted this side, if they can develop the appropriate policies, and when they get rid of the various complexes that have made it difficult for Armenians to think independently and without ideologically imposed mental constraints. An independent Armenia would be possible when Armenia can create normal relations with all its neighbors. Normal relations with all neighbors would constitute an essential dimension of Armenia's security.

Admittedly, such a position ran counter to (a) the consensus that had been achieved in the Diaspora, and (b) the ideology that had been forged around the role of Russia/the Soviet Union in Armenian history, built especially on the centrality of Armenian victimhood. That ideology had been sustained by Soviet Armenian historiography, as well as by the political discourse that had evolved in the Diaspora since the 1970s. In this new approach, we were dealing with the reversal of accepted wisdom. In other words, the second position constituted a revolution in Armenian political thought.

Armenia did become independent, and it did so with overwhelming support for the second position, at least in Armenia.

During the initial contacts between Armenia and Turkey, even before Armenia's formal independence, Turkey expressed the wish to normalize relations with Armenia, and expected that in return Yerevan would make sure the Diaspora would end its campaign for the recognition of the Genocide. Armenia rejected such a scenario, clearly and unequivocally.

The first administration of the independent Republic, from 1990 to 1998, under Levon Ter-Petrossian, developed a foreign policy that pursued the normalization of relations with all four neighbors, while developing a defense relationship with Russia, at least until such time as relations were normalized with Turkey. The Karabakh war, imposed by Azerbaijan, became a serious obstacle to the realization of the goal of normalization of relations with all neighbors, a necessary component of Armenia's security. The first administration sought normalization of relations with Turkey without preconditions. That was nearly achieved by early 1993, except for the widening Armenian-Azerbaijani war. Because of that war, Turkey balked at the conclusion of negotiations on the protocol for the normalization of bilateral relations. The Genocide did not play a role in those negotiations, neither in their progress, nor their failure. Turkey simply wanted to use its negotiations with Armenia to secure an advantage to its cousin, Azerbaijan, in the Karabakh negotiations.

In other words, the first administration (a) refused to make the Genocide the cornerstone of its relations with Turkey, and (b) was very aware of the dangers of making the Genocide a subject of bilateral or international negotiations.

Throughout these first years, the debate on the role of the Genocide in Armenia's foreign and security policies continued unabated. Critics maintained that the government was committing a grave error with its policies regarding Turkey, that the recognition of the Genocide and demands based on such a recognition should be a precondition for any relations with Turkey. That the absence of such recognition constituted a grave national security threat to the new Republic. That the Genocide was not merely a historical event, but a harbinger for things to come. The critics looked for any sign to prove their predictions right and could not find much. They exaggerated the significance of a statement made by President Turgut Özal of Turkey in 1993 following the Armenian occupation of Kelbajar.

The war in and around Karabakh continued until May 1994. During the winter of 1992-1993, the worst of these years, Turkey—the country that was ostensibly waiting for an opportunity to wipe out the Armenians of Armenia—opened its rail lines and border to move donated wheat from Europe to the Republic. The Abkhaz war had closed the rail line that came from Russia to Armenia through Georgia, and Armenia had no realistic alternative to receive that wheat. Thus, Turkey saved that same population from likely starvation.

Also, in 1992, Turkey became a member of the CSCE/OSCE Minsk Group, which was assigned the task of internationally mediating the Karabakh conflict. But as this went into planning in 1993, Armenia vetoed Turkey assuming a major role on the logistics and deployment of peacekeeping forces in the conflict zone.

The war ended successfully for the Armenian side—at least that particular phase of the war—in the summer of 1994, to the great dissatisfaction of not only Azerbaijan, but also of Turkey.

In 1995 Armenia commemorated the eightieth anniversary of the Genocide with a number major activities, including the founding and opening of the Genocide Museum and Institute.

Bilateral relations were not established, although informal and formal contacts continued. These resulted in the start of charter flights between Yerevan and Istanbul, which continue until the present. Turkey is accommodating a large number of citizens of Armenia who have found work in Turkey, and conducting trade between the two countries through Georgia. Even under the most adverse circumstances, Turkey did not attack Armenia.

This first phase of Armenia's independence closed with two significant events: (1) The Russo-Armenian Treaty of Friendship and Cooperation. And (2) the forced resignation of President Levon Ter-Petrossian over the issue of peace with Azerbaijan, which would have certainly unlocked the process of normalization of relations with Turkey.

Armenia's second administration, under Robert Kocharyan, formally reiterated the position of the first and stated that it was ready for the normalization of relations with Turkey without preconditions on either side. At some point, President Kocharyan, who had engineered Ter-Petrossian's removal, went as far as to state that the Republic of Armenia had no legal standing to demand territories from Turkey. Nonetheless, to the delight of critics of the first administration, he gave the Genocide issue such prominence that it was difficult to believe that he was continuing the policies of his predecessor. This apparent paradox is explained by the fact that for the second president, the Genocide issue was a bargaining chip against Turkey. Kocharyan believed that since Turkey is linking bilateral relations to the Karabakh issue, Armenia can use the Genocide issue as a weapon against Turkey, not because it was essential that Turkey recognize the Genocide, but expecting that Turkey would be intimidated by Armenia's taking the lead in the recognition campaign, that it would be scared, and would drop its precondition for the normalization of relations with Armenia, i.e., that it would remove the linkage of bilateral relations with the Karabakh issue.

During his ten years, Kocharian made some half-hearted attempts at the resolution of the Nagorno-Karabakh conflict, yet that too was not high on his agenda. Nonetheless, the debate on policy subsided once Genocide recognition was made part of the foreign policy discourse. Nonetheless, that discourse failed to persuade Turkey to untether the Karabakh issue from that of bilateral relations.

Independent Armenia's third administration, under Serzh Sargsyan, was widely expected to be a boring continuation of the second. However, we have witnessed two major surprises since 2008.

In 2009, Armenia and Turkey signed two protocols aiming at the establishment of diplomatic relations and normalization of relations, including the opening of the border between the two countries. Armenia signed the two protocols even though, at the insistence of Turkey, the second contained a clause that established a historical truth sub-commission, which was generally interpreted as questioning the Genocide. Since Armenia had brought the Genocide to the forefront of its foreign policy, Ankara insisted that the issue be dealt with in the protocols. In these protocols, Turkey seemed to be glossing over the issue of Karabakh, when in fact it had embedded that question, without naming it, into the preamble of the First Protocol.

Hardly signed, Turkey declared that the protocols could not go into effect until such time as Armenia had made serious progress in the resolution of the Nagorno-Karabakh conflict. On the Armenian side, the criticism, somewhat very vehement, focused on the historians' sub-commission. Having submitted the protocols for ratification by their parliaments, neither government demanded a vote, although it is questionable whether such was necessary in either country. And then, earlier this year, President Sargsyan withdrew the documents from consideration by the Armenian Parliament.

More ominously, last month Armenia's State Commission for the Commemoration of the 100th Anniversary of the Genocide issued a Declaration, dubbed Pan-Armenian, that (a) brought the Genocide to the center of Armenia's agenda, (b) considered the Genocide as the basis for reparations from Turkey, including territorial ones. The document refers to the Treaty of Sèvres and Wilsonian boundaries, claiming to some wider, though unspecified historic rights. President Sarsgyan, presiding officer of that Commission, reaffirmed the fundamental approaches underlying and expressed in that Declaration when he refused to consider the possibility of a presidential statement that might be based on some revisions of the text of the Pan-Armenian Declaration, a statement that would be more appropriate for a state with international obligations and less fraught with danger for its future. President Sargsyan continues to declare that Armenia has no preconditions for the normalization of relations between the two counties. Yet he has assumed the role of historian with a continuing barrage of statements and criticisms of Turkish officials' denialist declarations, while he has failed to address the tenuous and threatened state of the country's independence.

Sargsyan is a political figure who has been on the scene with some of the most important positions in the country, including defense minister, prime minister, and now president for seven years. His references to the subject of the Genocide can be counted on the fingers of one hand. It is difficult to resist interpreting this most recent barrage as a signal to Turkey that he does not care about relations with Turkey, and to assure Russia that Armenia's past overtures to Turkey should not be taken seriously or interpreted as a lack of complete devotion and loyalty to Moscow. Armenia's final shift to a "Russian orientation" was completed last autumn when Sargsyan unexpectedly announced that Armenia would join the Russian-led Eurasian Economic Union. Armenia had conducted four years of negotiations with the European Union leading to expectations that association agreements would be signed with the EU.

We can argue that by and large, Armenia is returning to the Soviet era's political and historical frameworks, abandoning the policies of the movement and founding principles of the republic's independence. It is obvious that we have already gone beyond the point of using the lack of recognition of the Genocide by Turkey as evidence of its genocidal intents toward the people of the Republic of Armenia. Now we are already developing a foreign policy agenda that would be characterized as aggressive by international standards—regardless as to whether our demands are justified or not. And we are doing so as if we are living in a vacuum, as if what we say and do have no consequences.

The role Armenian governments have assigned to the Genocide--and the change of focus that entail--has been transformed in a relatively short time. The engineering of that transformation has coincided with (a) Russia's policies to narrow down the boundaries of Armenia's sovereignty and (b) the extent to which authoritarian regimes in Armenia rely on Moscow for their legitimacy, a Moscow that has become more demanding. That is, these regimes have argued Yerevan has no choice but to seek Moscow's "protection," in view of the "imminent" threat of a renewed genocide.. While Moscow is chipping away at Armenia's sovereignty with the full support of the ruling oligarchic regime, leaders of Armenia and the media are discussing what to do in case of an invasion from Turkey, making it sound as if it was an imminent threat. The loss of sovereignty could not but also affect the resolution of the Karabakh problem; it is obvious, at least to me, that the future is slipping away from the hands of authorities in Armenia and Karabakh.

The more we bring the Genocide to the center of our perception of, and policies towards our neighbors, the more we will need to rely on Russia and be willing to cede sovereignty. And conversely, the more Russia wants Armenia to cede its sovereignty rather than seek other security options, the more the Genocide will be brought into play by Russia, by domestic forces supporting Russian policies, and by others, whether wittingly or not. The curious thing is that Russia's relations with Turkey, steadily constant and consistently friendly since 1923, have little to do with the Genocide. Yet in the current circumstances, in the minds of Armenian leaders in Armenia and the Diaspora, there exists a curious connection that has sustained irrational expectations for decades.

In other words, it is nearly impossible to turn the Genocide into the basic principle of foreign policy and territorial demands—without even a strategic concept as to how to achieve it, but still expecting an imminent attack from Turkey—and at the same time expect to have the minimal degree of sovereignty necessary to be called an independent state. Russia as our savior and "eternal friend" looms large in these unaccountable declarations and policies, just as the Soviet Union did in the minds of so many Armenian political leaders at home and abroad in earlier decades.

Two additional observations.

(1) The question of the search for external support by administrations that lack domestic legitimacy in Armenia becomes the mediating concept between what such regimes need and what Russia can offer, whatever the price.

(2) It is worth noting that the role assigned by an administration to the Genocide issue in Yerevan has been a critical, if not the determining factor, as to whether some domestic forces, and especially Diasporan elements, are willing to question the commitment of presidents and administrations to democracy, good governance, and human rights. If a president in Armenia talks about the Genocide loudly enough and makes it a cornerstone of the country's policies, all violations in these areas are permitted and the worst is ignored.

The purpose of this simple narrative has been to highlight some dimensions of Armenia-Turkey relations in view of the two approaches outlined earlier in this presentation, and the integral, but inverse relationship between rhetoric on the Genocide and the degree of sovereignty. If, as indicated above, Turkey is genocidal and Turks are criminal by definition, then it should not matter what we say or do. We are condemned to being a vassal state at best, and we participate in history not as actors with agency, but as the eternal victims who have no options.

One parliamentarian from the ruling party in Yerevan recently posited, "We have always been under someone's rule. It is better the Russians than the Turks." So, who needs independence? Who needs a foreign policy? And nothing we say or do matters so long as we can hide behind the big brother and maybe even challenge Turkey to a duel. That means we have no historical agency, in fact no history, just eternal victimhood and martyrdom.

Yet clearly during the past twenty-five years, Turkey did not behave as the essentialists had projected, even though one may fault that country for not being able to transcend its policy of favoring Azerbaijan and for its shortsightedness in regional politics.

The hold of the old perpetrator/victim paradigm might have been too deep in the Armenian political imagination, or the lack thereof, for an alternative framework to succeed.

The alternative offered by the 1988 movement may have already been replaced by the more comfortable and former paradigm. While at fault, Turkey has had limited responsibility in this change. On the other hand, Armenia and the Diaspora have taken positions, advocated platforms and policies regarding Turkey, that they themselves may not have taken seriously and which serve internal or domestic purposes, as if their words and actions do not matter to others, including to Turkey.

When these words and actions make a difference in Armenia's degree of independence, or in Turkey's policies in the future, it will be difficult to hide behind the original paradigm.

If we want to be part of the making of our own future, be agents in the making of our history, we must think, speak, and act differently than the eternal victims who have no responsibility in what has happened to them; a people who project to be victims in the future, and thus whatever happens to them has nothing to do with their own words and actions; victims who are more comfortable not assuming any responsibility. Victims who hide behind a big brother but, nonetheless, wave a sword at the designated perpetrator.

The Genocide has affected us in ways that we have not yet fully understood. It has affected deeply the development and evolution of our political thought. We have campaigned for its recognition by the international community and neglected to understand its full impact on us. We have found comfort in the collective memory of that catastrophe and failed to apply self-criticism that might have made it possible for us to distinguish between the historical event and the instrumentalization of the event, the role we assign it in our decision-making for the future, and the extent to which we want to take responsibility in the making of our future.

10

THE "GARBAGE BIN" APPROACH TO HISTORY AND ITS DISCONTENTS

2018

The following essay, with minor changes, was written at the request of the Böhl Institute website editors on the occasion of the 100th anniversary of the establishment of the First Republic of Armenia and was first published on that website in May 2018. The essay highlights the pitfalls of using historical events and assessing them at will according to one's current needs as the "lesson" of history, or as proof of one's ideological tenet of the moment.

For a people whose history covers a few millennia, the significance of the First Republic of Armenia far exceeds the number of years it lasted. Other than the Genocide that preceded it, I doubt that there is another period of two and one-half years that has received more attention by scholars, memoirists, and polemicists.

That may not be surprising since above all, the First Republic constituted the rebirth of Armenian statehood on a portion of historic Armenian lands after an absence of almost a thousand years, and doing so in the form of a modern republic.

On this occasion it is not easy to transcend polemics and controversies, especially for one who grew up reading and hearing about them, and then studying them, especially for one who had Simon Vratsian, the last Prime Minister of the First Republic, as a teacher and principal, and Garo Sassouni, the governor of Kars (then part of the Republic) as a literature teacher, as is the case of this writer. Issues can also be confusing, since just about everything about that republic—its genesis, development, leadership, policies, and demise—have been glorified by the dominant actor in the life of that republic, the Dashnaktsoutiun, and heatedly contested and harshly critiqued by the historians of the Second, Soviet Republic and the Dasnaktsoutiun's antagonists in the Diaspora, the Ramgavar and Hnchakian parties.

Now we are almost thirty years into the Third Republic. The political organizations that have appeared on the scene of Armenian history since the 1880s—at least those that have survived organizationally until the rise of the Third Republic—have all had their chance to present their current face and their case to the Armenian people of the Third Republic, and to all who cared to read or listen. They were able to offer their stories, their interpretations of the past, and their narratives.

In the early 1990s, so-called Marxist scholars of the Second Republic who had produced volumes against the First Republic and its main actor, the Dashnaktsoutiun, were suddenly transmogrified into the staunchest defenders of a new independence—and more. Meanwhile, the Dashnaktsoutiun, erstwhile the staunchest defender of independence, had a hard time recovering from its opposition to a new independence. The Hnchakians and Ramgavars had to adjust their policies to evolving realities, but always trying to find a way to accommodate their reflexive anti-Dashnaktsoutiun positions.

The remnants of the Second Republic's only political actor, the Communist Party, exited the stage in an agonizing act of irrelevance not long after the collapse of the USSR. The Ramgavars and Hnchakians were never strong in that part of Armenia which became the First Republic. Yet, as organizations contesting the power of the Dashnaktsoutiun in the Diaspora, they aligned with the Soviet position of the Soviet Republic. All three Diasporan parties returned to Armenia with great hopes. The Dashnaktsoutiun, exiled during the Second Republic, and having superior organizational traditions and skills, fared better when it returned to the Armenia of the Third Republic. Even then, in national elections in Armenia, that party has failed to garner more than ten percent of the popular vote during any election.

The narratives developed by each of these forces and the stories they told about the past, and especially about their pasts, changed conveniently, and as necessary.

It is said that when asked about what the future held, a Soviet politician replied, "The future is easy to predict. It is the past that cannot be predicted."

One only has to look at the school and university textbooks that have been prepared since independence in 1991 to confirm the volatility and precariousness with which the past—the most recent past since 1988, the makers of which are still around—to understand the troubling truth contained in that simple observation.

Regardless, by and large these organizations failed to capture the political imagination of the people of Armenia. Instead, the Third Republic was established and its history marked by forces indigenous to the Second Republic, to the surprise and general dismay of the three diasporized political parties. To that we must add the elements that acquired significance as a result of the Karabakh war forced upon Armenia and Armenians by Azerbaijan.

Beyond the politically and ideologically motivated accounts and assessments of the First Republic, we can certainly appreciate the serious efforts of the leaders of the First Republic to establish a modern, egalitarian, democratic society under the worst possible conditions. And that included the rights of women to vote in elections, before such a basic right was granted in the United States. These efforts would have been normal for European countries. Still, these dire conditions—domestic and foreign— which were exacerbated by the threat of a Bolshevik uprising in the country, also revealed the authoritarian impulses of the Dashnaktsoutiun that controlled the government.

All good intentions aside, that very precarious First Republic, populated by a huge number of orphans and refugees of the Genocide, engaged in wars with three of its four immediate neighbors.

Different historians and political forces can draw very differing lessons from history. President Levon Ter-Petrossian of the Third Republic, and a few around him who were historians, had drawn one set of lessons from history: they avoided three wars that brought an end to the First Republic.

We knew one war was what we could handle. Although it is not yet over, the first phase of the Karabakh war was won, while the First Republic lost territories to all three neighbors that it fought against.

During one of my daily morning meetings with President Ter-Petrossian, at a time when the Karabakh war was at its most intense, I found the president in a rather jovial mood. I had ready my list of items to discuss with him. The president waved his hand, as if to dismiss temporarily any other issue, and asked: "Do you know what today is?" I checked my mind and my notes and gave a very precise calendrical response, knowing full well he was not asking for the date. "Today," he said, "our Republic is a day older than the First Republic."

The question arises, what was the problem with the policy decisions of the First Republic? Or, as some would prefer to formulate it, what was the problem with the policies of the Third Republic's first administration under Ter-Petrossian? To critics of the Ter-Petrossian administration, the answer to the second formulation of the question has been that the first administration of the Third Republic did not have a "national vision." Meaning, that it did not make greater Armenia—the Armenia of the Treaty of Sèvres, and sometimes denoted by the term "Armenian Cause"—the basis of its foreign policy.

It seemed at this moment that simply put, the difference between the First and Third Republics was what one wished and what was attainable, and more significantly, between what was defensible on the ground and at the negotiating table and what was not. So, the answer to the first question asked at the start of the previous paragraph, on what was wrong with the First Republic, might be formulated in the following manner: the capabilities of the First Republic were not commensurate with its vision of the map of Armenia.

So, what is left to be said for an aging scholar who still has time to ponder, after more than fifty years of hearing, researching, writing, and all the while pondering about the First Republic and the two that have followed? And what is left to be said in view that this first, precarious, unlikely, yet juridically factual republic reestablished statehood in the millennial heritage of what we consider as our history?

I have been intrigued recently, what can I say, by a number of questions:

1. What causes change in Armenian history? What is the role of foreign powers and that of domestic forces?

2. Who manages that change, and with what tools? And what does one do with the change?

3. What is the role of statehood in Armenian history and why has it appeared and disappeared so often? As a corollary issue, what is the difference and the relationship between an Armenian "state" and an Armenian "nation," the latter implying a Diaspora or Diasporas? A state implies a territorially defined entity, while a nation implies an ethnic or religiously-based one, the elements of which can be found anywhere on earth. And, in the end,

4. What constitutes the nexus of Armenian history? In other words, what paradigm can we use to understand the history of a place and of a people where statehood was significant, but not always at hand? How did, let us say, the Armenia of 2300 years ago end up in the Armenia of today?

While it is neither the intention of this essay nor within its possibilities to answer them, it is possible to contribute to the understanding of that history by asking the right questions, since the wrong questions cannot provide good answers, while even wrong answers to the right questions can open pathways to a better understanding of historical and ongoing processes and, eventually, to the right answers.

I believe I can offer some thoughts along these lines on the occasion of the 100th anniversary of the establishment of the First Republic.

The First Republic encapsulates the dilemmas and challenges of Armenian history. It represents elements of continuity, but mainly change, the culmination of challenges and issues the Armenian people faced, at least as figured out by the political parties in the last thirteen decades or so, and by the Church for much longer.

As a paradigmatic model, it seems the First Republic, and much of Armenian history, can best be understood if we accept that what defined it was not its domestic programs and attempted achievements, as important as these were for that precarious state. Rather, it is the tensions it had to endure and resolve in the regional and international arenas, and the relationship of local forces with international ones. Much in Armenian history has been explained by the conflict between powerful neighbors and domestic forces. The better model, I have come to conclude, is seeing the interactions between competing domestic forces, each aligned with rival foreign powers. That alignment might be through direct collusion or indirect cooperation. Ideological, or very tactical. Or both. In other words, the domestication and internalization of regional and international rivalries, and the internationalization of domestic ones. And that places a good deal of the responsibility for the way Armenia's history has evolved on the shoulders of Armenian individuals and organizations who spoke and acted in the name of the Armenian people.

In the First Republic, the leading force, the Dashnaktsoutiun, aligned with the West, the anti-Bolshevik coalition, which delivered the dead-on-arrival Treaty of Sèvres, the ultimate achievement of the "Armenian Question," "Armenian Case," or "Armenian Cause" approach. The Bolsheviks in the Armenia of the First Republic obviously thought that the solution to that question could not be sought in the West, but in the ideals of the International Bolshevik Revolution, as manifested in the Bolshevik Revolution in Russia. Both sides believed in what they were saying—and died for it, too. More significantly, they killed each other for it. It may be worth reviewing developments our history of the last 2000 years under that light.

The Dashnaktsoutiun, the dominant force of the First Republic, ended up with far less territory than it started out with, and with far less than the Treaty of Sèvres promised. Promising is the easy part in history. And the Bolsheviks started with the Treaty of Kars.

On this 100th anniversary of that most important date of the rebirth of Armenian statehood, one last thought. More often than not, history has been treated as a garbage bin, where anyone can throw anything that one finds worthy of forgetting. Later on, anyone can go in and retrieve an item, as cats do, and market it again, recycled for new times and circumstances.

Sometimes, we need to rescue history from the damages the "garbage approach" can inflict on facts, processes, and critical perspectives.

11

HOW TO WRITE THE HISTORY OF THE THIRD REPUBLIC, OR HOW NOT TO WRITE IT

2015

The writing of history is, in itself, a difficult undertaking, if the historian is conscientious. Even under the best of circumstances a whole range of factors can obstruct the possibility of coming close to as objective a narrative as possible: to determine the theme of the project and formulate the questions to which the historian is seeking answers; to select and find sources and to understand them correctly; to verify the information in the sources; to organize the facts on the basis of a concept, framework or, preferably, as the evidence suggests; and, articulate the product, the narrative. The conscientious historian begins by recognizing and coming to terms with his/her own biases and prejudices, some evident, others possibly not so, that may obstruct her or his judgment during the difficult journey.

That journey will be filled with even more dangers when the subject of study belongs to contemporary times. That is the case of researchers who have already tried to write the history of the Third Republic or will try to write it in the near future.

This article is an attempt to identify the pitfalls that are already evident in some works or the historian should be aware of in the future. The original of the article was published previously in An Armenian Mediterranean. Words and Worlds in Motion, *edited by Kathryn Babayan and Michael Pifer and published in 2015.*

WHAT EVERYONE KNOWS

A few years ago, at a dinner following my lecture at an Ivy League University, a highly-respected scholar in a related field stated, "Levon Ter-Petrossian [the first president of the Third Republic] was the most corrupt man in Armenia in the 1990s." When I asked if he had reliable evidence for that statement—after all, we were all academics and scholars—he responded, "Yes, of course: everyone knows that." I suggested that if scholars base their judgment on "what everyone knows," we are all in trouble.

The writing of the history of any era presents challenges. The challenges increase manifold when that era is still unfolding. Paradoxically, those who could have been facilitating factors—eyewitnesses, actors, and decision-makers who are still living—can also be sources of complications. This statement, as it applies to the writing of the history of the Third Republic of Armenia (1991-present), may also seem strange, since the birth of that republic was followed immediately by a revolution in information technology.

Unless the historian is aware of the many pitfalls and takes immense precautions, they will face handicaps and problems that may be as difficult to overcome as those we face, say, when we try to write the history of a ninth-century social movement, or find the reasons for the collapse of an empire.

Problems in writing the history of the contemporary era in fact begin with the absence of open archives, and do not end with the evident need of living historical figures to justify their policies and actions and cover up their mistakes. There are so many ways for politicians and statesmen to act on the understandable instinct to control what is said and written about them: Destroying damning documents, not leaving behind archives, editing recollections in their memoirs, or even making sure some decisions do not have written records. Eyewitness accounts can, and are usually impacted by the loss of memory, wilful or unwitting, over even short periods of time. There are other factors affecting the accuracy of the writing of that history: propaganda wars that are waged by individuals, groups, and political parties to ensure the victory of their narrative and, indeed, of their political success, over that of opponents; the delay in making archives available; the biases the historian may have had when writing that history, while also being a citizen or interested party with pre-formed judgments regarding events he read about or saw on television or YouTube.

I am not even getting close to unchallenged preferences, prejudices, and ideological handicaps our historian may have even before starting to write that history. "I was there," "I saw it," "I read it myself," and such forms of logic are likely to give the historian a sense of security about his product that will lack a critical examination of documents and statements, and more significantly, will display an uncritical approach to one's own choice of documents and facts in developing an argument, a thesis, or a narrative for the history one is creating.

Without defenses against such possible dangers, we simply do not have the distance necessary to determine what event, policy, or statement is in fact important for the long haul, and ultimately, what is fact and what is propaganda or fiction. Certainly, it is extremely difficult to explain the "why" of any of these events, policies, and statements. For historians, what we must first decide is: What is to be explained?

In general, many historians are still writing modern Armenian history with the handicap of taboos created by a failed revolutionary movement to save Ottoman or Western Armenians; a genocide; a First Republic that was lost in two and half years; a Second Republic that lasted much longer than the first, yet which did not stand the test of time and was discarded by its own citizens. Now we are witnessing the life of a Third Republic that is faltering, and a Diaspora that becomes indifferent or indignant, when its prescriptions do not cure what it thinks are the ills of the republic.

THE DEBATE ON THE CENTRALITY OF STATEHOOD

The contemporaneity of the Third Republic which started in 1990-1991, but which can be traced back to 1988, may have induced some scholars who were personally acquainted with its leading figures to have a sense that what they know is what happened. How could it not? They were living witnesses. In many respects the post-independence period did not measure up to the expectations of its citizens, or of Diasporan Armenians. Though none of the latter group were ready for it, most welcomed it with trepidation, while some opposed it actively.

Additionally, many scholars in the Diaspora also write about the Third Republic as if it is in competition with the Diaspora. This may be a questionable but valid frame or reference, so long as it is not a clever way to elevate the status of the Diaspora over statehood, or to give short shrift to the history of that republic. For, statehood is what distinguishes the history of the Third Republic from the history of many periods of Armenian history or the history or histories of our Diasporas over many centuries. Let us not forget that in most of historic Armenia, there has not been an Armenian state for almost a millennium, with the exception of three republics encompassing but a small portion of its territory, and which combine for just a century of statehood.[1]

Indeed, it often appears to this writer that we are struggling with a paradigm in Armenian politics and history that first evolved in the fifth century. Ashot Sargsyan best defined that paradigm in 2004 in a paper presented at a conference at the University of Michigan-Ann Arbor. In that paper, the little known and too modest, but very important scholar, born and based in Armenia, juxtaposed the centrality of statehood in Movses Khorenatsi's *History of the Armenians* against Yeghishe's definition of Armenians as a community of Christians in his work about the Battle of Avarayr.[2] The question emerges: Are Armenians defined as a state, or are they a nation or people?[3] The first requires certain attributes, such as control over a definite territory and a government. As for the second, a people could be anywhere.

It is not all that clear to me that what we have here is a true dilemma.[4] A nation or people and a state are not incompatible concepts or structures, even if their confluence has produced the present system of an international community—however bloody and fragile. In fact, one can write a history of the world in the nineteenth and twentieth centuries anchored on the simple idea that nations should have states, and states will try to create nations out of the population they contain within what constitutes (or what they imagine to constitute) their rightful boundaries. And until recently, many histories were indeed based on that paradigm.

DIASPORAN CHALLENGES

This point is significant for two reasons. First, many historians of the Third Republic, or at least a good percentage of them whose works will be read by an international readership, are likely to be Diasporan Armenians who can read Armenian documents, though many who do not know the language have written very useful, as well as very ridiculous histories of Armenians in the modern and contemporary periods. The second reason this paradigm is relevant is that Armenia is still undergoing diasporization, while the existing Diaspora is changing its demographic centers and, accordingly, its definitions of Armenianness. Hence, the Diaspora is altering the forms, if not the substance, of "Armenian culture" it produces.

Armenians will continue to have different generations of Diasporans who will try to write history. The history written by Diasporans has many advantages. Yet it will also project the underlying problems that accompany being a Diasporan. Why do Diasporans write the history of the land they were not born in, or that they left and did not return to? As I have indicated elsewhere, being a Diasporan connotes a negative definition: You are not where you were supposed to be. And that matters when you write a history of the "homeland" or of "your people."[5] The result is often a "defensive" history, one that makes a contribution to or, at least, does not threaten the foundations of Diasporan "preservationist" ideology,[6] i.e., ethnic identity and pride, making sure all responsibility for failures are traced to external forces—often by choosing the question to be answered—and, ultimately, situating history within the victimization narrative.

We do have a generation of Armenians in the Diaspora who are distanced enough from "preservationist" or "defensive" impulses to integrate their sense of an Armenian identity as an initial mechanism of propulsion with their intellectual interests, and to focus on a historical problem in a manner that is both critical and significant to wider audiences and fields. This approach, in my opinion, is the most promising, because when used properly, this process requires the application of critical tools and standards that are often missing from histories that are ultimately intended to highlight communal identity and address its needs.

Yet it is easier to make use of these newer, more integrative approaches when writing about earlier periods. By and large, today's powers that be, whether in Armenia or in the Diaspora, do not feel as threatened when the critical approaches are applied toward ruling elites of much earlier periods, when it may be difficult for readers and audiences to transfer the analysis or conclusions from the study of a long-gone historical moment to the present. There are not many scholars and intellectuals in the Diaspora who are willing to endure the opprobrium, even wrath of the Armenian Church, the political parties, or the self-appointed guardians of orthodoxy by subjecting the recent history and policies of these institutions to a critical analysis.[7]

This is an important issue, since there are a number of elements that determine who writes history, why, and with what biases and taboos. I am not even speaking of party affiliations and ideological inclinations. There is a great deal of self-censorship, even when an independent Diasporan historian interprets Armenian history while trying also to be acceptable to the dominant community organizations, or to authorities in Armenia, lest she or he be ostracized, possibly attacked by name, or be called names.

When writing history, any history of any period, the historian must ask: What are the assumptions that she took for granted, what are the truths that he did not question and therefore did not need supporting documentation for, or even a footnote or two, because "everyone knows"?

It is intriguing that while we have seen an increase in the number of works published on the complex ways in which the question of Armenian identity is analysed, I am unaware of any monographs that study, even if not so critically, the transnational institutions and organizations and individual leaders who often govern such institutions and organizations for decades. After all, these categories constitute the leadership of the organized segment of the Armenian Diaspora, a leadership that claims to represent Armenians and Armenian interests, and which attempts to define and determine "Armenianness." In essence, we are lacking a critical perspective of the institutions and elites that determine Armenian orthodoxy: Good or bad, the good and the bad.

Even from a strictly utilitarian point of view, a century into the major modern diasporization process, it is impossible to determine what has or has not worked as far as the stated goals of these institutions are concerned, assuming one accepts uncritically the stated goals of these institutions and elites. When doing their own accounting, these institutions have determined that the Armenian nation has survived due to the fact that they, these institutions, continue to exist. Has anyone counted the numbers of Armenians who faded away, for any given reason? It would not be an exaggeration to state that over the span of Armenian history more Armenians belong to this latter category. Does that constitute a failure of our institutions? Should not that invite investigations into the larger policies followed by Armenian elites beginning in the nineteenth century, at the very least? Analysis of elites in the earlier periods, especially the fourth and fifth centuries when the dominant paradigm evolved, would certainly be enlightening as well.

In brief, to some degree or another, most Diasporan scholars of Armenian origin share with the broader community what one might call the "survival syndrome." This syndrome tends to treat with kid gloves every institution or organization that existed prior to the Genocide, as if these were relics with a sanctity about them. "Preservation of identity," followed in recent decades by the campaigns for Genocide recognition, the two Holy Grails of Diasporan existence, invite the withholding of critical analysis and judgment with regard to these institutions. Consciously or otherwise, scholars of Armenian origin often share the assumptions underlying such reflexes. They may not wish to antagonize the major forces who lead the larger community, and who can ostracize an academic in many ways, although most academics are, technically speaking, independent of communities and protected by academic freedom.[8] Such ostracism can reach the level of intellectual terrorism when scholars are subject to organized and vehement attacks for their unorthodox views.

SOME EXCEPTIONS

There are two broad exceptions to this general comment in the post-Genocide period. Soviet Armenian historians did their best to critique the policies of the Dashnaktsoutiun, the party from which they had wrested power, then expelled from Armenia in 1920-21.[9] The Dashnaktsoutiun responded with equal force from the Diaspora. Also, the post-Soviet Diaspora was engaged in an internal battle between those who, on the one hand, supported Soviet Armenia for various reasons and, on the other, the Dashnaktsoutiun that opposed it. This conflict reached its heights with the international Cold War and produced much interesting and useful analysis of Armenian institutions, including of the church. Unfortunately, setting aside the more sober style of the first category, these debates were largely polemical, ideologically motivated, and vitriolic in nature. It is difficult to assign them labels of scholarly and intellectual discourse.[10]

Generally speaking, non-Armenian scholars do not have much interest in the internal functions of Armenia or the Armenian community, except when it relates to geostrategic considerations, international dimensions of the "Armenian Question" and, more recently and generally, the Genocide recognition issue.[11]

Obviously, I am referring to specific institutions: The Armenian Church, including its two Catholicosates and two Patriarchates; and the Armenian political parties, i.e., the Hnchakian Party, the Dashnaktsoutiun (with its affiliate cultural, educational, sports, relief, and youth organizations), and the Ramgavar Party. To these we now must add the remnants of the Armenian Secret Army for the Liberation of Armenia (ASALA), which claimed the status of a new party in the Diaspora, and whose ideology and actions had serious consequences; the Armenian General Benevolent Union; and possibly others. While useful, histories of institutions or organizations commissioned by the subjects themselves, or authored by members of the subject institutions, cannot be considered as critical accounts of the history of and historical roles played by these institutions.[12]

If Diasporan scholars and intellectuals cannot, or are not willing to tackle the problems immediately surrounding them, if they have no willingness to be critical of institutions that have defined the Armenian world in which they function, how can they be trusted to weigh in and measure the challenges, processes, and, ultimately, the history of the Third Republic?

The problem I see here is not different from the problem I noted in the early 1990s: How can the Hnchakians, Dashnaktsakans, and Ramgavars, who had displayed little knack for democracy—i.e., open accountability to the Armenian community and transparency of their operations and decision-making processes regarding their major policies and shifts in such policies—go to newly-independent Armenia and teach its citizens democracy, citizens who had brought down the Soviet Union and were already democratizing the country, whether successfully or not? How can a few Armenian scholars suddenly become specialists in state-building? That is the same question I had to ask regarding some international scholars who suddenly became experts in the understanding of international terrorism, including Armenian terrorism, in the 1970s and 1980s.[13]

One is tempted to qualify the liberties Diasporan scholars often take concerning events in Armenia as a form of internalized orientalism. Scholars allow themselves to study and make judgments about individuals and policies by standards that would not hold when applied to non-Armenian issues.[14]

Much is taken for granted in the histories that are written: Assumptions that are not discussed; biases and prejudices that the authors hold, but of which they are unaware. And in a historian's work, what is taken for granted and not questioned is what they present as facts which underlie their interpretation.

SCHOLARS IN ARMENIA AND THEIR CHALLENGES

This is not to say that historians in Armenia do not have their problems. In fact, they do, and some of these problems may be as prohibitive as those in the Diaspora. Scholars in Armenia had to live and write in an environment created by a one-party, ideologically-organized political system. That changed with independence, or at least during the first ten to fifteen years of independence. In fact, the change was so radical that a historian who had made a career of writing about the political and ideological bankruptcy of the Dashnaktsoutiun, and who had exposed that party's links to the United States Central Intelligence Agency (CIA), ended up becoming a member of that party.[15] A Communist Party ideologue who had occupied the important position of Second Secretary of the Communist Party of Soviet Armenia ended up writing a history of the Ramgavar Party, a history requested by and paid for by that party.[16] The window that was opened in 1991 has been closing slowly since the end of the 1990s, although there is still some room for a relatively wide spectrum of historical interpretations. Still, historians must find ways to sustain research and then publish their works, especially independent ones, and also those who disagree with a regime that is developing a kind of orthodoxy reminiscent of the Soviet period, and which may not be welcome in established or state institutions. Here too, more often than not, self-censorship becomes important, as economic survival is a major issue. Additionally, scholars in Armenia, especially the older generation, defined professionalism in terms of its Soviet context. Accessing primary or secondary sources outside the USSR was not a common practice, and most Armenian historians trained in Armenia and the USSR did not command foreign languages other than Russian (with the exception of some also trained in philology or specialists of the "oriental" languages).

Yet, there is a fundamental difference between these two categories of historians. Historians in Armenia usually do not have the underlying burden of concern about their Armenian identity and what they "owe" to the nation. And this is an important distinction that might mark the difference between a good or a bad historian, all other things being equal. Diasporan Armenian scholarship has yet to produce the equal of Ashot Hovhannisian's work on the origins of Armenian liberation ideology and its development in pre-modern and even modern times.[17]

Non-Armenian scholars may not have the same challenges as those of Armenian origin. Yet most, particularly those who do not know Armenian, weave their narratives by relying on non-Armenian sources such as reports from foreign correspondents and embassies in Armenia, or the works of Armenian scholars and the rare, usually poorly translated texts.[18] They are then likely to miss the nuances and possibly major issues. In the South Caucasus, as in many other parts of the world, to miss the nuances is to miss everything. This is also likely to lead to policies that produce disastrous consequences, for which external forces are not likely to take responsibility.

This is also true in the sense that one must select which documents to read. The problem of translation—and choice of documents to be translated—is predominant in embassies of foreign countries in Yerevan. Who decides what article from which newspaper is relevant to be translated or summarized or even referred to, when the absolute majority of foreign diplomats stationed in Armenia do not know the language or know it enough to make such a determination? Unless, of course, the diplomat has a sense of what questions to ask from other sources and/or with regard to a specific matter on hand, and in addition to general directives, accordingly gives instructions to the translators to look for relevant material in the media. Additionally, more often than not, non-Armenian scholars focus on any relevance Armenians or Armenia have to the region or the wider international community. Consequently, many of their works address the concerns of the international "security" problem, their initial motivation to the study. The internal developments and domestic forces, and their relation to external forces and factors, matter only to the extent that these are relevant to these scholars' concerns, a sure recipe for short-changing the agency of Armenians in Armenian history.[19]

DO WE KNOW, OR NEED TO KNOW ABOUT THE FIRST AND SECOND REPUBLICS?

It should be evident that no informed and intelligent history of the Third Republic can be written without an adequate review of the histories of the first two. The value of the First Republic for understanding the story of the Third lies in (1) the significance of the adoption of its symbols and, more importantly, (2) the attempt of the leaders of the Third Republic—many of them historians or highly educated personalities who had studied that history for at least a couple of decades—to avoid its mistakes.

The significance of the Second, Soviet Republic is a different story. First, obviously, chronologically it precedes the Third. More importantly, the Third Republic is more organically related to the Second, since the members of the Yerevan-based Karabakh Committee that led Armenia to its independence opted for the legal way to achieve that goal. That means all steps and actions were in compliance with existing Soviet laws—both USSR and ASSR (Armenian Soviet Socialist Republic)—and all changes were introduced by the use of the legal mechanism, i.e., the existing legislative process. Thus, Soviet Armenian laws remained valid until changed by the ASSR Supreme Soviet, later the National Assembly, beginning in the summer of 1990. Furthermore, there is continuity from the Second to the Third Republics not only in the legislative process, but also in personnel at high levels of government. One can also not ignore the unseen ways in which having been brought up and educated in the Soviet period, even the most democratically inclined and pro-independence leaders bore the stamp of that period, in both the positive and negative senses.[20]

HOW MUCH, THEN, DO WE KNOW ABOUT THE FIRST TWO REPUBLICS?

For the First Republic, we have the pioneering works of two of its four prime ministers, Simon Vratsian[21] and Alexander Khatissian,[22] and the assessment, memoirs, and analyses of many major actors, including the critical appraisal of its first Prime Minister, Hovhannes Kachaznouni.[23] Unfortunately, while the archives of the republic are open at the National Archives of Armenia, the republic archives collected by the Armenian Revolutionary Federation (ARF) and currently housed in Watertown, Massachusetts, remain under restricted access at best.[24] However, we have the monumentally detailed, four-volume work of Richard G. Hovannisian, who was able to benefit from these rich sources.[25] Other historians too have written about the period and added their own assessments. All interested researchers have had access to the archives of non-Armenian governments that had relations with, or interest in the Republic of Armenia.

In contrast to the First Republic, which spanned only two and a half years, the Second Republic, which lasted seventy years, does not yet have its own historian or historians. No doubt the Second Republic produced much more raw data than the first. Its institutions published a large number of official histories on anniversaries of Sovietization extolling the industrialization of the country, the mechanization of its agricultural sector, and progress made in education, health care, housing and social services, all made possible by the Soviet status of the republic and the leadership of the Communist Party of Armenia. The statistical figures and assessments offered in these volumes are valuable, as long as they are looked at with a critical eye, given the nature of the centrally-planned economy and the need of authorities to constantly prove the successes of five-year plans. One need only look at the state of the infrastructure in towns and villages outside Yerevan, when the Third Republic inherited the former Soviet economy, to question if it is possible to accept these numbers as representative of the country's actual conditions.

Other than such official sources and histories, the Second Republic has had little attention. There are some exceptions: Mary Kilbourne Matossian's pioneering research,[26] Ronald Suny's brilliantly interpretive volume,[27] Claire Mouradian's work,[28] and a few other specialized studies. There also exists a number of surveys on Armenian history written or edited by scholars, and all, to one extent or another, cover the Soviet Armenian Republic.[29] Yet none of these works are based on the kind of primary source research and secondary literature that would make it possible to portray what would be accepted as the history of those seventy years. Only recently have articles and even volumes been published that study specific aspects of Soviet Armenian history using archival documentation or oral histories—the kind of work that will make it possible to imagine a history of the Second Republic as a whole.

It is possible to argue that twenty-five years after independence, historians in Armenia have not produced a history of the Second Republic.[30] In general the Soviet regime has not been scrutinized in independent Armenia. Suffice it to state that this is largely due to the delicate relations independent Armenia has maintained with post-USSR Russia.[31] Excepting two publications, even the Stalinist regime that destroyed the intellectual and cultural elite that Soviet Armenia had managed to produce has not had its due assessment.[32]

Since independence, a number of players have produced memoirs that should make significant contributions to writing the history of that republic. The last Communist Party Prime Minister of Armenia, Fadey Sargsyan, as well as leading academic Sergey Hambardzumyan, amongst others, have published memoirs chronicling their participation in public affairs. So have players in Moscow such as Anastas Mikoyan and former KGB agents. However, very few of these memoirs contribute to a historical understanding of the Second Republic in terms of how decisions were made during various decades, shifts in the distribution of power between the center and periphery, or the actual ways in which the formula "national in form, Marxist-Leninist in substance" was applied and worked (or did not work), with the exception of Suny's work. We certainly have not come to terms with the Great Purges and smaller incidents which cost Soviet Armenia most of its elite intelligentsia. Equally important, the Second Republic lacks a serious study of the economic changes that were introduced and the industrialization that characterized it, just as is the case with other periods of Armenian history. Occasional articles by, and interviews with Soviet Armenian officials published after 1991 offer more insights and leads, but are hardly sufficient. Most revealing regarding the history of the period in question are the memoirs of high-ranking Soviet KGB officials concerning the USSR's relationships with Diasporan Armenian parties, memoirs which were published in the West.[33]

During my tenure as Director of the Armenian Studies Program at the University of Michigan in the early 2000s, we undertook an oral history program aimed at recording the memoirs of political decision-makers of the end of the Soviet period, the period of transition (1988-1991), and the first phase of the independence period that followed (1991-1998). Our interviewers were able to get to a few of the Soviet era leaders who were still alive, but most were dead, or had died while we were planning the interviews. In most cases, we were too late.[34]

In the case of Western and even of many non-Western countries, scholars and serious journalists produced book-length studies and biographies of important personalities who shaped an era within a few years after a leader's tenure, or even during that tenure. We have some article-length profiles of a few of the leading figures of the First Republic, though as far as I know, none of them were dominant leaders in Soviet Armenia over the ensuing seven decades.[35]

In other words, *we do not have a critical and comprehensive accounting of the period in Armenia's history that gave birth to the Third Republic.*

One way to create a distance between researcher and subject is to determine, at the start, the issues that should be examined. Otherwise, it becomes very easy to be overtaken by chatter and gossip. It is always possible to change direction and find new areas to explore new issues, once research suggests as much. I will dispense with suggestions for a list of themes that might help a researcher make sense of the twenty-five years of the history of the Third Republic, as well as possible sources for such.[36] But a few concluding remarks are in order.

CONCLUDING REMARKS

We need different ways (or even in some cases, simply scholarly ways) to analyze the history of the Third Republic. The problem of writing a history of the Third Republic has significance beyond Armenian Studies alone, as it would have potential implications for broader regional studies that want to incorporate an "Armenian" model, but have to rely on non-scholarly material to do so. In this way, a more rigorous assessment of the republic's history would also shed new light on other fields, such as a history of the Caucasus, the Mediterranean, or even "world" history.

There is a general relaxation of standards of scholarship when it comes to the politics and policies of small nations, standards which would be otherwise unacceptable if applied to big countries. The writing of Armenian history, especially of the modern and contemporary periods, has been afflicted by biases and a partisanship that is more fundamental than would be the case if a scholar simply belonged to, or sympathized with an Armenian political party or faction (as is sometimes the case). That history has been largely uncritical and rarely endowed with a conceptual framework. The exceptions may be narratives built around the Genocide and concomitant "Russian orientation," and even then, these present their own problems.[37]

Additionally, history is being distorted, even though most participants who made or witnessed that history are still alive. Many of them are already revising their own recollections and even creating new facts and narratives.[38] As is the case of many other post-Soviet states, and even post-Soviet authoritarian states, the scholar has to be careful not to assess major players by their best-known roles alone. So many major players became secondary or insignificant within only a decade or two, while so many minor ones became major actors themselves. And so many shifted allegiances from one set of principles to another.[39] Such migrations and transformations are important to keep in mind because any of these players may appear in the headlines at some point, but the scholar should not allow the news cycle to dictate the significant moments—moments that "everyone knows" but which are rarely examined critically—of a different kind of modern Armenian history.

As indicated earlier, if and when writing the history of the Third Republic, the most likely nexus that will connect it to a broader history of Armenia is its fundamental character as a state, and therefore its place in a chronological narrative about Armenian statehood (or the absence thereof). A history of Armenia does not delegitimize a history of Armenians. These are simply different categories. The relationship between the two varies with time. Sometimes diasporas are totally irrelevant to Armenia, at other times they are significant in the creation of an Armenia, or in their role once an Armenian state existed.

It would be revealing to flesh out the heterogeneous relationships between politically defined factions of Armenian nobility—when applied to very early periods—, or those between various forces, factions, and parties within an Armenian state and society, later. These multifaceted relationships might then be put into a more nuanced framework which accounts, as well, for the external forces and powers that tried to influence, if not control differently, Armenian state policies through actors in Armenian state or society, within and without the territory of Armenia.

In other words, as far as the story of Armenian statehood is concerned, that which will explain the most in the recent past, and in even ancient and pre-modern histories as well, is a more complex relationship between domestic and foreign actors.[40] On many occasions, geopolitical rivals have used raw military power to occupy the region. And yet, if we study carefully that history, we will see that often the greatest rivals for the control of the region have acted through domestic (that is, Armenian) players who internalized the discourse of foreign powers, and presented that discourse as if doing so was in Armenia's interest. And many did, believing fully that they were doing so in the interests of an Armenia and Armenians, and that it was them who were using foreign powers to achieve these goals.

Statehood and its absence—and the reasons for its absence—could be construed as the nexus of what differentiates the history of Armenians from the history of Armenia. That is not the only valid nexus, of course, as some have argued. But that is what the periodization of the history of Armenia indicates: the term and era of a Third Republic that we are bound to consider, compelling us to make statehood and its characteristics the core of both what we write as history and how we relate it to the rest of Armenian history. Useful and necessary as a nexus for the history of the state, such an approach could hardly produce an adequate history of the Armenian people over the past thirty years, not only because the Diaspora has been relevant to that republic on so many levels, but also because it has its own dynamics and logic.

Ultimately, the real and perceived roles of Armenia for the Diaspora, and also of the Diaspora for Armenia, easily challenge the method of writing history, taking the state—the nation-state—as the sole nexus of the history of the Armenian people. As fluid and possibly ephemeral as the Armenian Diaspora may be, it represents a powerful magnet for Armenia, and is powerful enough to make an impact on the state of Armenia itself. Ideas and programs conceived in the diaspora are easily transposed into Armenia, and Armenia's issues readily become the issues of the Diaspora, though the latter will incorporate Armenia's problems into its own agenda in its own way.

Much more than many other diaspora-homeland relations, in the case of a small nation such as the Armenians (and even a smaller state like the Republic of Armenia), given the organic relations between the two, it is not possible to write an intelligent history of the republic with the Diaspora as an addendum. Historians may very well look at the Armenian case in order to develop more adequate models for the writing of history, especially since more and more states are ending up with diasporas, and not all of them are as passive as the French or the Italians in the United States.

There are those who have written that history constructed around the church.[41] Others have imagined the history of Armenians as the history of political parties.[42] Then we have the great works on the Armenian Genocide that describe, and even try to explain why that catastrophe happened.[43] Yet none of these situate what happened to the Armenian people—and why—in the context of a long-term history of this people: That for different reasons, the depopulation of the indigenous Armenian population from the Armenian homeland—the process of Diasporization—goes back nearly a thousand years.[44]

Such a history need not be antithetical to the push to write "world" history or "Mediterranean" history. Indeed, it would have to be consistent with regional and wider history. Instead, it would shed needed light on lesser-examined processes of modernization, nation-state building, and nationalization. Not only scholars of Armenian history, but scholars of world or Mediterranean history may have yet to explain how it was that a people who were a majority on the Armenian plateau, who had enough resources to create a few dynasties of their own and maintain long periods of autonomy, were in the end reduced to a numerical minority in most areas of historic Western Armenia, incapable even to defend themselves against genocide.

---

1. Historic Armenia corresponds roughly to most of the eastern half of Turkey, in addition to the present Republic of Armenia, the Karabakh region, Javakheti, and Nakhichevan.

2. Ashot Sargsyan is a historian and senior researcher at the Matenadaran in Yerevan. He edited the reissue, Stepan Malkhasyants, *Movses Khorenatsi* (Yerevan: Haykakan KhSH GA Hratarakchutiun), 1991, which is

regarded by many as the definitive critical edition of that most significant early chronicler, who is considered the father of Armenian history.

3.   Either term can be used as the opposite of "state." The Armenian term for people is *zhoghovourt* (zhoghovourd); the one for nation is *azk* (azg). The latter term was part of the terminology of Armenian chroniclers as early as the fifth century. At the time, this term referred to a clan or a large family, especially one that had landholdings and was part of the nobility. Increasingly, the term was applied to Armenians as a collective.

4.   One should not be surprised, perhaps, that no scholar studying the rise and impact of Armenian nationalism—of Armenian or any other origin—has ever referred to significant works by a number of leading intellectuals of the early twentieth century who defined Armenian nationalism or were often actors in its development. For example, one could mention three leading intellectuals of the Dashnaktsoutiun party who had a dominant role in the development and consummation of the idea of nation: Karekin Khazhak, *Inch e azkoutiunu* [What is Nationhood], originally published in Constantinople in 1912 and reproduced in Beirut in 1974; Levon Shant, *Azkoutiunu himk martgayin ungeroutyan* [Nationhood as the Foundation of Human Society], originally published in *Hairenik Monthly*, 1922; H. Kachaznouni, *Azk yev Hayrenik* [Nation and Fatherland], published serially beginning in 1923 in *Hairenik Monthly*, Boston, and published as a book in Beirut, 1974. Whether or not one agrees with the concepts and opinions expressed in these and other such works, ignoring or being ignorant of the conceptualization of the nation in works published just before and after the Genocide, otherwise available for the serious-minded scholar, constitutes a mortal sin (so to speak) in academic, if not intellectual terms.

5.   Here I make a distinction between Diasporan Armenians and Armenians who, at best, feel as part of an ethnic community in a country other than Armenia. The first assumes a definite sense of identity with an "Armenian homeland;" the second refers to those who may have a sense of ethnic identity but no mental, political, or other commitment to an Armenia, real or imagined. Other varieties exist, but this is not the place to expound upon them.

6.   The term is "azkabahbanoum," literally "the preservation of the nation," indicating, roughly, the desire to maintain a distinct culturally identity.

7.   Interestingly enough, many historians are more than ready to take liberties when describing or analyzing institutions of the Armenian state.

8. The use of the term "intellectual" in the Armenian context varies somewhat from the more general use in Western literature. In the Armenian context, specifically since the nineteenth century, the term "intellectual" refers to anyone involved in public discourse. Writers and poets, principals and teachers of community schools, editors and journalists of community papers, party leaders and orators, medical doctors and lawyers promoting or affiliated with a cause, all more often than not were considered intellectuals, regardless of the level of discourse or of the education or experience of the individual.

9. This party has been the best organized and dominant one in the Diaspora since its expulsion from Armenia in 1920-1921.

10. The exception in Diasporan historiography may be sociologist Sarkis Atamian's *The Armenian Community* (New York: Philosophical Library, 1955). Although written in support of the Dashnaktsoutiun position at the height of the Cold War, the study is a serious attempt at analyzing the differences, from a sociological point of view, between the Dashnaktsoutiun and its main Diasporan adversary, the Ramgavars.

11. While we in the West will be more familiar with what is written by non-Armenian, Western scholars, the bulk of historical work will be written in Armenia, and in Armenian. This is not a comment on the quality of the works produced there, some of which is still quite admirable. Additionally, it is what is produced in Armenia and in Armenian that will determine the impact of history-writing on the general population of Armenia.

12. Maghakia Ormanian's *Azkabadoum* ["National History" or "Story of the Nation"] may be as close as can be found to an exception.

13. Here, I am referring to Michael M. Gunter, Gwynne Dyer, Kamuran Gürün, Justin McCarthy, and others.

14. For example, see Stephan Astourian, "From Ter-Petrosian to Kocharian: Leadership Change in Armenia" (Berkeley Program in Soviet and Post-Soviet Studies Working Paper Series, 2000). This is an oft-quoted paper which, in my view, does not support its assertions about the first administration with sufficient evidence. Also see Simon Payaslian's *The Political Economy of Human Rights in Armenia: Authoritarianism and Democracy in a Former Soviet Republic* (London: I.B. Taurus, 2011), a monograph over 400 pages which argues that the administration of Levon Ter-Petrossian was not different from the administration of Soviet Armenia.

15. Lendrush Khurshutyan, *Spyourkahay kousaktsoutyounneru zhamanakakits edapoum* [Diasporan Armenian Parties in their

Contemporary Phase] (Yerevan: The Institute of History of the Armenian SSR Academy of Sciences, 1964).

16. Karlen Dallakyan, *Ramkavar azatakan kousaktsoutyan patmoutyoun* [*History of the Ramkavar Liberal Party*] (Yerevan: The Institute of History of the Armenian SSR Academy of Sciences, 1999).

17. Ashot Hovhannisyan, *Drvagner hay azatagrakan mtki patmoutyan* [Episodes from the History of Armenian Liberation Thought], 2 vols. (Yerevan: The Institute of History of the Armenian SSR Academy of Sciences, 1957 and 1959).

18. Rarely do non-Armenian scholars read and understand Armenian at a level of proficiency necessary for any serious claim to use documents in Armenian—speeches, press conferences, etc. Such scholars must rely on Diasporan representations of such primary and essential sources often selected on the basis of partisan and political-ideological preferences. There is no organization or institution that has taken on the task of translating all that is relevant.

19. Thomas de Waal's *Black Garden: Armenia and Azerbaijan through Peace and War*, revised edition (New York: New York University Press, 2013) may be an exception to this general comment, although it contains many factual errors. Philip Remler's *Chained to the Caucasus: Peacemaking in Karabakh*, 1987-2012 (International Peace Institute, 2016) is more limited in scope, but presents a factually more solid study.

20. In 2006 while at the University of Michigan, Ann Arbor, I invited the fourth—the first three had not lasted long—Prime Minister of independent Armenia, Hrant Bagratyan, to visit our campus and deliver a public lecture. Bagratyan was prime minister for three years; he was thirty-three when he assumed that position and undertook the fundamental transformation of Armenia's economy from the centrally-planned, Soviet-style economy to the free market model. In addition, I invited him to attend one of my lectures in a course I was teaching for the first time, "The Third Republic of Armenia through Primary Sources." The lecture and discussion that day, by coincidence, concerned economic changes. At the end of the lecture and class discussion, I introduced the guest who had been sitting with the students, not having revealed his identity, and invited them to pose questions to the former Prime Minister. Bagratyan was totally honest and provided full answers. The last question a student asked was, "What was the most difficult legislative initiative to pass by the parliament?" Bagratyan did not hesitate. "We had some, but not much difficulty in getting laws passed," he said. "The most difficulty we had was with people who were supposed to implement the new laws."

21. Simon Vratsian, *Hayastani Hanrapetoutiun* [Republic of Armenia] (Paris: The ARF Central Committee of America, 1928).

22. Aleksandr Khatissian, *Hayastani Hanrapetoutyan tsagoumn u zargadsoumu* [The Rise and Development of the Republic of Armenia], 2nd edition (Beirut, 1968).

23. Hovhannes Kachaznouni, *Dashnaktsoutiunu anelik chouni aylevs* [The Dashnaktsoutiun Has Nothing to Do Anymore] (Vienna: Mkhitarian Press, 1923.) A thoughtful and rare critique on ARF policies and events of the party to which he belonged, this critique elicited responses from pre-eminent leaders of the party such as Simon Vratsian, Roupen Tarpinian, and others.

24. Originally comprised of documents sent by the government in Yerevan to the Armenian delegation to the Peace conference in Paris, these archives were enriched by a massive effort by the Dashnaktsoutiun to collect all possible material on the revolutionary movement and the First Republic. With the advance of German armies into France during World War II, these archives were moved to Boston. They are currently housed in the Hairenik building of the party in Watertown, Massachusetts.

25. Richard G. Hovannisian, *The Republic of Armenia*, 4 vols. (Berkeley: The University of California Press, 1971-1996).

26. Mary Kilbourne Matossian, *Impact of Soviet Policies on Armenia* (Leiden: E. J. Brill, 1962).

27. Ronald G. Suny, *Looking Toward Ararat: Armenia in Modern History* (Bloomington: Indiana University Press, 1993).

28. Claire Seta Mouradian, *De Staline à Gorbatchev: Histoire d'une république soviétique, l'Arménie* (Paris: Ramsay, 1990).

29. See volumes of survey histories by Richard G. Hovannisian, George Bournoutian and Simon Payaslian, among others.

30. The state has produced official textbooks for school and university classrooms. But it is not possible to consider these as part of the writing of history. These are best regarded as political statements from the government in power.

31. Unlike Georgia and Azerbaijan, Armenia did not gain its independence through anti-Russian rhetoric.

32. It was in 1992, I believe, that the "intelligentsia" of Yerevan organized a roundtable discussion at the National Academy of Sciences to present their issues. President Ter-Petrossian was invited to participate. Ter-Petrossian was unable to accept the invitation, however, and asked me to attend in his place. The mostly privileged intelligentsia, led by the poetess Silva Kaputikyan, presented its core case for almost two hours. Their problem was simple: Why wasn't the government continuing to subsidize

them as the Soviet government had? They had done very well under the Soviet regime and now they had fallen on hard times. Although most of the population was in the same situation, most likely worse, the elite felt entitled to favors. It was clear that they were trying to bargain. Unless the government restored their privileges and subsidies, they would become a new opposition to the Ter-Petrossian government. When it came my turn to speak, I asked two questions: (1) Was not the role of the intellectual in society to ask fundamental questions? Questions that could explain the past and the present, and then consider the impact of the answers on the issues society is facing? (2) Would it not be part of such a critical analysis to assess the impact of Sovietism on Armenia and on Armenian society, independent of any government subsidies? For the most part the members of the audience received my comments as if I was trying to sell cows in the Opera house.

33. For example, see works by Oleg Kalugin, former head of the First Directorate of the Soviet KGB. These memoirs are significant and they explain, with circumstantial evidence in support, the shift in the Dashnaktsoutiun's policy with regard to the USSR and Soviet Armenia, all this being relevant to the history of the Third Republic, especially in its relations with the Diaspora and the position taken by the Dashnaktsoutiun, mostly dictated by its leader Hrayr Maroukhian, with regard to the Karabakh committee and independence.

34. The tapes of these interviews, more fruitful as far as the transitional and post-independence are concerned, are preserved in the offices of the Armenian Studies Program at the University of Michigan, Ann Arbor. Copies are deposited in the President Levon Ter-Petrossian archives in Yerevan, Armenia.

35. Incidentally, it is necessary to write that the same can be said of the Third Republic, after 25 years of its founding.

36. Hopefully these materials will manage to find their way elsewhere.

37. The "Russian orientation" narrative was developed by Soviet Armenian historians, although it had its roots in earlier writings. The narrative indicated that Armenian liberation activists may have tried to get European/Western assistance to create a new Armenian state on Armenian soil, but that they all ended up realizing that Russia is their only hope. That approach was made easier, even legitimized as a result of the Genocide in Western Armenia. That formula has returned to the political agenda of Armenia in the past few years.

38. The aforementioned historian Ashot Sargsyan who best defined the Khorenatsi vs. Yeghishe conception of the Armenian nation and Armenian history has recently authored a booklet that presents the

framework for, and the actual distortions of the history of the republic in texts approved under the Kocharyan administration by the Ministry of Education of Armenia for different levels of teaching of Armenian history to the next generation of citizens in the republic. Ashot Sargsyan's work, although brief and with lapses of its own, is a devastating indictment of the work of historians in Armenia who had anything to do with that history, revisionist at best.

39. Just to cite two significant examples from two different arenas: A leading member of the Karabakh Committee, Vazgen Manukyan formed his own party, the National Democratic Party, and became the candidate for the combined opposition against Ter-Petrossian's bid for a second term as president. He continued in opposition, lost some of his close allies within his party, and eventually joined the staff of the third President, Serzh Sargsyan, an ally of the second president Robert Kocharyan who forced Ter-Petrossian to resign in 1998. He is still serving as Chairman of the Citizen's Advisory Council, which is appointed by the president. Rubik Hakobyan was first a member of the Armenian National Movement, the continuation of the Karabakh Committee, next a member of the Dashnaktsoutiun, then a member of Raffi Hovhannisian's Heritage Party, and more recently alienated from that as well.

40. This argument can be construed as an amendment to the geopolitical interpretation of Armenian history. The latter argues that there has been an Armenian state when the two neighboring superpower states have both weakened. Such a formula presumes that an "Armenian" factor, or agency, is relevant only at times pre-determined by others, and only temporarily. In this case, Armenian history should be seen as a footnote to the histories of empires and not as history of a people, unless that history is seen as one of victimization. The rise of the Third Republic, while Turkey to its west was and is a powerful state, is one example where such generalizations do not explain the rise and fall of Armenian statehood. This comment does not apply to the first millennium of Armenian history in the common era, when, with or without a king, a statehood survived and acted under the regime of powerful landowning families, the nobility or the Nakharars.

41. Maghakia Ormanian, *Azkabadoum*.

42. Mikayel Varantian, *H. H. Tashnaktsoutyan badmoutiun* [History of the Armenian Revolutionary Federation], 2 vols. (Paris and Cairo: Dbaran "Husaber," 1932, 1950); Arsen Gidour, *Badmoutiun S. D. Hnchagian gousagtsoutyan* [History of the S(ocial) D(emocratic) Hnchakian Party], 2 vols. (Beirut., 1962-1963).

43. See the large body of works produced by Vahakn Dadrian, Taner Akçam, Richard Hovhannisian and Raymond Kevorkian, and interpretive works by Irving Horowitz, Helen Fein, Robert Melson, and others.
44. Sporadic massacres and migrations, forced or compelled by economic conditions over time are the better-known processes of diminution of the numbers of Armenians in their own homeland.

12

FROM HISTORIAN TO DIPLOMAT: THE WRITING OF HISTORY BEFORE AND AFTER PARTICIPATING IN ITS MAKING

2011/2021

The essay below is based on my last public lecture (November 8, 2011) at the University of Michigan, Ann Arbor, before I left my position as professor of Modern Armenian History, in May 2012. It explores the difficult but essential relationship between knowledge, in general, but more specifically knowledge of history and the practice of diplomacy.

"What is the difference," asked my interlocutor, a former student turned journalist, "between what you were doing as a historian and what you do now as a diplomat?" That was in mid 1994, I believe, my fourth year of working in the government of Armenia and third year of direct and active involvement in diplomacy. At that moment I had dual positions as advisor to president Levon Ter-Petrossian and First Deputy Minister of Foreign Affairs.

After some thought, I offered an answer in the form of an example.

As a historian, you wake up one day, read the newspaper. A news item triggers in you the question, what caused the collapse of the Roman Empire? When the question refuses to disappear from your mind over the next couple of days, you spend a few hours a day in the library in the following weeks, to see what historians of that empire have to say, and decide that you are not satisfied with the available answers. So, you decide to dig into original sources and do thorough research. You take meticulous notes, look at causes of collapse of other empires, think about it over wine and discuss it with colleagues over whiskey. Now you are almost a month into what has become a major project.

You spend the next couple of months writing an essay. Then, you wait another couple of months for an opportunity to present your essay as a paper at an academic conference, while refining your text and doublechecking some sources. After listening to your paper at the conference, a few of the 15 or 20 colleagues raise questions which you will need to address and some suggestions which you gracefully welcome, and you thank your colleagues. Now we are three or four months since the inception of the project.

Then you go home, turn your paper into an article, submit it to a scholarly journal for publication, wait for the peer reviews, rework your piece, assuming the editors found it worthy of publication. After you submit the article, you wait only a few more months, if you are lucky, for your article to be published. Your article announces to the world that the reason for the collapse of the Roman Empire was the gradual elimination of the ruling classes due to their slow poisoning by the water that lead pipes carried to the homes of the privileged.

A few colleagues and family members know about the article—because you have told them—a number of them will even read it; regardless, many will congratulate you and thank you for your insight. Now more than a year has passed since that fateful morning coffee.

The article is added to your curriculum vitae and will count as a plus in the file you submit to get a promotion at your institution.

For sure you have added precious knowledge about empires and privileges and the impact of lead. Maybe some wise statesman will see your article and decide that technical and scientific progress could have adverse consequence, unintended ones, on the course of history or the future of a state. Maybe.

Not much else happens as a result of your long journey; nothing else changes; no one is practically affected.

Now comes what I do now.

You get a call at 4:00 o'clock or so in the morning from an assistant in the office doing night shift who says the Iranian ambassador called and demanded an immediate meeting, that the ambassador will not wait until regular hours later in the day, and that he will show up at 6 am in your office, no reason given. You call the chief of the staff of the presidency, who was ready to call you. He informs you that Karabakh anti-aircraft guns had shot down an Iranian cargo plane that was flying over Karabakh territory; the technician manning the radar assumed it was an Azerbaijani attack plane. In fact, the plane was transporting families of Iranian diplomats and military personnel stationed in Moscow; the passengers were returning home for Nowruz, Iranian New Year celebrations. All 33 or 34 aboard are dead.

And the Iranian ambassador demanded the meeting to get an answer to this "hostile and unacceptable act."

And you have less than two hours to do the equivalent of hours, days, weeks and months of research, deliberation, weighing of options, formulation and articulation, with little resources on hand, to dissolve or minimize the impact of a rare situation. At best, you have the telephone.

And what you say and don't say, the way you listen to an angry ambassador, and the way you respond at that moment, will matter: Iran may choose to respond militarily when Armenians are at war with Azerbaijan; or Iran may close its border with Armenia, thus eliminating the only border that has kept Armenia going during harsh economic times, exacerbating the shortages of consumer goods in the marketplace and causing an inflation that may even sink the newly implemented and fragile economic reforms.

That, my friend, is the difference between what a historian does and what a diplomat may end up doing. That happened in 1993.

In the telling of this story, the historian and the diplomat seem to be engaged in completely unrelated endeavors.

Yet the relationship between history and diplomacy, or statecraft in general, is more intricate and complex than the above differentiation represents. Furthermore, this telling is not an exercise in using one's experience to illustrate history. Rather, it is an attempt to locate points of intersection between diplomacy and history, identifying how historical knowledge, a virtual experience, and practice, an actual experience, are related to and affect each other.

At one level, all diplomats and statesmen have some connection to history. Whether once professional historians, history buffs or history-averse politicians, when analyzing or making decisions, diplomats have some idea of how to asses the parties to a conflict or who they are dealing with as the interlocutor, the antagonist or the enemy. The less they know, the more chances there are that they will make the wrong decision and the less likely it will be that they will realize that they made a mistake until it is too late.

The diplomat may know history, but that knowledge may be superficial or, more likely, politically or ideologically determined, thereby compromising the analysis and the likely scope of reaction.

Or, as is the case with the real incident above, history can fill, even if partially, the vacuum created by the lack of time and resources. Knowing Near Eastern history and cultures, one of my areas of specialization, having studied European diplomatic history, another area of specialization, and having thought about my contacts with Iranian diplomats during the previous 14 months or so made it possible for me to bring to mind incidents in history where conflict was averted or exacerbated. History offered a number of formulations as responses that could be tested mentally. These elements of history helped significantly to better understand the words and formulas used by the interlocutor, to assess the degree of antagonism reflected, the openings in the interlocutor's discourse that were not so obvious, and thus calibrate the words and tone in the response.

Being a historian does not guarantee, of course, that you will have learned lessons that will be of use to get a resolution to a tight situation. If, for example, after reading history a diplomat has concluded that the goal of Turkey is to commit a new genocide of Armenians, then it is difficult to imagine that s/he can be receptive to words or signals that are contrary to his/her beliefs, and thus the diplomat will have done a disservice to his/her mission, unless the mission is to perpetuate enmity, tension, and conflict, for whatever reason. Knowing history or being a historian will only guarantee, then, that the diplomat can use a lot of historical data to calibrate and later justify what s/he will be doing.

Clearly, in my case the historian did not disappear when the diplomat appeared. The historian, it seemed, was always there, at varying levels of intensity and consciousness, observing, marking moments, noting events and documents that the historian would consider pivotal or noting changes that became shifts in paradigms.

* * *

Now, let us see what makes this historian, so we can be a little more specific regarding the role that being a historian played in my approach to policy implementation through diplomacy and policy making itself while working in the administration of the first President of the Third Republic, Levon Ter-Petrossian, from 1991-1997.

First, my areas of interest as a student of history have included the histories of the Middle East, Africa, the Soviet Union, China and the North and South Americas. During my graduate studies I focused on Islam from the 7th to the 15th centuries, modern European diplomatic and military history, Armenian history, and African history. As a graduate student, I produced major research papers on the 652 AD "treaty" signed between the then leading Armenian nakharar Theodoros Rshtouni and Mo'awiya, the leader of the Arab/Muslim armies, later founder of the Omayyad dynasty. The details of that agreement, related by the 7th century chronicler Sebeos, manifested, in my view, an imaginative diplomacy aimed at consolidating a degree of statehood against not just Arab power but also the Byzantine policy of attrition of Armenian statehood. Another paper I wrote analyzed the fear of war in France, 1870-1914 (indicating the corrosive nature of fear on the body politic and the inevitability of war under some circumstances). A third major paper focused on the French vested interests in the transatlantic slave trade of Africans in the 17th and 18th centuries (the dominance of economic interests over moral principles). In one project under Professor Richard G. Hovannisian, a group of students looked at documents related to the Armenian Question in the US State Department Archives (an example of strategic considerations hiding behind humanitarian concerns). As part of an enlarged group, I also participated in one of the first Genocide survivors' oral history projects (confirming, if such was needed, that people forced out of their homes do not easily forget).

While a graduate student I started teaching Armenian history at the university level in Los Angeles. While still in that city, I also taught a course on fascism in another college. When living in the state of Washington for a short period, I taught a course on the relationship between religion and politics in Sub-Saharan Africa (understanding the intricate relationship between the two in obtaining and maintaining authority and power).

Although I started writing my doctoral dissertation on the Armenian revolutionary parties, at the end I wrote it on the "Ideology of Armenian Liberation, from the 16th through the 19th centuries," hoping to explain the evolution of Armenian political thought that led to the rise of the

Hnchakians and then the Dashnaktsoutiun as revolutionary parties. That dissertation, incidentally, if ever published after some editing, will be titled "In Search of the Savior," and that should give some idea of its contents. If nothing else, the research and reflection involved in that work led me to have serious questions regarding the internationalization of Armenian issues and the inevitability of the use and abuse of the Armenian Question by the Great Powers, our saviors of the time.

Following the completion of my studies, I wrote on the evolution of Armenian political thought, the Armenian revolutionary parties, the Armenian Question, the Genocide, the Diaspora and Soviet Armenia.

Just as my interests have been wide and not limited by the usual academic disciplines, my career as a historian has not been a conventional one. My forays into teaching, editing, writing and archival work have been interspersed or accompanied with political engagement: in electioneering in Lebanese parliamentary elections as a teenager, and later in the United States, as an anti-Vietnam war protestor, as a black and native American civil rights activist during university years, and as a Hay Tahd activist for many years until the mid 1980s.

The introduction to the historian is not complete, though, without the starting point, the original sin, so to speak. That starting point was when my grandfather told me stories about his experiences during the massacres and deportations, while teaching me the game of backgammon. He was a master player; but he was unable to answer the innocent question I had as a boy of 13 or 14, Why? Why the massacres and deportations?

I did not know then that the answer to that question could make or break a Third Republic of Armenia.

***

I could not argue that every item I listed above, either as an area of study and research or as a field of action, became directly, immediately relevant during my seven or so years as a diplomat, or subsequently. I can argue, that the totality of these meanderings did shape a worldview where human behavior, in all its nobility and barbarity, needed to be understood on both the personal and collective levels; and that understanding the other became a foundation on which to build dialogue and, eventually, negotiations. At some point or another, I brought into play one moment or another of the histories I'd worked on, and one reflection or another they had inspired in order to shape a diplomatic discourse and achieve a policy goal. For a small and vulnerable state such as Armenia, with few resources at its disposal, a diplomat can garner support from the vast field of knowledge that is history, the history of humankind, as "lived" experience. History can act as an advisor to the diplomat, if the diplomat will allow it to do so in all its complexity.

Researching, reflecting on, writing, and articulating history, Armenian and other, led me to reassess key moments in our history, and the evolution of that history. I ended up questioning strongly held beliefs about Armenian history and decided that unproven assumptions and taken-for-granted conclusions turned our history into something closer to a folktale, even a legend that closed doors to reflection. That reassessment was fundamental in the underlying analysis of today's strategies and options and, as a result, to my approach to diplomacy.

The diplomat can be an agent who changes the future; they seek to change—the situation of their country, in the opponent's country or in both, by working out a change in relations between them.

Just as the diplomat benefits from the political imagination of historical figures, the historian must have a particular kind of appreciation for what may be called the diplomatic imagination. But imaginative diplomacy is not the same as diplomacy based on imagined facts and assumptions.

Diplomacy requires some wisdom too, not just a cleverness with words or casuistic arguments. Wisdom to recognize and respect differences as well as commonalities. Wisdom can be reached through different paths. Understanding one's kind and the way we have behaved at different times and in different places is one of the paths, and one of the more useful ones. States and societies are different and, at times, function in opposing ways. Yet they are all made of humans, and humans, in their infinite varieties, share certain fundamentals.

To have any hope for success, diplomacy requires a clear purpose and a solid foundation in the form of sane and feasible foreign and security policies. It is not as if you walk in on any situation and do a good or bad job. The best prepared and experienced diplomat cannot produce a miracle in negotiation if they are assigned a goal that is otherwise impossible to achieve, if the policy underlying diplomacy is not based on realistic assumptions and calculations. Demanding the impossible is likely to reward the diplomat and the policy makers behind it with failure and possible disaster rather than any positive results which the pursuit of feasible goals may produce. Clarity requires adaptation to changing circumstances.

And the diplomat will appreciate constructive ambiguities in a text that is being negotiated, if that will allow creating a more positive environment which, in turn, may, in the future, make acceptable to one side or the other what is not acceptable at the present time; in some cases, insisting on certainty may do more damage than good and close a door to long term progress. When necessary, the diplomat—and the statesman—must be able to live with long periods of uncertainty. In contrast, the historian seeks to be as clear and precise as possible.

Regardless, good diplomacy begins with good policies. Despite the odds, it became possible for me to work for seven crucial years with the leaders of the Third Republic because (a) they had reached the same conclusion as I had with regard to the political/historical roots of the Young Turks' genocidal policies, and (b) the leader who emerged, Levon Ter-Petrossian, was a historian himself, as were other leaders of the Karabakh movement and later the independent republic, such as Hambardsum Galstyan and Vahan Papazyan, while still others, such as Babken Ararktsyan and Vazgen Manukyan (mathematicians), and Vano Sirateghyan (writer), had a strong sense of history and agreed where wrong interpretations had (mis)led our people.

Being a historian gave me the habit of having the long view, made me more sensitive to core issues underlying the more numerous and interesting details, to compel colleagues, allies and adversaries to have discussions on the fundamentals.

Practically speaking, knowledge of history—details in history, not just general outlines—came in handy in achieving stated goals in diplomacy but also avoiding major mistakes.

- In 1993 some patriotic enthusiasts, even a few in the top echelons of the government, argued that it was feasible, even easy, for Armenia's army to take Nakhichevan within a few days. The historians in that group had to explain to them that the status of Nakhichevan as an autonomous republic within Azerbaijan was an internationally guaranteed one; it was set in a special section of the Treaty of Kars in 1921; that that Treaty was signed by Russia, Turkey, Azerbaijan,

Georgia and Armenia and these five countries were also guarantors of that status; that any move against Nakhichevan would bring Turkey immediately into the war, just as Turkey had acted in 1974 in Cyprus.[1]

· At moments of super-patriotism and irresponsible "strategic" thinking, some advocated, even if half-jokingly, driving our armies all the way to Baku to compel Azerbaijan to concede Karabakh's independence. The same strategists had supported the occupation of more Azerbaijani districts around Karabakh with the same purpose in mind. Although the occupation of the seven districts became inevitable, even if not necessarily sanctioned, the historians were able to disabuse the super-patriots of their illusions with ample examples in history of the ultimate failure of such strategies and the fact that while going in may be easy, getting out is not so easy. Of course, there were many other perfectly good reasons to dismiss such an insane suggestion.

· The situation was similar to politically inspired demands that Armenia assist Javakhk Armenians achieve their goal of uniting that district in Georgia with Armenia. Considering the history of relations between the two countries, that would have been a massive and fateful error.

· In 1993 the critical railroad from Russia through Abkhazia to Armenia was disrupted due to the Georgian civil war and Russia made a formal request from CIS countries, including from Armenia, to send peacekeeping troops under the CIS flag to Georgia. Despite the temptation to do so, for reasons other than the purpose as formulated by Russia, Armenia decided not to do so for, among others, historical reasons. During their first period of republican independence in 1918-1920 Armenia and Georgia had fought a war, and the issues involved in that war were still simmering, making current relations fragile. The presence of Armenian troops in Georgia could have easily caused incidents that would bring old and new grievances to the surface, endangering Armenia's indirect and crucial transport route to the Black Sea.

Intimate knowledge of the history of Ottoman Armenians and of the First Republic of Armenia and of their experiences with the Great Powers led the government NOT to overestimate the willingness or ability of Western powers to assist Armenia in critical times or to rely on their promises, written or otherwise. These experiences included the Great Powers' numerous promises to compel the Ottoman Sultan to implement reforms in Ottoman

Armenian provinces; the promise by France to ensure independence for Cilicia if Armenians fought on the side of the Allies; the sad experience of the Armenian Legion and France's withdrawal from Cilicia in 1921; and, the reneging of the 1920 Treaty of Sèvres by the Treaty of Lausanne in 1923.

Thus, knowledge of history played a central role in the determination of an Armenia-centered policy, rather than using the pro-West or Pro-Russia "orientation" paradigm as the method of formulating and gauging foreign policy options.

***

There are many instances where I was simply inspired or encouraged by history to act in an unconventional manner. The most telling example was my trip to Jalalabad, Afghanistan, for crucial talks with then Prime Minister Gulbuddin Hekmatyar.

In May of 1994 the Russian Ambassador to the OSCE Minsk Group, the very capable Vladimir Kazimirov, engineered a cease-fire to bring an end to the hostilities in the Karabakh war. That cease-fire, nonetheless, was seen by the parties as a temporary halt in military operations. Baku was on the losing side in that war: the Armenian side had taken control over Nagorno Karabakh and seven surrounding districts. Leaders in Baku were wary of freezing the situation on the ground, lest that led to the permanent or, at the least, the long-term Armenian control of these territories. Baku planned to resume the war relying on a large number of Afghan mujahid mercenary fighters it had recruited. Some Afghan mujahids had, in fact, already participated in the war that had just stopped. The Armenian side had no reason to continue the war. The only way to prevent a restart of the war was to dissuade the Afghan government from deploying mercenaries and to withdraw the fighters they had already sent.

There was a decision for me to travel to Afghanistan and talk with the then Prime Minister Gulbuddin Hekmatyar;[2] it was one of his advisors who had signed the agreement regarding the mercenary force. The idea seemed outlandish at first. Since Afghanistan was in a civil war, the logistics of getting there was another major problem; the UN had declared the Afghan air space a no-fly zone. But then I remembered King Hethum I of Cilicia who first sent his brother, Smbat the Constable, to Karakorum, the capital of the Mongol Empire, and later he himself traveled there to talk with Möngke Khan and signed an agreement, a treaty. Each trip had been an adventure and lasted 18 months. But there was a precedent, an act of diplomatic imagination. I had heard about it in the Palanjian Jemaran (high school) in Beirut and explored the incident later as a historian.

Getting to Jalalabad in June 1994 was one big ordeal. But deciding on an approach was far more complicated. How do you convince the Prime Minister to go back on his lucrative deal with Azerbaijan? One of the tools I had was my knowledge of Islam and the history of that religion: when I eventually met him, I spent some time discussing some historical events between historic Armenia and Islamic empires. I also ventured into the tenets of the Quran that I considered relevant and useful for the occasion. I proved that the Karabakh war not a religious one. The respect that I showed his religion by having studied it was one of the factors that led Hekmatyar, in fact, to reverse his position. There were, of course, other dimensions to our two-hour meeting. The mujahids already in Azerbaijan were withdrawn and the remainder were never sent. (I will discuss my other arguments and approach on another occasion.)

The loss of Afghan fighters made it just about impossible for Azerbaijan to restart the war. The second element of our approach was to work on a new ceasefire document, this time through direct negotiations, that still maintained some ambiguity but made the cease-fire permanent until the signing of a grand political agreement. Obviously, we did not have too many tools in our toolbox, so every little bit helped.

I cannot argue that had there not been a precedent in history or had I not known about it I would not have undertaken the journey to Jalalabad. I do not know. I do know that the precedent made the trip to that distant land less outlandish and less implausible.

It is possible that someone else might have achieved the same results without intimate knowledge of history, through some other logic or experience.

***

Discussing diplomacy related to Armenia—as a historian, a mechanical engineer, or a shoe maker—we must first determine whether there is need for one.[3] The answer to that question depends on the answer to the question I innocently asked my grandfather: Why the Genocide? As implied above, it turns out that there are two possible answers.

Simply put, one answer is this: Turks and their state Turkey are genocidal by nature, that it is in their genes to want to kill Armenians and to kill Armenians whenever they can. As discussed in detail in this volume and elsewhere, the fear of being massacred again is the fundamental and only factor to be considered; and the answer to the fear is to find a savior protector. In this case you do not need diplomacy; all you need to know is how to beg, to lobby, and to invite pity and protection. The rest is detail.

The second answer is that massacres and deportations constituted tools in the hands of the Ottoman rulers; what amounted to a genocide was a policy designed to solve a particular political problem or a set of related problems, therefore they are historically defined and historically limited in application, unless the same or similar problems arise. In this case you need diplomacy in order bring a sense of normalcy to relations with Turkey so as to minimize, if not eliminate, any real or perceived threat or resolve pending issues.

In the case of the first answer, you are likely to surrender your sovereignty to buy protection. That means someone else will define your interests and determine the level of Armenians' involvement in the management of their own affairs. In the case of the second, you are likely to rely more on diplomacy than you bargained for.

What emerges from the two narratives presented above is the centrality of Turkey not just in our minds but also in the actual future of the Third Republic.

1998-TO PRESENT: IMPACT OF DIPLOMAT ON HISTORIAN

Transition back to "civilian" life at the end of 1997 after seven years of intense work was not easy but it was a welcome relief. Throughout these years, especially beginning in 1992, I felt more responsibility than power. Upon my return to Cambridge, Mass., I had no idea what I would be doing with my life. Those seven years were critical for any conventional academic career, since I had spent them on a project that did not involve what it takes to get a decent position at a decent university.

During the first few months after my return, I was unable to concentrate on anything that required mental exertion; I could not even read a newspaper. I spent time doing repairs on the house, watching old, black and white movies—color movies seemed too crowded to my mind—and returned to my desk slowly and with some trepidation. I guess those months were also useful for me to sort things out, at least start to, even if I did not think I was thinking.

Eventually I returned to teaching and writing history. While my fascination and love of history had not changed, my relationship to it had, after having taken part in its making.

Teaching was not the same anymore. I was reluctant to make generalizations, and my writing became more tentative. In my mind I went over the policies I had supported and implemented, the major decisions I had made, and methodologies I had deployed to complete one task or another, to achieve one goal or another.

As I started writing and teaching again, I found myself changing the aspects of our history that I emphasized or covered. The day-to-day formulation of policies and choices made by historical figures made details of strategies and outlines of tactical moves as important as the larger perspectives and goals.

Participating in the making of history was, at least for this writer, a humbling experience above all. The sense of responsibility—to identify issues and face crises, to make the mechanics of weighing options and decision-making with the leadership work, and in some cases when waging the battles of diplomacy alone—was much more of a determinant than any sense of contentment or of power than is usually attributed to high positions. To meet that responsibility required harnessing all the mental energy and knowledge I had.

Back in academia and under less trying circumstances, I now had to contend with a heightened sense of the historian's responsibilities. Having been so close to power and decision-making, I still do not have the answers to many questions; the picture I have is more complete in some areas and less so in others. I no longer have the certainty some historians and essayists display when writing about this period, while proudly displaying much ignorance. In the case of some, the less informed they are, the more confidently they write.

As far as the Third Republic was concerned, my views of the fundamentals in its founding and evolution during the first years did not change with my experience in government.

I had started with some clear ideas regarding the larger issues, the strategic ones: Armenians in Armenia should have independence if that is what they want; we should help, if possible; but not fight them, if we disagree. The goal of diplomacy should be to strengthen Armenia's sovereignty, create options for the future, and provide for its security through normalization of relations with all neighbors. And, for that to happen, Armenian diplomacy should begin the analysis of any issue or crisis by determining clearly Armenia's interests, and then look at how the interests of neighbors, allies and enemies could relate to our own.

The fundamentals survived my experience; but the policy-to-practice process came to life and moderated the certainties of the past.

Inevitably, my deepened sense of subtle, often unseen changes along with the obvious ones in real time and of leaders as living and evolving personalities making and struggling with decisions was not confined to the immediate present time of action; it led me to perceive earlier Armenian history differently. I started questioning decisions and policies of historical figures that I had accepted as normal or as the best possible outcomes. It was humbling to realize how little we know of those historical figures and the real circumstances under which they made decisions, how few questions we have asked, how many options we have disregarded, and how much evidence we have ignored or misinterpreted.

The following are some of the observations that complicate the writing of history, whether of the Third republic or of history in general, that invite historians to be less sure of what questions to ask, where to find answers, what possibilities to consider, how to read documents and determine what these sources reveal or conceal, to be more cautious when making generalizations, and less certain about causalities they ascribe to events and motivations to decision-makers.

- The problems and challenges facing the Third Republic of Armenia were bigger than the old and new institutions that were supposed to deal with them. Personalities became more dominant and significant than institutions in defining policies and strategies. As indicated above, I have been wondering to what extent this perspective could affect the way we analyze other periods in our history, including the times when royal and nakharar institutions prevailed. How were policies developed and implemented in the past? Were there, actually, policies in place? And, how were unanticipated problems dealt with and, in fact, could such problems have been anticipated and better dealt with?

- There are limits as to how many revolutions you can carry out at the same time without bloodshed. This limitation matters when you have too many problems to resolve and there is no perfect scenario.
- Independence is the beginning of travails: it requires everyday work, a tremendous effort to focus on the challenge on hand as well as the long term. Independence changes the agenda and the country is in trouble when political forces do not rise up to the challenge of managing a state; and a state is not a corporation, a political party, an aesthetic project, or a luxurious monument.
- Archives will not be sufficient to explain why any decision was made, what might have been behind the decision that is not reflected in the records. So many of the critical discussions in which I was involved were held and decisions taken during late-night informal meetings; this was not usually by choice; rather, because the problem required an immediate solution and there was no time to gather a formal meeting and we did not have the luxury of time and of resources to record such proceedings. Unless participants write their memoirs, reveal these instances in interviews or otherwise share them with others who might record them, moments precious to history will be lost forever and, in fact, are being lost.
- In assessing actors and policies, what did not happen that could have happened is as important. Would it not be important for historians to ask the question, Why did Turkey not support Azerbaijan during the first war to the extent that it did during the 2020 war? What questions could be asked in assessing our historical figures and their policies that have not been asked?
- Policies create their own dynamics: what starts as a bargaining chip, or a test of the opponent's intentions and vulnerabilities, may become a solid demand. What causes the start of a conflict or a crisis is not necessarily the reason why the conflict or the crisis is not resolved.
- The details of implementing a policy or a strategy is as treacherous as the process of developing them. There are so many pitfalls that may cause failure, from incompetence to domestic opposition, obstacles within and without the state. To succeed, the best policies as well as the best-intentioned reforms require management skills, a decent degree of competence, and the ability to foresee obstacles and be prepared to deal with them. Often, the scope and success of a policy is limited by the availability of human resources with commensurate capabilities.
- Power impacts individuals differently; for some, a high government position is primarily a source of power; for others, it is the sense of

responsibility that weighs more. Individuals change when they acquire or are given a position of power, and those changes can be much more fateful than the celebrated aphrodisiac effect.

- Appointments to positions and promotions are a very tricky business. Competence is not a constant quality in an official. A good manager of five subordinates is not necessarily a good manager of 50. A good doctor will not necessarily make a good health minister. A minister who starts well may easily become unproductive, even detrimental, over time for a number of reasons. Not all officials improve with experience or learn from their mistakes; some have no capability to recognize or admit to mistakes. Some will grow and develop. Others may even regress; power will release ambitions and negative traits that had been controlled or suppressed. Thus, to characterize a historical actor in simple terms may miss the reason for the most important change in or impact of that individual.
- Some political leaders excel as opposition leaders but will fail as government officials when they come to power. The two stages present different kinds of agendas and not everyone is capable of transitioning successfully and productively.
- Having an education, expertise, and intelligence are not the same as having good judgment, or being wise. These attributes can and have been used to pursue and justify policies and practices that are less than noble. The impact of the conjunction of personality, dedication to a cause, ambition, and opportunity is difficult to assess but impossible to deny.

***

At the end, whatever the reader thinks of the value of history for diplomacy and for policy making, I cannot escape one comparison that summarizes my tentative argument.

The first president, Levon Ter Petrossian, who was, as indicated, a historian, could not but see his work as the continuation of history, as if history was a lived experience.[4] He often refused to make statements on situations if he thought the statement might come back to haunt him and the country in six months: he "imagined" the present as the past of the future.

Robert Kocharyan, the main conspirator in forcing Ter-Petrossian's resignation and the second president of the republic, stated privately and, I believe publicly, that he does not read books and does not want to know history. "Knowing history will be an obstacle to my way of making decisions," he said to me. His decisions came from "here," he said, indicating his stomach. Vazgen Sargsyan, Defense Minister and later Prime Minister, was Kocharyan's main co-conspirator and the real power that shifted the balance against Ter-Petrossian. He was not as sanguine as Kocharyan when he thought about history. He thought policy making through history and a rational process was useful only up to a point. Vazgen looked at history as a good playing field that should be explored to produce great literature, especially epic stories and heroic figures. "Your generation," he said two days before I was to leave my positions in the government in late September 1997 and after we had a few drinks, "Your generation worked a miracle during these years. Levon [Ter-Petrossian], Babik [Ararktsyan, a close ally of Ter-Petrossian and at that time Speaker of the parliament], and you made policy on the basis of rational thinking and history. But your time has passed. Now the time has arrived to act by *dukh*, a Russian word meaning spirit, used here to indicate daring, gutsiness, chutzpah.

For one thing, if anyone, it was Ter-Petrossian who had "won" the first Karabakh war that had been initially launched against the Armenians; and he was close to reaching an honorable peace with Azerbaijan on the basis of mutual concessions; he understood the limits of what a military victory could deliver; and he knew the best time to negotiate peace is when you are in a relatively strong position. Kocharyan and V. Sargsyan obstructed that peace and established a fruitless and eventually disastrous policy that lasted until 2020, pitiful to say, because they and their successors thought with their stomach and were led by their dukh. That policy made the second war in 2020 inevitable, a war for which they were not prepared and that was lost.

There is a simple truth about Armenian history—whether of a thousand years ago, the last two centuries, or the Third Republic—that explains the significance of history and the value of being critical about it. With rare exceptions, Armenian political thought and policies have resulted from our history, often inspired by certain paradigmatic patterns established in the fourth and fifth centuries of our common era, and have been reinforced throughout history by clergymen/chroniclers and pious lay leaders. Those patterns favored belief-based instead of fact-based solutions to problems. Not knowing or ignoring that history and its problematics means using that belief-based process, since that is, so to speak, the default process.

The general lack of diplomatic experience and tradition weighed heavily on policy making and diplomacy in the Third Republic, giving history an inordinate level of significance in the context of a political culture that was already dominated by history or for what passes for history. One way or another, history will be a major determinant of current policies; but history will be useful if knowledge of history is not haphazard and selective, if it is understood critically rather than dogmatically, and if that understanding is of actual history and not legends and illusions derived from them.

---

1. Other than the independence of the island, the 1960 Cyprus treaty included also provisions regarding the rights and participation in government of the island's Turkish minority. Great Britain, Greece and Turkey, the signatories of that treaty, were guarantors of all the provisions of the treaty. Turkey invaded the island and occupied one third of the land when nationalist Greek Cypriots sought to unite the island with Greece, violating the terms of the 1960 treaty.

2. I cannot remember who came up with the idea. The intermediary of the meeting was to be Abdul-Haq, a highly respected Afghan anti-Soviet mujahid leader. Abdul-Haq's family was very influential in the east of the country. His brother Qadr was governor of Jalalabad province. I had become acquainted with Abdul-Haq in Europe under circumstances to be related on a later occasion. First Abdul-Haq and then his brother were assassinated in connection with the US-Taliban conflict.

3. The late great diplomat and beloved colleague Rouben Shugarian wrote a whole book on the subject, *Does Armenia Need a Foreign Policy?* (London: Gomidas Institute, 2016).

4. See this author's "Ընթերցողի նշումներ Լեւոն Տէր-Պետրոսեանի 'Խաչակիրները եւ հայերը' գործի Բ. Հատորի կապակցութեամբ" [Notes from Reading Volume II of Levon Ter-Petrossian's 'The Crusades and Armenians'] work in *Sնունագիր. Գիտական Ժողովածու Լեւոն Տէր-Պետրոսյանի 75-ամյակի առթիւ,* [Festschrift on the Occasion of Levon Ter-Petrossian's 75th Anniversary], Yerevan, 2021. In this article, I argue, with examples, that the first President's careers as a politician and statesman had a deep impact on the writing of his monumental work on the Crusades and the Armenians. Upon reading my article, following the publication of the Festschrift, Ter-Petrossian called to inform me that my argument was absolutely valid.

EPILOGUE

To understand a confrontation, a conflict, or a war, political or other, a good historian explores all possible explanations from the point of view of all involved parties before reaching a conclusion. Those capabilities then allow the historian, when turned a diplomat, to understand and think as his/her opponent thinks, as an essential component of preparing for negotiations. And that, in turn, helps the diplomat appreciate the other side's concerns, the source of differences, the problem the other side is trying to resolve, and move more easily toward solutions.

Of course, for this to be true, a historian must have gotten rid of ideological restrictions, unexamined assumptions, blind beliefs and "accepted wisdom." The good historian does not leave any assumption unchallenged.

And if the historian had the opportunity, luck or misfortune to have become a diplomat and then returned to writing history, that history is likely to be richer. That history is likely to be closer to what happened in the past and why; because the diplomat has seen how policies are made and executed. Or bungled.

This is so, of course, if the historian is a good one and then became a good diplomat.

That, my friends, is what it seems I have been aiming to achieve for decades. I am not sure I am there yet, but I know I have tried my best, regardless of the cost.

A significant segment in most societies prefer to believe in stories, legends and myths instead of an examined history. That is also the case with Armenian society. One can even argue that elites in Armenian society may be speaking the language of these legends and myths. The difference is that in politically mature societies, the elites know that what they are promoting are legends and myths; most members of Armenian clerical and political elites are fervent believers in our legends and myths; more often than not they base their legitimacy as elites on sharing that belief system. These elites act as the guardian of a certain orthodoxy. Many intellectuals and academics do recognize myths and legends when they find them; yet for the most part critical thinking remains within the walls of academia or private discussions, rarely intruding into the sphere of public discourse and decision making. That explains why Armenians' participation in the making of their own history has often not led to positive results.

The thought that I did my best both as a historian and a diplomat does not comfort me. I have learned to live with doubts and questions, including about my own path and contributions to history and diplomacy. I am satisfied, though, that throughout I tried to remember that both history and diplomacy are about people, real people. It is their lives that must be explained by a historian and saved by a diplomat; their lives and the quality of their lives. And to explain their deaths when caused by human failure.

Placing people at the center of history and diplomacy is not so simple; institutions, starting with the state, act as intermediaries. It is also not easy to answer a simple question: have states served to defend people or caused their demise?

So, at the end, it appears that the historian negotiates history and the diplomat helps write it. A continuum rather than a conflict, albeit a complex one, a dialectical continuum that alternated between reflection and action, which explains the structure of this author's public life.

ABOUT THE AUTHOR

Gerard Jirair Libaridian is a retired historian and diplomat. He has taught and written on Armenian history and authored numerous books, articles and reports on contemporary Armenian, Middle Eastern and South Caucasus politics and international relations, (published in a number of Western and Middle Eastern languages).

Libaridian was a co-founder of the Zoryan Institute for Contemporary Armenian Research and Documentation (Cambridge, Massachusetts, 1982) and served as its Director until 1990. During that period he also was editor of the *Armenian Review* (1983-1988) and Director of the Dashnaktsutiune Archives (1982-1988).

From 1991 to1997, Dr. Libaridian served as advisor to the first President of Armenia, First Deputy Minister of Foreign Affairs, Secretary of the National Security Council and negotiator with Azerbaijan and Turkey, among others.

He has taught and lectured extensively in institutions of higher learning in the US and internationally. Most recently (2000-2012) he was Alex Manoogian Professor of Modern Armenian History at the University of Michigan, Ann Arbor, where he also served as Director of the Armenian Studies Program.

Libaridian is currently working on a number of book projects.

Other English language works by the author relevant to the themes discussed in this volume:

Editor, *A Crime of Silence, The Armenian Genocide: Permanent Peoples' Tribunal*, Zed Books Ltd., London, 1985.

Editor, *The Karabagh File: Documents and Facts, 1918-1988* (ed.). Zoryan Institute, Cambridge, Mass., and Toronto, 1988.

Editor, *The Sumgait Tragedy: Pogroms Against Armenians in Soviet Azerbaijan*, Caratzas, New York and Zoryan Institute, Cambridge, Mass., 1990.

— *Armenia at the Crossroads. Democracy and Statehood in the Post-Soviet Era: Essays, Interviews and Speeches by the Leaders of National Democratic Movement in Armenia*, Blue Crane Books, Watertown, Mass.,1991.

— *The Challenge of Statehood: Armenian Political Thinking Since Independence*, Blue Crane Books, Watertown, Mass., 1999.

— *Modern Armenia: People. Nation. State.* Transaction Books, New Jersey, 2004.

Guest editor, *Demokratizatsiya* (Washington, DC) Spring 2006 special issue on Armenia.

— *A Precarious Republic: The Third Republic, the Karabakh Conflict, and Genocide Politics,* Gomidas Institute, London, 2023.

See also, *www.libaridian.com*

A PRECARIOUS ARMENIA

The Third Republic, the Karabakh Conflict, and Genocide Politics

G. J. Libaridian

Does Armenia Need a Foreign Policy?

Rouben Shougarian

Hambardzum Galstyan

UNMAILED LETTERS

ALSO FROM THE GOMIDAS INSTITUTE

Web: *www.gomidas.org*
Email: *info@gomidas.org*